MOURNING THE NATION TO COME

MOURNING THE NATION TO COME

Creole Nativism in Nineteenth-Century American Literatures

JILLIAN J. SAYRE

Louisiana State University Press
Baton Rouge

Published with the assistance of the Rutgers Research Council

Published by Louisiana State University Press

Manufactured in the United States of America
First printing

Designer: Laura Roubique Gleason
Typeface: Garamond Premier Pro
Printer and binder: Sheridan Books

A modified version of Chapter 1 was first published in Elizabeth Fenton and Jared Hickman's *Americanist Approaches to the Book of Mormon* (London: Oxford University Press, 2019).

Chapter 2 appeared in a different format as "The Necropolitics of New World Nativism" in *Early American Literature,* 53#, no.3 (Fall 2018): 713–744.

Portions of chapter 4 appear here, in modified form, courtesy of the *Papers of the James Fenimore Cooper Society* (2011).

Library of Congress Cataloging-in-Publication Data

Names: Sayre, Jillian J., author.
Title: Mourning the nation to come / Jillian J. Sayre.
Description: Baton Rouge : Louisiana State University Press, 2020. | Based on the author's dissertation (doctoral)—University of Texas, Austin, 2010. | Includes bibliographical references and index.
Identifiers: LCCN 2019030783 (print) | LCCN 2019030784 (ebook) | ISBN 978-0-8071-7189-9 (cloth) | ISBN 978-0-8071-7284-1 (pdf) | ISBN 978-0-8071-7285-8 (epub)
Subjects: LCSH: Nationalism in literature. | Death in literature. | Grief in literature. | Indigenous peoples in literature. | American literature—19th century—History and criticism. | Latin American literature—19th century—History and criticism. | Brazilan literature—19th century—History and criticism.
Classification: LCC PN56.N19 S39 2020 (print) | LCC PN56.N19 (ebook) | DDC 809.9/897—dc23
LC record available at https://lccn.loc.gov/2019030783
LC ebook record available at https://lccn.loc.gov/2019030784

The paper in this book meets the guidelines for permanence and durability of the Committee on Production Guidelines for Book Longevity of the Council on Library Resources. ♾

For Nathan and Lewis, *in memoriam*

Contents

Acknowledgments

During the long process of planning, researching, writing, and rewriting this book I have accumulated more debts than I can possibly acknowledge here. I beg your patience, dear reader, as I mention a few.

This book originated in my doctoral work in Comparative Literature at the University of Texas at Austin. To Elizabeth Richmond-Garza and all the faculty who supported me there I send my unbounded gratitude. I owe particular debts to Martin Kevorkian, Neville Hoad, Jossianna Arroyo-Martínez, Josh Gunn, Diane Davis, and Nicolas Shumway, who all shaped in their own ways the foundations of this book. I thank the Graduate School at UT-Austin for the dissertation fellowship that allowed me to complete much of the research that remains central to this study. Thank you to Walter Edwards and the Humanities Center at Wayne State University for providing space and community to work on the project while it was still in its early stages. This project has also received support from the Rutgers Research Council, and I would like to thank the council and the Rutgers community for helping grow the work of early career scholars like myself. Rutgers-Camden is a wonderful home for me and my work and I am endlessly thankful for the support I've received here both in general and for this project in particular. Special thanks to Tyler Hoffman, Lisa Zeidner, and the whole English Department, as well as to Kris Lindenmeyer and Howard Marchitello in the College of Arts and Sciences.

I would also like to thank James Long and everyone at LSU Press for all their work in making this book a reality. Jo Ann Kiser has been a patient and thoughtful copy editor, and I am so grateful to have been paired with her. A book is nothing without good readers and this project owes all of its current success and none of its shortcomings to a litany of generous scholars who have lent their time and expertise to the work. The project took a decisive turn at the First Book Institute at the Center for American Literary Studies at Pennsylvania State University. To Sean Goudie, Priscilla Wald, and all the participants at the First Book Institute I thank you for your insightful responses to the project. I would also like to thank Jared Hickman, Liz Fenton, and the reviewers for the *Americanist Approaches to the Book of Mormon* for helping me reshape chapter 1. Kirsten Silva Gruesz, Rodrigo Lazo, and the reviewers for the *Early American Literature* special issue on the Spanish Americas have made a lasting impression on chapter 2. To all the organizers and audiences at conferences for the Society of Early Americanists and C19 where I've tried out some of the ideas in this book, I thank you for all the ways you have helped me think in new and more generous ways about these texts. Thanks to Brooke Hunter, Erin Hurt, and the Philly writing group for helping me think about how I framed the project. Kathryn Hamilton Warren and Alberto Varon offered me sympathy, encouragement, and margaritas at a difficult time in the process and for that I am forever grateful. At Rutgers, Holly Blackford, Carol Singley, and Howard Marchitello all provided generous feedback on my writing. Robert A. Emmons Jr. helped me digitize images for the manuscript. Kevin Bourque implanted the earworm of "John Brown's Body" so many years ago, which I could only expel by taking the joke seriously and writing about it endlessly. Molly O'Hagan Hardy has been my guide in and out of the archives; she is an invaluable source for new and better ideas, and a most amazing friend. For letting me mull endlessly over two dead mothers, for his generous readings and generative responses, for his continuing mentorship and faith in the project, and of course for pointing me to Emerson's return to his wife's casket so many years ago, I owe Martin Kevorkian a second round of thanks. And where would I be without Lindsay DiCuirci's help with my writing, my research, and my conference anxiety? I don't know and I don't care to find out.

Finally, and in a helplessly inadequate way, I want to thank my families for all their love and support. To my Mom, Dad, Judi, Jim, and Janet, all I can say in the end is thanks. To my sisters and nieces, I likewise extend my gratitude. You all are a fierce bunch of women and inspire me every day. To Linus, it has been a delight—and a challenge—watching you grow. Thank you for teaching me patience and the ukulele. You are an amazing kid. And to Jim Brown, for all the ways you have and continue to support my work. You make my life and my writing better. Thank you. This book is dedicated to my brother, whom I lost when I was quite young, and my stepfather, who passed while this project was just getting off the ground. I inscribe them here as a memorial of sorts, one that recognizes their (continued) impression upon my work and upon me.

MOURNING THE NATION TO COME

Introduction

The Book Is a Grave

> That is the gods' work, spinning threads of death
> through the lives of mortal men,
> and all to make a song for those to come . . .
>
> —Alcinous, *The Odyssey*

Guardian of the Graves

In the opening of *Imagined Communities,* his famous study linking print and national cultures, Benedict Anderson traces the "cultural roots" of nationalism by first pausing at memorials of loss, the forceful "cenotaphs and tombs of Unknown Soldiers."[1] It would be more accurate to say that Anderson and his study *are taken hold of* by these memorials, a passive structuring of the encounter with the tomb, one that more closely attends to the affective power of what Anderson calls the "*arresting* emblems of the modern culture of nationalism."[2] Anderson's historical narrative, and so its author and readers, are detained by the tomb because the memorial hints at the possible origins or sepulchral foundations of national communities. "It may be useful," Anderson says, hedging in advance of the claim, "to begin a consideration of the cultural roots of nationalism with death."[3]

Anderson makes this connection because the monuments invoke a shared loss, one that affectively interpellates the citizen as the subject-who-is-called-to-mourn. While the remains are unknown, the inscriptions on the tombs ask for the bodies to be claimed within an economy of mourning, an organizing structure of community that predicates the ability to mourn for another on a prior shared identity that can be recognized and affirmed in the experience of its *dis*connection. Those who "feel the force" of these sites, in other words, those who feel *arrested,* emerge as recognizable subjects within the "*national* imaginings" that "saturate" the tomb itself, imaginings that are notably intuited or felt rather than announced.[4] Anderson notes that because the cenotaph testifies to nationalism's concern with death, it suggests the nation's "strong affinity with religious imaginings," another way of organizing shared identity through the consumption in kind of a prior sacrifice. Arrested by the tomb, that is, the modernity of the nation touches on prior ways of knowing the self, of being together.

But despite its proposed (although only possible) utility, Anderson does not make more of this moment of arrest, the captivation that creates a public out of those of whom it takes hold, those who feel together its arresting power. Death is quickly categorized as but one form of suffering that first religious and then national communities render significant by the "transformation of fatality into continuity, contingency into meaning," a coincidence that Anderson's progressive history undermines in positing at the outset that the "dawn" of nationalism occurs only subsequent to the "dusk of religious modes of thought."[5] The memorials themselves, Anderson carefully notes, and the nations they affirm, are pressingly modern, emblems of the "modern culture of nationalism" that has "no true precedent"; their modernity itself is *forceful.*[6] This rupture of modernity, Anderson argues, is grounded in a "fundamental change . . . in modes of apprehending the world, which . . . made it possible to 'think' the nation."[7] For Anderson this change is a historical movement away from the Messianic simultaneity of religious communities and toward the secular, calendrical development of "homogenous empty time," the disappearance of narratives marking that which *will have been* in favor of those structured instead by a "meanwhile."[8] We can only "'think' the nation," Anderson argues, through the flat chronology of a shared present, and that can only be accomplished once we have progressed beyond the *pre*scribed narratives that yoke present and past under the sign of a future fulfillment.

Anderson's formulation of nationalism as a cultural artifact, predicated as it is on a modern organization of time and space, remains a significant critical contribution to literary, cultural, and historical studies, allowing scholars to shift their attention to the nation form as the object of critical analysis rather than as an inert organizing principle separating histories and traditions. The growing supralocal fields of hemispheric and oceanic studies, those that highlight networks of relation and influence in international contexts, as well as regional and hyperlocal comparatist work that traces fractions and distinctions belied by the idea of community coherence all build from Anderson's work in this way.[9] But they also gain momentum from work in postcolonial theory that has put pressure on Anderson's imagined community and in particular on his location of it within modernity's "empty time." Partha Chatterjee has suggested that this very division of the modern from the premodern consigns in advance other experiences of time to the realm of the "archaic or backward." "I believe this view of modernity," he writes, "or indeed of capital, is mistaken because it is one-sided. It looks at only one dimension of the time-space of modern life. People can only imagine themselves in empty homogenous time; they do not live in it. . . . The real space of modern life is a heterotopia. . . . Time here is heterogeneous, unevenly dense."[10] Chatterjee's critique offers a way to think critically about the universalizing declarations of the nation, attending to sites of resistance or unbelonging from within the particular lived experience of those gathered under its name. But even in its skepticism Chatterjee's heterotopia of "real space" still retains a tacit acceptance of the empty time of Anderson's imaginary through which the modernity of the nation is produced. Even in acknowledging the diversity of experienced temporality within its subjects, "that word Benedict Anderson has taught us to be so sensitive to—the word *meanwhile*" persists as the organizing term of the nation itself.[11]

Mourning the Nation to Come returns to that opening tomb to reconsider the temporality required by Anderson's theory of the nation, to rethink the stark division Anderson argues between religious and national communities. I ground that revision in precisely the work of death that arrests Anderson at the start of his study, following the lead of scholars like Sharon Patricia Holland and Joseph Roach in refocusing our critical attention on this proffered (and ultimately withheld) consideration of death in his work.[12] But unlike Holland and Roach, who see death as an opening onto a critical understanding of those excluded from the imagined national subject, I offer this reconsideration from within the organizing work of what Priscilla Wald calls the "official stories" of the nation itself. These stories, as Wald defines them, "are narratives that surface in the rhetoric of nationalist movements," narratives that are saturated with authority both grounded in and buffered by their ability to "articulate a cultural identity." "Official stories," Wald says, "constitute Americans."[13] *Mourning the Nation to Come* investigates these constitutive narratives, showing how Euramerican settler colonists become nativist patriots, but it also shifts the attention to national rhetoric in order to better account for the *when* of these Americans, describing how their stories don't just call subjects into being, but call them into *being-in-time* and so *being-in-place* through their distinctly "arresting" narratives of mourning. The current study explores the "chronogeopolitics" of national narratives, a term Mark Rifkin defines in respect to settler states like those that serve as the focus for the current study as the mechanism through which "the nation-state and its coherence serves as the background against which to register forms of temporal feeling and fields of possibility."[14]

To begin a consideration of the nation with death, as Anderson tempts us to do, requires us to rethink the temporality to which it is attached. The tombs Anderson remarks upon are spaces for the nation to mourn together, to affirm a sense of community through a shared loss. But this mourning radically disrupts a flattened temporality; to be called, to be hailed by the memorials of mourning, shatters the "meanwhile" on which Anderson conceives the modernity of national imagining. In *Arranging Grief,* Dana Luciano describes the way loss creates a "psychological experience of time" affiliated with nonlinear temporalities that she connects to the cyclical time of private life.[15] Grounding her study in detailed readings of nineteenth-century consolation literature, Luciano argues that this "pull of the mournful moment" effectively "slowed or suspended ordinary time," allowing those affected to linger on or in the past.[16] Following Luciano, we can understand the "arresting" moment of the cenotaph as a dislocation in time. The experience of commemoration in the present is shot through with a heavy sense of the past, a retrospection in which the present subject feels the full weight of her loss—experiences the encounter with the tomb as loss—only in recalling a prior union. In this way, we can say that the narrative structure of mourning is analeptic, an irruption of the past into the field of the present.[17] Moreover, as an affective discourse, this fractured temporality exceeds the conscious, voluntaristic imaginings Anderson ascribes to the "empty" shared present. Mourning insists instead on a prehistory of the subject, a haunted affective landscape experienced in the present as the pressing reaffirmation of a relation upon which the emergence of the subject is predicated. That is, the commemoration of loss in mourning is *responsive,* a response-ability to the dead, who, while lost to us, do not cease to call upon—to arrest—those who *will have* paused, like us, at the tomb. Despite Anderson's insistence on modernity's absolute rupture with a prior conception of "simultaneity-along-time," then, the "ghostly national imaginings" that haunt the opening of his study perform precisely that work of bringing together those passed (or, the past) with the present, those upon whom they call.[18]

A Second Life

This haunting is made further manifest in Anderson's revised edition of *Imagined Communities,* an afterlife of the text in which he appended two new chapters, including a new ending, "Memory and Forgetting," that would reconcile his insistence on the newness of nationalism with its popular historicist narratives. In the first edition, he writes, he had failed to articulate why, despite the declared lack of precedent, "new-emerging nations imagined themselves antique."[19] To address this question, Anderson turns again to monuments raised in commemoration of the dead, although in this new concluding chapter he and his readers pause over books instead of tombs, History instead of the cenotaph. There, he locates the source of this apparent contradiction, that of modern historical forms narrating their origin in an immemorial past, in the work of nineteenth-century historians like Jules Michelet (1798–1874), whose writing, Anderson says, "exemplifies the national imagining being born, for he was the first selfconsciously to write *on behalf* of the dead."[20] Michelet's history structured the present as endlessly entangled with and by a past that functioned as a prepolitical genealogy, rewriting present national identity as a culmination of previous sacrifice and so a debt owed to the dead, a debt acknowledged and addressed through the shared consumption of these figures as the narrative of national history. But Anderson ascribes this "particular historical emplotment," this return of the dead, this work of death upon the living, to the same calendrical movement he claims for the regional newspaper. In doing so, Anderson overlooks the deep resonance between Michelet's conscription into the service of the dead, his vision of History as a durable and perduring monument to their work of producing the present, and the arresting tombs and cenotaphs that initiated his study.

For Michelet, the work of History, what Anderson describes as the origins of national imaginings, is indeed deeply rooted in a relationship to the dead and ultimately to death itself. In the passage Anderson cites as "characteristic" of this new history, Michelet envisions the historian as acting upon a responsibility to the dead, as arrested by his duty ("ce devoir") as a guardian of the graves ("gardien des tombeaux"). History itself is preoccupied with, taken hold of by the demands made by the dead as part of a patrimony they leave for the future ("chaque mort laisse un petit bien, sa mémoire, et demande qu'on la soigne . . . les morts sont . . . ces *miserabiles personæ* dont le magistrat doit se préoccuper").[21] Michelet sees the grave as a page upon which to write the history of the nation, and so his texts become the production and reproduction of venerative or commemorative spaces, the cenotaph printed and distributed among a sometimes far-flung reading public, through which the dead return to occupy the space, minds, and hearts in the present. But Anderson's assessment of this nationalist historiography as "empty time" not only disregards the analeptic voice of mourning, the return of the past, but also the important ways in which this writing sacralizes a secular political identity through a proleptic structure as well, turning the dead into prophetic figures who speak the present into being. Anderson describes Michelet's writing as a presentist "ventriloquism" through which the historian writes "*on behalf* of the dead," but Michelet himself calls his methodology an *exhumation* through which the dead themselves return to live and speak again ("Je les ai exhumés pour une second vie"). The dead in Michelet's history are renewed, resuscitated: "L'histoire," he writes, " . . . donne nouvelle vie à ces morts, les ressucite."[22] Thus revived, these figures transform the conscious declarations of national allegiance into an affective economy by calling the present reader into their community, much like the inscription of the tomb circumscribes its audience by providing a space to feel together, to feel as one. The community that gathers through the text is one that is *prescribed* by its narrative, spoken into being by these resuscitated dead who narrate how their work *will have* produced these future readers. The nation emerges in these texts as the creation of the dead, nationalism as a sense of responsibility for this gift. In his history, Michelet is not arguing for a calendrical progression in which the present is separated irreparably from the past (and equally from the future), but rather an experience of the present as an afterlife, a realization or fulfillment of prior sacrifice. In writing the nation as an experience of mourning, Michelet produces national identity not within an empty sense of a "meanwhile" but rather within a tension between the analeptic voice of loss, narrating a disconnection with those passed and thus mobilizing an affective striving after union, and the proleptic voice of fulfillment, producing a community as the legacy of that past by which they feel themselves arrested, to which they feel themselves attached.

In his study of early national temporalities in the United States, Lloyd Pratt locates this haunting as a "temporal heterogeneity" within the historical romance, "a kind of double-timed modernity in which synchronic simultaneity subsists alongside simultaneity-along-time" that is further complicated by a "revolutionary messianic time" through which the narratives address the foundational violence of their histories.[23] Pratt locates these Messianic moments in prefigurative gestures in the text, a character's "forebodings," a mother's "warning spirits," and signs in the sky taken as providential messages.[24] But while he identifies this work in accounting for national history, Pratt nonetheless characterizes it as a "supernatural alienation of time from its familiar measures" through which new possibilities of affiliation can emerge that contest the unequal terms of national belonging.[25] I argue that as a popular form of historiography, this Messianic mode in the historical romance aligns more closely with the organizing work of national history as imagined by Michelet. If we cease thinking of the nation as produced solely or even primarily in an empty present, we can see these prefigurative moments instead as locating the present community within the fullness of time. In searching out the "very very deep roots" of nationalism,[26] these histories foresee the present, anticipate the nation as the inevitable realization or fulfillment of a prophecy buried in the past, overwriting the rupture of revolution in their revelation of an antique teleology that *prescribes* the nation.

The Living and the Dead

I start with these two moments, the tomb and the book, because in bringing together these inscriptive devices we can better understand the emotional life of nationalism, particularly for those New World nations that reside at the center of Anderson's study.[27] These mournful inscriptions call the living into communion with the dead, a shared consumption that becomes the mechanism for that particular form of group psychology we call nationalism. Michelet writes that in giving new life to the nation's dead, history brings together those whom time has separated ("associe ainsi ceux qui n'ont pas vécu en même temps"). This, he says, is how you make one family, one common state between the living and the dead ("ainsi se fait une famille, une cité commune entre les vivants et les morts"). It is this figure of the national family, produced through a synchronic relationship to the dead, a relationship made possible through the haunted mechanism of print culture, that *Mourning the Nation to Come* takes as its focus.

What Michelet describes as the "justices" of History, what arrests Anderson as the work of the tomb, is what this study will call the *scryptural economy* of nineteenth-century nationalism. The monumental writing it describes functions as an apparatus for the nation, making space for an emotional tie that emerges subsequent to the nation but is nonetheless asserted as its foundational principle. This idea of nationalism takes as its foundation Michel de Certeau's theory of the scriptural economy, the organizing structure of inscription that produces the subject through the fabrication of the text, both on the page and on the body, instantiating itself violently as a disciplinary scripture and lovingly as a supportive structure of recognition. My shift to a scryptural economy emphasizes this structure's connection to and deployment of the affective energy of loss, of disruption or disconnection as a way to consolidate not just the subject in the singular but the body politic writ large.[28] In the scryptural economy of early national historical writings, from religious texts to epic poems to the increasingly popular historical romance, the book functions as the durable inscription of the tomb, one that reproduces the experience of loss for a community of readers who are made to feel themselves responsible to the dead commemorated in these monuments. In this way, the scryptural economy described here does not depart from Anderson's argument about the centrality of print culture to early nationalism, particularly for North and South America, but rather refocuses our attention on print as participating in a material culture that cannot be flattened out in time, seeing print objects not simply as shared objects in the present but rather as objects shared between the past and a pending future.

The book and tomb, as inscriptive devices, are both untimely objects, predicated upon a chronological gap between the 'now' of the making and that of its consumption. Both the book and the tomb perdure in time, so if the affected subject, she who feels herself arrested, requires us to reconsider Anderson's theory of homogenous empty time, his central mechanism does as well.[29] Indeed, even this binary location of then and now is further fractured by the doubled sense of making, as both the narrative time of storytelling and fabrication, the material conditions of production, distribution, and even preservation. Certeau focuses his work on inscription in part on this dispersed work, the "faire" that is required in the production of a page not simply as an ideological figuration (the body of the other, as he notes, is produced as the blank page upon which to write the history of the nation), but as a physical space via printing that becomes "both the support and the incarnation of the model."[30] If we amplify our understanding of making to include the material environment of the text, then we can no longer insist on a simple dualism between the time of the story and that of telling it. Consider Anderson's favored artifact, the regional newspaper.[31] While Anderson grounds his theory of communalizing effect on the shared date on the page (we are all reading Wednesday's news, and we all share Wednesday just as we will all share Thursday), the events that it describes are historical, distant by at least a day, and, for the period he describes, often longer. Their preparation for print, the writing, the typesetting, the act of printing, might come close to the "now" of a shared present but these textual formations nonetheless resist the "meanwhile" upon which Anderson grounds his idea of shared identity.[32] Instead, the dead letter, the voice of the past, arrives in the future to tell you who you will have been, a "constellation" of time, as Benjamin described it, a simultaneity across time made possible by print language. "While the relation of the present to the past is purely temporal," Benjamin writes, "the relation of what-has-been to the now is dialectical: not temporal in nature but figural," what he explains elsewhere as "not progression but image, suddenly emergent." For this reason, we might understand historiography as a form of what Benjamin called the dialectical image, "wherein what has been comes together in a flash with the now to form a constellation" and perhaps better understand Benjamin's insistence that "the place where one encounters [dialectical images] is language." "The image that is read—which is to say, the image in the now of its recognizability," he writes, "bears to the highest degree the imprint of the perilous critical moment on which all reading is founded."[33] The book, the newspaper, the pamphlet are all produced in the past for a pending audience, a reader to come; the printed text is in this way a material artifact of temporally divergent actions of writing, printing, reading, and preserving texts.[34]

The scryptural economy functions as an effective apparatus for national community because it exploits not a modern shift away from prescription, what Anderson describes as the religious mode of prolepsis, but rather a finitude shared between the living and the dead (and those yet to be born) that announces itself as that which *will have come,* the very structure of fulfillment from which Anderson distinguishes the nation. If the dead will have been resurrected in the text of his national history, then this anticipation of a return recalls Michelet to (and in advance of) his own mortality. The historian insists that his work on behalf of the dead requires him to consider the necessity of his own future inscription. He has done this work on behalf of the dead because he himself will have needed the same assistance. "Je n'ai perdu de vue de devoir de l'historien," he writes; "j'ai donné à beaucoup de morts trop oubliés l'assistance dont moi-même j'aurai besoin."[35] In an earlier draft of the essay, Michelet prefaces this need for assistance with a more straightforward admission: "Je mourrai bientôt et moi-même, avec mes longs travaux, je serai un souvenir, un fait du 19e siècle dont j'écris l'histoire [I will die soon and myself, along with my long labors, I will be a memory, a fact of the nineteenth century of which I write the history]."[36] Michelet's relation to the dead, a relation that he revives in his writing, is thus marked by a consideration of his own mortality, understood here as a text to come. In bringing the present subject into relation with the dead, the scryptural economy mobilizes death itself as an external narrative that gives the subject form, the "mass ceremony of reading" functioning as a form of transubstantiation in which the reader, feeding on the dead crying out from the dust, is incorporated into the national body. But this incorporation is driven by a futurity in that it also recalls the subject to his own death, which he cannot know and must likewise be written (and consumed) by another. Witnessing (to) the death of others, recalling (in advance) his own mortality, Michelet accounts for his own "petit bien" that he leaves for the future, his existence outside of himself, the shared finitude of the subject that drives his obligation to the past, giving to it the assistance that he himself will have needed.[37]

In order to clarify the relationship outlined here between death, print culture, and the event of incorporation, I offer the reader a Prolegomenon that examines this work through an interrogation of a single cathected figure, the abolitionist John Brown, a critical reading that introduces the theoretical framework of the study separate from its more detailed investigation of the chronogeopolitics of creole nativist rhetoric on which the remainder of this study focuses. "Working through John Brown's Body" recalls both the psychoanalytic goal of working through a neurotic entanglement and an active engagement with an object that is both a historical body (John Brown) and a textual corpus: the many odes, reflections, songs, and translations in which that body circulated, expanding beyond the strict generic boundaries of History to include a variety of cultural forms that ground national feeling in curating particular understandings of the past. In *Metahistory*, Hayden White called his study of the narrative structures in historical writing—structures that not only describe dominant historiographical patterns but also prescribe epistemological limits for identifying possible archives and communicating meaningful events—as an investigation of the "poetics of historiography." The current study shifts this approach in order to address what we might call the historiography of poetics, seeing the writing of history as crucial for the development of national feeling but also as a dispersed apparatus that includes religious writings, political declarations, songs and anthems, paratextual writings, personal correspondence, essays, and journalistic accounts alongside the standard categories of poetry and fiction. As functions of the larger apparatus, these diverse writings produce and respond to a discursive horizon against which the possible pasts of History emerge from the disorganized morass of things that have simply passed, pasts that prescribe the individual's relation to the community and so to the state. Through a close reading of several of these artifacts, I demonstrate how the scryptural economy conscripts the reader, enlisting her in its affective project of identification. In drawing this work of death and the dead, I expand upon the necrogenic foundations of narrative, the generative work of death and the responsibility of mourning that Robert Pogue Harrison has described as the "humic foundations" of culture.[38] I develop this reading as part of the book's overall project of identifying the constitutive work of loss itself, the experience of which acknowledges a shared finitude at the heart of the socius.

Building on this understanding of incorporation, in the remainder of the book I turn my attention to the social work of death in the popular historical romance in novel and verse, as well as in contemporaneous religious writings with which it shares its tropes. In elaborating the particular position of New World nationalism, I focus on the genre of historical writings often gathered under the title of "Indianist romance," those writings that take account of Native American history, and in particular Native American and European contact, in order to translate Indigenous claims to the land as an iteration of creole nativism, a patriotic attachment to a historical legacy made legible in the memorials that mark the landscape, the cenotaphs and tombs that call the reader into mourning. These historical romances came to prominence after the creation of the state as a way to affirm in retrospect the deep roots of Euramerican nationalism, discovering a genealogy for the nation that extends far beyond political arguments for independence and so establishing a chronogeopolitics that give place to the nation as a prophetic fulfillment, allowing the settler state to emerge as "a given in which to set the unfolding of events."[39] In shifting our attention from the revolutionary ruptures that gave rise to independence and toward the consolidations of the early national period, I follow the strong critiques of Anderson's history of creole nationalism offered by scholars of Latin American history and letters. Anderson locates the origins of the imagined national community in the itinerancy of the colonial creole functionary and the spread of local newspapers leading up to independence.

But Latin Americanists have taken issue with this idea of the nation's priority, arguing instead that national imaginings and the print culture to support it can be more strongly characterized in its latency, the work of creating a territorialized identity that arrives *after* the declarations of a state.[40] While, as John Chasteen asserts, "every successful independence movement in the hemisphere played the nativist card," these national identities, imagined as more expansive than the province of a particular birth but also disconnected entirely from a European heritage, were shaped by the independence conflict itself and continued evolving up to the mid-century. The "americanidad" that emerged in this period became a creole identity grounded in a general nativist opposition to foreign power,[41] a rhetorical position exploited by "members of the native-born white minority who sought not to remake colonial society, but to assume control of it themselves."[42]

In *Constituting Americans,* Priscilla Wald describes this work in the United States as authors being "called upon to make Americans culturally just as the founders had made America and Americans politically,"[43] and by putting this US project in conversation with Spanish American and Brazilian authors engaged in the same work we can see how it relies on a "nativist formula—America for Americans" that emerges in the national romance as an extension of settler colonial occupation. In connecting these national narratives to death and mourning instead of to love and devotion, I draw on the structure laid out in Doris Sommer's *Foundational Fictions,* which locates the work of the national novel in its libidinal investments, its union of erotics and politics,[44] but I also shift this focus to better account for the constitutive work of loss, a loss that does not confound but rather grounds the nation through commemorative acts of mourning. In turning our attention to death rather than love, mourning rather than marriage, I draw out the ways that the loss of shared love objects creates a feeling in common among early national readers, making possible an emotional tie that emerges prior to the voluntaristic bond of citizenship. By conscripting their readers into the affective space of love and death, these romances create a sentimental connection between the body of the reader and those of the historical characters through an erotics of mourning itself, of loving the dead as a way of claiming a cultural inheritance. This argument builds in many ways from Peter Coviello's idea of national mourning that he sees tying together disparate moments in American literary history. Coviello forwards that "the sense that loss, the affects of suffering and bereavement and the attachment to others they invoke, can be of central importance to the fellow-feeling of which American nationality is made."[45] I place this "affect-nation" in the context of nativism as a way to see how the communalizing effect of mourning is specifically deployed as a way to connect the suffering body to the land, that which holds the (lost) love object that these communities desire. In placing this "feeling together" of mourning within the context of an American nativism, *Mourning the Nation to Come* offers this national discourse as an extension of what Patrick Wolfe identifies as the "elimination logic" of settler colonialism. That is, even in the affectionate discourse through which it laments the foundational violence of colonial history, this national mourning functions as a form of settler colonial territoriality that "destroys to replace" Indigenous identity.[46]

The first chapter, "Books Buried in the Earth," builds on the Prolegomenon's exploration of our relationship with and through the dead to consider how the post-Revolutionary present was understood as a revelation or fulfillment of a previously inscribed text, a prophetic structure that connects national imaginings to that simultaneity across time that Anderson refuses in the opening and closing of his book. I trace this narrative structure through close readings of early Mormon writings, including *The Book of Mormon* (1830), texts that emerged concurrently with the national romance in the United States and that imagined the nation laden with scripture ripe for exhumation. I highlight the connection between body, land, and book in early church writings and put that work in conversation with contemporaneous interest in and theories about the ancient burial mounds as a way to understand how this religious community, attached so strongly to a larger national identification, imagined itself in relation to the dead. In *The Book of Mormon,* a book discovered buried in the hills of New York, the narrative of the Nephites and the Lamanties lends an antique grandeur to the American landscape, a history that calls upon the reader to mourn for the men and communities it describes. The reader is hailed by the dead who speak from this grave, called by bodies so familiar in their social identifications that they function as an anticipation of the reader herself. But even as the reader volunteers identification by mourning this familiar form, she has already been spoken into the text by its prophets. The structure of prophecy in *The Book of Mormon* and other early Mormon church writings foretell the reader in her contemporary situation, thus making of the post-Revolutionary subject a historical inevitability emanating from the land itself.

Chapter 2 turns from the self-consciously religious nationalism of early

Mormon church writings to secular histories, showing how they follow the same narrative structure. "Sovereign Tears, or, The Indian Is History" outlines the ways in which these early national historical writings cleared the ground of rival claims by giving death to the Amerindian. I work through the violence of the "Vanishing Indian" trope in national romances as a form of what Achille Mbembe calls necropolitics,[47] tracing the ways texts like Catharine Maria Sedgwick's *Hope Leslie* (1827) and Henry Wadsworth Longfellow's *Hiawatha* (1855) render the Indian representable only through his pending extinction that is itself historically displaced. In thus disavowing a present culture or living people, the narratives incorporate the already-dead or already-dying Indian into a national history as the lost love object for a community of creole mourners. In these romances, there are no Indian remains or monuments save for the reader's tears, tears that assure her simultaneously of her survival (as she of whom the dead are "survived by") and thus her own sovereignty. I connect this discourse of "vanishing" so popular in early national literature in the United States to that of creole patriotism in Spanish America. At first glance creole patriotism seems to distinguish itself by presenting a relationship to Indigenous America that promoted continuity instead of disappearance, celebration instead of lamentation. But through close readings of prominent texts from this tradition, including Vicente López y Planes's anthem "Marcha patriótica" (1812), José Joaquín de Olmedo's "La victoria de Junín" (1825), and the anonymously published *Jicoténcal* (1826), I show how these ideas of resurrection and restoration belie a prophetic structure of substitution or translation that connects the seemingly disparate nativist rhetorics in the United States and Spanish America through their necropolitical structure. These writings give death as a means of affirming the presence of a survivor, highlighting the ways in which the erasure of "vanishing" goes hand in hand with an affirmative materialism that *gives space* to the national community *in time* by commemorating these removals as foundational deaths.

The "vanishing" explored in chapter 2 describes the scryptural method of producing a vacancy or blank page upon which to inscribe a national *nativist* identity. The following chapter, "The Shadow of the (m)Other," attends to the generative work of mourning as *making place* for that national identity, inscribing the narrative of national continuity beyond the rupture of the Revolution upon the blank page it produced through the popular historical romance. In contrast to the Vanishing American, the Native American who leaves no trace, I show how these national novels imprint the landscape with memorial markers that "arrest" the reader, recalling them to the foundational work of the more familiar bodies of the creole elite. In doing so, I shift our understanding of the communalizing work of the historical romance away from sexual coupling and toward the mournful work of the *hic jacet,* the "here lies" of the memorial inscription. These venerative material spaces of page and grave produce the present community by making locatable a shared identity predicated upon—instead of riven by—the experience of loss. That is, these memorials give the dead "une second vie" as texts that will-have-been consumed by a future reading community produced as the inheritor of the (one day) antique inscription.

In order to explore this work of mourning and identification I study the ways in which death and mourning make impossible interracial relationships in the historical romance. From James Fenimore Cooper's Leatherstocking novels (1823–41) to Lydia Maria Child's *Hobomok* (1824) and José de Alencar's *Iracema* (1865), I show how Indian-white couplings seem to ameliorate the violence of colonial history by displacing a purely European or imported heritage. But competing with the companionate or sexual work of these foundational families is the spectacle of death and the generative work of mourning. Refocusing our critical attention on the figure of the dead mother in these romances, I argue that we can better understand the historical romance as a Freudian family romance, in which new identifications emerge from the revelatory space of the maternal body. This reverses in an important way the conclusion Marc Redfield draws from Anderson's opening consideration of death in *Imagined Communities.* The Tomb of the Unknown Soldier, he says, demonstrates that "from the perspective of nationalism per se, only male citizens can die . . . all a woman will ever be able to do is mourn. She mourns . . . furthermore, above all as a mother."[48] In attending to the inscriptive space offered by her corpse, the romances argue for the necessary death of the mother in order to establish an affective attachment to the land, a nationalism effected by the mournful assertion of the memorial inscription of both the page and the grave. Redfield argues that "mourning is her destiny . . . because continuity is her function," connecting her (re)productive role to the feminine national iconography in which she becomes "the national iconic signifier for the material, the passive, and the corporeal, to be worshipped, protected, and controlled."[49] In chapter 3 I relocate this objectification, the mother's passive material, her capacity as the space for inscribing the nation to her cenotaph, the worship, protection, and control to the evocations of mourning *for* her, not *by* her. In attending to the inscriptive space offered by her corpse, the romances argue for the necessary death of the mother in order to establish an affective attachment to the land, a nationalism effected by the mournful assertion of the memorial inscription of both the page and the grave. The nation, I argue, will be written over her dead body. This mournful work illustrates how these romances used the interlocking discourses of gendered desire, mourning, and ultimately identification to create the nation as a site of desire whose objectification is made possible by the intervention of death.

Tracing the movement from loss in chapter 2 to attachment in chapter 3, chapter 4, "Mother Tongues: Translating the Nation," focuses on the tension established and maintained between these two points by attending to the collecting and translating of Indigenous languages in the national romance. In *Imagined Communities,* Anderson argues that print language acquires a "darkening varnish," a deep sense of its own antiquity because the "fixity" it lends to language has an attendant archival function. That is, the stability of print language makes accessible the past and thus develops the relation between the present reader and her history. But while focusing on this historical sensibility in print language Anderson also elides language projects in the Americas that sought to distinguish—at the level of language—American cultures from their European heritage. "Language," he declares, "had never been an issue in the American nationalist movements."[50] In this chapter I show this claim to be false, tracing the ways in which American writers in North and South America developed a "darkening varnish" for distinct American languages via the incorporation of Native American names, terms, and traditions into the national romance. Following Eric Cheyfitz's formulation of translation as foreign policy, that is, as a way of organizing and making available sites of otherness for exploitation,[51] I focus this question of appropriation on the mediatory figure of the translator who simultaneously makes Indigenous languages available for consumption while at the same time overwriting Amerindian speakers. Revisiting several of the romances addressed in previous chapters, including those by James Fenimore Cooper and José de Alencar, as well as the writings of Joseph Smith, I put these works in conversation with the national language projects of such contemporaneous thinkers as Noah Webster, Antônio Gonçalves Dias, and Andrés Bello. In thinking critically about the figure of the translator, I show how the romancers appropriate Native languages, authorizing their use only as historical artifacts, as dead languages, presented to an audience that remains at a social, geographic, and (in this structure) temporal distance from the *indio.* It is through an interrogation of this mediatory figure, I argue, that we can better understand national language projects in the Americas as connected to the cultural work of death in literary life.

The Coda, "What Remains," brings together the arguments of the previous chapters through the sustained study of a resistant figure, the Pequot preacher William Apess. Mirroring the Prolegomenon's working through of a single cathected figure, the Coda connects Apess's engagement with print culture to this instantiating, identificatory work of the text as witness to death, but it importantly pivots to consider the Native American as that witness. Moving through Apess's reiterated fear of death in his autobiography to his spectacle of Native American mourning in his "Eulogy for King Philip," I elaborate on how we can understand his substantiating use of print culture, what Philip Round locates as his engagement with proprietary authorship,[52] as connected to this larger psychic structure of identification. But I also study the provocative trace of an oratorical "here" in Apess's writing, a shifting instantiation that gestures to an unincorporated remainder that resists the objectifications of print. This reading brings together the concerns of vanishing, mourning, and language in the book and offers a way to understand Apess's performance as an example of what Derrida named "impossible mourning," a commemoration that resists the incorporative violence of identification by leaving space for the other to speak.[53] I show this by meditating on the polyvocal and historically dispersed use of Algonquian in Apess's "Eulogy," the arresting presence of Indigenous language that in its connection to popular early national Indian biographies and colonial translations of the Bible bears witness in turn to allohistories of the nation, narratives that resists the incorporative violence of national identity.

Mourning the Nation to Come tells the story of how nations come together not through simple narratives of union but rather by the evocation—and invocation—of disconnection and dissolution. The dead that bring the living into relation and the inscriptive space of the memorial, the scryptural apparatus of national histories, gather the community to feel as one. But while this study traces histories of the nation it is not itself a comprehensive history of national feeling circumscribed by a beginning and end of nativist incorporation. Not only does its comparatist project address uneven timeframes of national formation, but also, and more importantly, the mournful bond described in this study as emergent with the development of national feeling in the nineteenth century continues to impinge upon contemporary social and political formations.[54] The nation, and in particular the creole nativism that territorializes American identity, is born from an attachment that is also a foundational disavowal, one that forecloses the possibility of Indigenous presence and an Indigenous present. Insofar as the nation institutes and repeats this primary dislocation of Native subjects "outside temporality and presence" in the narratives of its origin, it creates a bind at the center of its liberal structures that requires the continued colonization of Indigenous peoples. Because of the centrality of concepts such as the nation and citizenship to ideas of personhood, this bind remains salient beyond historical considerations of national formation. Jodi Byrd writes, "The emphasis in international law on nation-state formations predicates that indigenous peoples remain still colonized liminally within and beside the established geopolitical and biopolitical borders and institutions of (post)colonial governance as stateless entities. As a result, the breakaway settler colonialisms that produced the global North, and particularly the United States, have created internally contradictory quagmires where human rights, equal rights, and recognitions are predicated on the very systems that propagate and maintain the dispossession of indigenous peoples for the common good of the world."[55] In offering a way to understand how this bind is produced as the very condition for the nation's possibility, *Mourning the Nation to Come* maps the necropolitics of the cultural imaginary, the violent consumptions of identification, as a new way to understand those arresting tombs and cenotaphs of community.

Prolegomenon

Working through John Brown's Body

Unfortunately, nothing can be said which in [the historians'] opinion has not been said before, and truly the same prophecy applies to all future times; for since human reason has for many centuries speculated upon innumerable objects in various ways, it is hardly to be expected that we should not be able to discover analogies for every new idea among the old sayings of past ages."

—Kant, *Prolegomena*

The Meteor, or, Writing the Event

The history of December 2, 1859, begins for us in 1865, with a novelist-turned-poet who, being struck by the imminent victory of the Union, takes up his pen to draw. Herman Melville had not published in eight years when he started his *Battle-Pieces*, and it was the urge to paint an elegy for the war, to render in words the scenes of struggle and death, that brought him back to storytelling. The poems attempt to document "the terrible historic tragedy" by resurrecting its ghosts and presenting them in an aggressively visual manner.[1] Battle-pieces were then better understood as a genre of painting and the poems' evocative presentations of bodies and lands mimic the sketches and paintings to which the title refers.[2] Melville's was a history made present to the reader, or rather the reader was made witness to the events of history, a method that not only served a documentary process but also a cultural mourning that attempted to reconcile a broken community by forcing it to relive, once again, its own pain, suffering, and dissolution. Melville ends the book with just this meditation on the (re)constructive work of mourning. "Let us pray," he says, "that the terrible historic tragedy of our time may not have been enacted without instructing our whole beloved country through terror and pity; and may fulfillment verify in the end those expectations which kindle the bards of Progress and Humanity."[3] This healing process that Melville enacts in his poetry is instructional, teaching the subject the acceptable way to feel, as well as providing the correct objects toward which to direct this feeling, objects that represent a progressive mourning. Through such a purging, an externalization and communalization of internal experience, the community overcomes the strife of individual passions and ambitions.[4] In this way, the poems work to produce a communal affect, a cathartic feeling together and a feeling as one, through the sentimental experience of history itself.

Presiding over the book, marking the stark rhythm of its verse like a pendulum "Hanging from the beam, / Slowly swaying," is John Brown's body.[5] "The Portent" is Melville's record of Brown's death and its impact on the war:

> Hanging from the beam,
>   Slowly swaying (such the law),
> Gaunt the shadow on your green,
>   Shenandoah!
> The cut is on the crown
> (Lo, John Brown),
> And the stabs shall heal no more
>
> Hidden in the cap
>   Is the anguish none can draw;
> So your future veils its face,
>   Shenandoah!
> But the streaming beard is shown
> (Weird John Brown)
> The meteor of the war

The poem is set apart from the rest of the collection: a blank folio intervenes between it and the rest of the text, it is the only poem set entirely in italics, and it is the only poem to address an event prior to the war.[6] But even as the poem insists on its singularity and difference, its subject, Brown's body, sets history in motion, making possible the war that Melville is about to recount and also giving space for that telling. John Brown's body provides a material foundation for Melville's narration of events because Brown intercedes between the situated author (Melville in 1865) and the abyssal past, making writing, and here the writing of history, possible. Historiography, Michel de Certeau asserts, depends on the "rupture between a subject and an object of the operation, between a will to write and a written body."[7] This writing is only possible when the historian can differentiate past from present, finding in such a separation the "absent figure" onto which he can write.[8] This possibility of narration is what leads critic Robert Pogue Harrison to assert that society and culture are necrogenic, that, insofar as we inhabit the world historically, the dead provide the material basis for new and emerging life. The world, in this structure, is built upon what he calls a humic foundation, "one whose contents have been buried so that they may be reclaimed by the future."[9] This burying (*humando*) humanizes (*humanitas*) the ground (humus), plants our history at our feet, ready to be dug up, and so temporalizes spatial awareness: it gives us a place, both a space and a time, in which to dwell, from which we can write history and through which we can pass on our dead, bequeathing a heritage for those to come. When Melville calls for Progress and Humanity from the theater of death, this foundational work of the dead provides the material for his project, serving as the object for a conciliatory mourning.

Melville's history relies on the mediatory figure of John Brown, whose death renders narratable the events of the war and whose body speaks in the place of the author. The wounds of the nation, the scarring of the land and the people that are presently described in the poems about the war are already writ large on Brown's body itself, in the cut on his crown, in the stab wounds unable to heal. Brown is coequal with and cause for the history that has yet to occur. The addressee of the poem, the "you" of the Shenandoah Valley destroyed by the war, is simultaneously darkened by Brown's person ("Gaunt the shadow on your green") and confused and made one with the executioner's victim. It is Brown's head that is "Hidden in the cap," even as it is Shenandoah whose "future veils its face." Finally, with Brown's "streaming beard" made the "meteor of the war," he is rendered as both symbol and sign of the war, its meaning, a catastrophic event, and its language, a message in the sky. Brown's body thus overcomes the muting forces of the veil, the "hidden . . . anguish none can draw," and becomes not only the material of the past but also its narrator. The seer, blinded by the "cap," tells the future of the war, his beard the "meteor" that sets its trajectory. The poet makes of Brown—painted as the meteor, the portent, the sign from heaven—a symbol of fatalism, transforms him into a prophet and so brings into doubt the question of individual culpability or authorship. As divine ordinance, the prophet lives in service of the message, the future foretold and directed by an external hand. Brown, in this poem, is medium, not man. John Brown, "weird" as the sisters in Macbeth,[10] translates and testifies to a divine, proleptic history that elides Melville's own position as author and the connection between history and fiction, between the truth of the event and the (re-) creative work of the author. This intervention makes historiography, according to Certeau, "a discourse of the dead . . . a discourse in the third person";[11] the mediation of the speechless body allows the historian to occult his own narrative responsibility, the interested nature of his discourse. History, in this construction, is a religious text that can only be accessed through its prophet, who is already dead.

On December 2, 1859, John Brown was executed; he was left to hang for a few minutes, quietly placed in a box, and taken to his wife in Harper's Ferry; the guard opened the coffin twice before it left the state, just to make sure the body was still there. The body of the abolitionist, would-be insurrectionist, and convicted traitor was a source of anxiety for the State of Virginia and for the nation at large. His execution was closed to the general public; the witnesses consisted mainly of the military guard ordered by the governor to attend Charles Town with the goal of diminishing the rebellious potential of the spectacle. No "unrecognized citizens" were allowed, nothing "done for show" as one of the officers observed.[12] The State of Virginia effectively censored the event, believing that the danger resided in physically witnessing Brown's death, that the event, as a single instant, could not be effectively reproduced. The historical instant of his death, though, is preserved as text in letters guarded in the archive at Virginia Military Institute; in them Brown's lonely execution finds an audience in letters home and military reports. One of the officers, "Stonewall" Jackson, wrote to his wife of John Brown's body in a "battle piece" reminiscent (in advance) of Melville's work. "Brown fell through about 25 inches," he writes, "With the fall his arms below the elbow flew up, hands clenched, and his arms gradually fell by spasmodic motions—there was very little motion of his person for several minutes, after which the wind blew his lifeless body to & fro."[13] In the letter, Brown's body provides material for the intimate communication between man and wife. Jackson paints Brown's death in this aggressive detail in order to make Mary Anna present, so that she can, through his words, through this body, see the act as if she were there. In this communication, Jackson testifies to his wife, making the unicity of the instant, as Derrida calls it, exemplary but also, in turning testimony into text, prosthetic and thus repeatable.[14]

This textual experience of Brown's death, this communion through his body, is only one in an entire corpus of Brown writings, both by the man himself and his supporters in the North, a scryptural economy that rendered ineffectual the state's attempt to secure his physical body. Several of these texts, like Melville's poem, were composed as historical reflection, but a surprising number of them were written previous to that fateful day in December. In fact, Brown had been dying for years, the man's body circulated in sermons and speeches, put on display in newspapers and pamphlets. Even though Virginia attempted to control the event, it had already been seen by hundreds of readers, it had already come to pass, making the event itself the realization of a text, a fulfillment of prophecy.

John Brown's body had been in circulation in Northern homes for years previous to his execution. After gaining notoriety, if not fame, in the bloody struggle for Kansas, Brown returned to New England to relate his experiences to sympathetic audiences. Brown used tales of his own combat and experiences with death to solicit material support for his militant abolitionism, testifying to the violence that had left free Kansas "a vast sepulchre."[15] His dark testimony, the voice coming from the grave or sepulcher, painted a moving picture and transformed Brown himself into a folk hero who intervened on behalf of the helpless but also, as an actor, on behalf of those ideologically connected to his cause yet physically distant from the struggle. One trope that illustrated Brown's connection to his New England supporters was the figure of the Puritan. Julia Ward Howe, the prominent author and social reformer, remembers Brown appearing in her home for a conference with her husband, Dr. Samuel Gridley Howe. In her *Reminiscences* she describes Brown, remarking, "He looked a Puritan of the Puritans," connecting his body to an important American religious heritage.[16] Lydia Maria Child called Brown "a Psalm-singing, praying old Puritan,"[17] and Ralph Waldo Emerson also made this comparison, calling Brown "a fair specimen of the best stock of New England." "Our farmers," Emerson remarked, "were Orthodox Calvinists, mighty in scripture" and John Brown was a reminder of that shared cultural inheritance.[18] Brown himself reminded his readers of his historic character, recalling his ancestor "Peter Brown from the Mayflower" and his grandfather, Captain John Brown, who died during the Revolution.[19] As the incarnation of a national body, John Brown places himself in historical continuity rather than violent rupture with present-day citizens, arguing for their shared values while reminding them of debts owed to the dead.

Howe also remembers her husband laying claim to a much greater religious body for Brown, comparing his devotion to emancipation to Christ "who had willingly offered his life for the salvation of mankind."[20] Brown's work was a salvation that necessitated sacrifice and, like Christ, the sacrifice was his own body. This comparison also appeared in the writings of Emerson and Victor Hugo. Months before Brown's body caught the wind on that field in Charles Town, Emerson caused a stir by proclaiming Brown "the new saint awaiting his martyrdom," one who "will make the gallows glorious like a cross."[21] Brown's death was not only foretold by these writers but also integral to their conception of the man himself.

One of the most famous of these John Brown elegies was Henry David Thoreau's "A Plea for Captain John Brown," in which Thoreau "[pleads] not for his life but for his character—his immortal life."[22] In this plea for Brown, written over a month before the man would be executed, Thoreau declared that he "is not Old Brown any longer; he is an angel of light."[23] Because of this transformation, the author finds himself speaking of Brown in the past tense; "He was," Thoreau says, "the most American of us all."[24] This tendency, he says, to "anticipate a little," to "[think] and [speak] of him as physically dead," comes from Brown's relation to death itself.[25] "This event," Thoreau declares, speaking of the instant of Brown's death that has not yet occurred except in text, "advertises me that there is such a fact as death."[26] It is through Brown that the community rediscovers death and so, like his contemporaries that likened the abolitionist to Christ, Thoreau writes a necessary sacrifice onto Brown's body: "I almost fear that I may yet hear of his deliverance, doubting if a prolonged life, if any life, can do as much good as his death."[27] In a sermon Henry Ward Beecher delivered for Plymouth Church, the minister ordered that "no man pray that Brown be spared. Let Virginia make him a martyr. . . . [A] cord and a gibbet would redeem all that, and round up Brown's failure with a heroic success." John Brown agreed with Beecher. When he was given the sermon to review, he returned the text complete with his own marginalia. Next to this passage asking for his death, the abolitionist simply wrote "Good!"[28]

Brown often found himself "anticipating," speaking of himself in past tense. In his letters from prison, he addressed his wife as "my poor bereaved widowed wife" and compared himself to martyrs like John Rogers and the Apostle Paul.[29] He wrote from prison: "I think I feel as happy as Paul did when he lay in prison. He knew if they killed him it would greatly advance the cause of Christ; that was the reason he rejoiced so. On that same ground 'I do rejoice, yea, and will rejoice.'" He concludes his citation by making an even greater comparison, taking the words of Christ in his own mouth. "Let them hang me," he says, "I forgive them, and may God forgive them, for they know not what they do."[30] For Brown, it is this inscribed death that brings him into cultural life, and it is the textual spectacle of his body, an instant testified to over and over again that rallied Northerners in support, much as the Virginia governor had feared from the actual execution. Like Christ's death, Brown's execution was necessary, premonitory; like Christ's, Brown's cultural work was and is predicated on the destruction of his own body. Writing and reading these texts, composed in the future anterior (he will have died for us), consuming the body of the aged abolitionist, acted as a communion that consolidated a community of supporters.

Even those who did not support Brown's cause would acknowledge his sacrificial economy. Three weeks after Brown's execution, John Greenleaf Whittier published his Ossawatomie poem that argued Brown's "guilty means" were cleansed by "the Christian's sacrifice."[31] Nathaniel Hawthorne's famous rejection of Brown, "Nobody was ever more justly hanged," demonstrates the author's understanding of Brown's necessary death and its affective potential. "He won his martyrdom fairly," Hawthorne tells his readers, changing the adverb "justly" from a condemnation to a sense of balance or justice that Brown wins instead of suffers. Being "justly hanged" is a fair exchange of action and consequence, the forfeiture of "the life which [Brown] had staked and lost." Hawthorne's understanding of Brown's death gives new light to Melville's body "Slowly swaying (such the law)." The "law" here implicates both a secular legal system as well as a natural one (gravity) and in both the poem and Hawthorne's statements death is responsibly given ("such the law") rather than unfairly imposed. But even though Hawthorne admits Virginia's "right to take the life," he also looks back with an eye to the future, seeing Brown's body in 1862 as the portent Melville introduces in 1865. "It would have been better for [Virginia], in the hour that is fast coming," Hawthorne writes, "if she could generously have forgotten."[32] The hanging of Old Brown is an event that, once realized, threatens to return as death itself.

Stonewall Jackson was also moved by Brown's connection to death. After testifying to the instant of death, his thoughts turn inward. The Southerner and future Confederate General is strangely affected by what he has just written, about what he has just seen, and he goes on to ruminate on death in general and the spiritual life that must follow. "I was much impressed," Jackson writes to his wife, "with the thought that before me stood a man, in the full vigor of health, who must in a few minutes be in eternity."[33]

Being Impressed and Other Signs of Conscription

In this writing of the event, Jackson is moved, notably, by what he sees, affected by the confrontation with *der Tote,* the dead one who, in this religious construction, will have lived on. "I was much impressed," Jackson writes, describing for his wife the event in the passive structure in which the subject is marked upon (impressed) but also drawn in. This is an act of impressment through which the subject is made subject to an-other. The passive structure of the affected note hesitates between a subject who feels and one who is made to feel, an experience of the world that comes from an outside that already exists internally. This "incisive excision," as Jean Luc Nancy and Philippe Lacoue-Labarthe call it,[34] is evident in other writings from the John Brown corpus. Addressing the attack on Harper's Ferry, Julia Ward Howe states that "none of us could . . . approve an act so revolutionary in its character . . . yet the great-hearted attempt enlisted our sympathies very strongly."[35] Ward's description of enlistment, like Jackson's impression, hesitates between voluntarism (I enlist!) and a demand to serve (I was enlisted). Even Hawthorne, who declared that in Brown's case "nobody was ever more justly hanged," witnessed himself feeling otherwise. Directly after his disavowal of Emerson's "gallows" statement and his assertion of an unsentimental "intellectual satisfaction" regarding Brown's death, Hawthorne admits that "my Yankee heart stirred triumphantly when I saw the use to which John Brown's fortress and prison-house has now been put. . . . The engine-house is now a place of confinement for Rebel prisoners." Conscripted as he is by his own sense of citizenry, Hawthorne identifies with Brown himself. "What right have I to complain of any other man's foolish impulses," he asks, "when I cannot possibly control my own?" Such rhetoric indicates that the relationship to the object is not simply an act of consumption but also infringes upon the autonomy of the subject who is threatened with being herself consumed or overwritten. Even Thoreau feels impelled to speak. He argues that though sympathizers "wear no crape,"[36] their very thoughts are possessed by Brown and his fate. Thoreau himself resorts to a kind of automatic writing, attempting to engage rather than exorcise this spirit. "I put a piece of paper and a pencil under my pillow," he says, "and when I could not sleep, I wrote in the dark."[37] "I do not wish to force my thoughts upon you," Thoreau says of his plea, "But I feel forced myself."[38] This affective structure connects the heteronomy of historiographical discourse, the discourse on the silent other body,[39] to an ontology; this is not mere conquering of space, a writing on the other, but also a recognition of a vulnerability or exposedness attached to the self, an opening up of the self to the possibilities of being marked in turn.

The gift of death, that he will have died for us or in my place, carries with it the acknowledgment of a shared finitude that one can only articulate through the figure of death, the death of the other, of the others.[40] Jackson's impressment, Ward's enlistment, imply the shared condition that exists outside of and prior to any voluntaristic political relation, as "He will have died for us" becomes "as I one day will die." Robert Pogue Harrison argues that it is in this liminal place, the link between a past and a future, in which the living exist; we are called to answer for a past and in this to prepare the way for those to come. Harrison states: "In the human realm the dead and the unborn are native allies, so much so that from their posthumous abode . . . the former hound the living with guilt, dread, and a sense of responsibility, obliging us . . . to take the unborn into our care and to keep the story going."[41] This story, arriving from and for futures past, is narrated in the future anterior, the will-have-been. This structure does not describe a conditional or possible future, but rather a backward-glancing prognostication, what Harrison asserts as the pastness of the future, the continued presence of the dead that we gift to the unborn. What Harrison describes is a hauntology, the ethical demand of a speech from no where/one that both invites and resists acts of identification and appropriation, forcing us to question the autonomy, indeed the sovereignty, of the subject. These statements hint at an exposedness of one body to another, possibility, through the experience of "an outside which affects from within,"[42] of being effected through affect.

How Do I Speak My Own Death?

The work of mourning effected by these authors and readers is not simply a discourse written on the dead, but one that takes in or incorporates the reader. These texts transformed the sometimes ambivalent Northerners, bringing forth a group now willing to engage in armed struggle as if they were John Brown himself. Through Brown, Thoreau argues, "we aspire to be something more."[43] If John Brown's body is, as Melville wrote, the meteor of the war, this is in part because it prepares the way for war by making possible the event of one's own death. In his "Reflections on War and Death" Freud noted that "no one believes in his own death." "We cannot, indeed," he says, "imagine our own death."[44] John Brown is a figure that intervenes and makes articulate the connection between subject and the aporia of his own death.

One can witness this incorporation of the subject through one of the most popular John Brown texts that appeared during the Civil War. The martial anthem "John Brown's Body" carries with it the acknowledgment of shared finitude even as it seems to deny death itself. In its lyrics, the song eulogizes Brown and his work but also inscribes a substitution and a continued work in death.

> Oh, John Brown's body lies a mould'ring in the grave,
> While weep the sons of bondage whom he ventured all to save;
> But tho' he lost his life in struggling for the slave,
> His soul is marching on.
>
> Chorus
> Oh glory hallelujah
> Glory glory hallelujah
> Oh glory hallelujah
> His soul is marching on.
>
> John Brown was a hero undaunted, true and brave;
> Kansas knew his valor when he fought her rights to save;
> And now tho' the grass grows green above his grave,
> His soul is marching on.
>
> He captured Harpers Ferry, with his nineteen men so few,
> And he frighten'd "Old Virginny" 'till she trembled thro' and thro';
> They hung him for a traitor, themselves a traitor crew,
> But his soul is marching on.
>
> John Brown was John the Baptist for the Christ we are to see,
> Christ who of the bondman shall the Liberator be;
> And soon throughout the sunny south, the slaves shall all be free,
> For his soul is marching on.
>
> The conflict that he heralded, he looks from heav'n to view;
> On the army of the Union with its flag red, white and blue,
> And heaven shall ring with anthems o'er the deeds they mean to do,
> For his soul is marching on.

> O soldiers of freedom, then strike while strike you may
> The death blow of oppression in a better time and way;
> For the dawn of old John Brown has brighten'd into day,
> And his soul is marching on.

The song, sung lustily by Union troops on the march and headed into battle, called forth men to action by reminding them of what and who lies "a mouldering' in the grave" and still manages to go "marchin' on." The men sing that John Brown's work continues, that although it is done by other hands, it is possessed by the same spirit. As Franny Nudelman notes, "As Brown's body decays, his spirit is reborn and, in turn, donates new life to the army and the nation it serves."[45] Brown's time has not ceased but rather, because of his death, matured, "brighten'd into day." In the full light of day, we see John Brown as another John, John the Baptist, but we also see Brown the insurrectionist coming again, being transformed into Christ "who of the bondsman shall the Liberator be."

The lyrics thus echo the hagiographies written by Brown's supporters, and the original lyrics and melody, a Methodist hymn,[46] reflect the religious tone of this prose as well.

> Say brothers, will you meet us?
> Say brothers, will you meet us?
> Say brothers, will you meet us?
> On Canaan's happy shore?
>
> Glory, glory hallelujah!
> Glory, glory hallelujah!
> Glory, glory hallelujah!
> For ever, evermore!

This religious investment represents the transformation from individual to plural, a process of communal identification that transfigures the many into one or reveals the multiplicity that the "one" occults in the assertion of its autonomy. The proper name John Brown replaces the address "Say, brothers" in the original verse (Say, brothers will you meet us?), an act of communion that unites the community in the figure of Brown, in his death, in his continued life (in them). As a rallying cry and an apologia for the war, Brown mediates between powerful and troublesome bodies. He asks the reader to remember the white victim of white aggression, a strategy of identification that re-places the (black) body at the heart of the dispute. John Brown fought for the slave; John Brown's body asks that you fight for it (the mediating figure), and in turn, for yourself. But the song also reminds the soul-dier, the soul that goes marching on, that it is he who goes marching on into death, and, perhaps, as a martial anthem, into the face of death itself. In this transubstantiation in which brothers, the Union soldiers, become John Brown, the present disappears with the subject and we are left, instead, with a past that is projected into the future. This responsibility is revealed as a response-ability as the guilt that hounds the living, a call from no place that is at the same time "my" place. The voluntaristic, affiliative act of political identification is in fact produced by a conscription of feeling. This affective structure, as Mikkel Borch-Jacobsen points out, "defines the primal authority as 'ethical,' 'moral' authority and not as political authority" because this feeling of response, of guilt is not about social anxiety but rather a submission to an internal authority.[47] A "me that is not me and yet is still me."

This progression is aped by the evolution of the John Brown song itself, in that it is only after Ward hears soldiers singing themselves into John Brown's body that she rewrites the song as "The Battle Hymn of the Republic," transforming John Brown into the nation itself. In her verses, Howe transforms Brown's body into the Lord himself, who calls upon the citizen to respond:

> Mine eyes have seen the glory of the coming of the Lord:
> He is trampling out the vintage where the grapes of wrath are stored;
> He hath loosed the fateful lightning of His terrible swift sword:
> His truth is marching on.
>
> Glory, glory, hallelujah!
> Glory, glory, hallelujah!
> Glory, glory, hallelujah!
> His truth is marching on
>
> I have seen Him in the watch-fires of a hundred circling camps,
> They have builded Him an altar in the evening dews and damps;
> I can read His righteous sentence by the dim and flaring lamps:
> His day is marching on.
>
> I have read a fiery gospel writ in burnished rows of steel:
> "As ye deal with my condemners, so with you my grace shall deal;

Let the Hero, born of woman, crush the serpent with His heel,
Since God is marching on."

He has sounded forth the trumpet that shall never call retreat;
He is sifting out the hearts of men before His judgment-seat:
Oh, be swift, my soul, to answer Him! be jubilant, my feet!
Our God is marching on.

In the beauty of the lilies Christ was born across the sea,
With a glory in His bosom that transfigures you and me:
As He died to make men holy, let us die to make men free,
While God is marching on.

He is coming like the glory of the morning on the wave,
He is wisdom to the mighty, He is succour to the brave,
So the world shall be His footstool, and the soul of Time His slave,
Our God is marching on.

Howe maintains the same structure and melody as the Brown song, but God notably replaces Brown as the celebrant at the center of the work and it is God's truth now, instead of Brown's soul, that is marching on.[48] God, like Brown, makes possible the violence of the war because it is He who has "loosed the fateful lightning," ripping through the sky like a meteor with "His terrible swift sword." This is a sword notably borne by Brown himself as he wrote in a letter from jail, "Christ the great Captain of liberty . . . who began his mission, as foretold of him . . . saw fit to take from me a sword of steel after I had carried it for a time."[49] But even as the song seems to make the same move from Brown to Christ as do writers like Emerson and Thoreau, it complicates this substitution by triangulating the relationship with an "I" who testifies to God/Brown's work. "Mine eyes have seen the glory," "I have seen Him," "I can read," the voice insists in an open first-person that takes in the reader with its insistence on "Our God." The penultimate verse declares that Christ "transfigures you and me," and that "As He died to make men holy, let us die to make men free." In these verses, you and I become the objects to be impressed upon, we are enlisted by the guilt felt over the suffering of one who stood in our place and so we recognize, in the face of death, our own shared finitude. The political demand of the patriotic anthem arrives from the affective demand of the dead Father, the audience drawn in as actors through the debt that is owed to the dead. "So your future veils its face," Melville's poem declares, confusing the reader with the Shenandoah Valley, itself hidden by the line break. The supple possessive pronoun thus renders the "Shenandoah!" alternately the reader's own cry of lament or invocation of an elsewhere. In conjuring this "aspect of war," the reader can ask: what is owed to the dead in that valley?

Melville's mournful project in his *Battle-Pieces* may be considered a failure. The book did not sell in large numbers and the critical reviews were, if not negative, nonplussed.[50] In his *Atlantic Monthly* review, William Dean Howells famously declared that Melville's poems were too original, that they had lost any genuine historical reference, any claim to the actual dead, and had consequently lost the ability to incorporate the reader into or through the memorial verses. "Mr. Melville's work," Howells writes, "possesses the negative virtues of originality in such degree that it . . . reminds you . . . of no life you have ever known." "Is it possible," he asks, ". . . after running over all these . . . verses—that there has really been a great war, with battles fought by men and bewailed by women?"[51] Melville's aestheticized war is unrecognizable, overly mediated by an insistent author that distances the reader from the event instead of making it present. The conjure work fails and Melville's pieces have a feeling of "remoteness" that renders the bodies in his sketches "impalpable."[52] Melville's "originality," his "skill," instead foregrounds the creative work of the historian, what originates in Melville himself, the interpretive or manipulative work of the artist upon the canvas. His paintings offer up the artist for consumption instead of the object of his art. "Is it only that Mr. Melville's inner consciousness has been perturbed," Howells asks, finding only singular and not communal experience in the text. Instead of witnessing and being affected by the event itself, the reader witnesses the inscription of the poet himself, Melville's own incorporation and personal mourning. Melville's body, at least for audiences in 1866, is not an object that can be shared, and so the reader is distanced from the dead and made to realize the intervening voice of the poet himself. Howells objects that it is not Brown who testifies, the flesh of the words, but rather Melville, the writer, who crafts the story out of "not words and blood, but words alone?"[53] "There is not much of John Brown in this," Howells says of "The Portent," "but . . . a good deal of Mr. Melville's method." Instead of the conciliatory mourning Melville imagines in his "Supplement," his readers find instead a phantasmagoria of mourning, a drawing back of the veil that foregrounds the production of affect through writing, and that in doing so it loses the magic, the affective potential of the event. Melville "fails to move us,"

Howells claims, or, as another review criticized, "[Melville's originality] removes him from the sympathies of a large class of readers."[54]

These objections highlight and yet refuse to address how Melville's imposition testifies to another event, the event of incorporation itself. This second event revises the heteronomy of prophecy, written on Brown's body in the opening poem. What appears at first to be a proleptic voice, one that foretells the future, is complicated by the analeptic position of the author, who selects from the past an event to tell his story. The meteor (the prophecy that functions as history and as history's effects) is revealed as a participatory construct, a prophecy that is not given but created in the act of interpretation and ritually recreated in the act of consumption. The meteor is not simply John Brown but Melville as well.[55] It is this recognition, the recognition of the chronicler's voice, that Walt Whitman offers in his own record of John Brown's meteoric death. In "Year of the Meteors," the poet works through a testimony of the event only to find his own writing and thus his own death in the end. "As I flit through you hastily," the poet asks, "soon to fall and be gone, what is this book, / What am I myself but one of your meteors?" In Whitman's *Leaves of Grass,* the dead cease to be separated from the reader both spatially and temporally as the poet calls them forth in the blade of grass, the inspiration/transpiration of dead young men, women, and the children "taken soon out of their mothers' laps."[56] These dead, for Whitman—including Whitman—are the American subject.

I

Books Buried in the Earth

> I went unto the angel, and said unto him, Give me the little book. And he said unto me, Take it, and eat it up; and it shall make thy belly bitter, but it shall be in thy mouth sweet as honey. And I took the little book out of the angel's hand and ate it up: and it was in my mouth sweet as honey; and as soon as I had eaten it, my belly was bitter. And he said unto me, Thou must prophesy again before many peoples, and nations and tongues, and kings.
>
> —Revelation 10:9–11

> There were four major people who abridged the Book of Mormon. They were all qualified to address the future because they had seen it.
>
> —Monte S. Nyman, *I, Nephi, Wrote This Record*

The Sky Falls over Zion

In the very early morning of November 13, 1833, the sky came crashing down. A meteor shower lit up the midnight sky, heavenly bodies falling in such large numbers that night became day and clocks useless.[1] Many of the witnesses thought the spectacle presaged the end of time; some thought it was the apocalypse itself and fell to their knees in penitence, while others declared it to be a sure sign of God's anger and could only wait anxiously for the "fearful calamities [that] would probably speedily follow."[2] The itinerant preacher Samuel Rogers remembers, "One old lady was emphatic in the statement that it was certainly a 'token of some sign.' . . . Some men declared that they saw great balls of fire. . . . Others thought they saw these great balls of fire bursting among the tree-tops." It was a sign. Or perhaps a burning bush. God was speaking and the world was ending; one need only read the sky through the Text. These witnesses, Rogers declares, all "undertook to prove out of the Scriptures that this was one of the signs of the coming Son of Man." But despite cries that "the world is surely coming to an end," the witnesses survived to see the event itself memorialized in newspapers as "The Night the Stars Fell," aestheticized in poetry and painting, and preserved in autobiographies and chronicles of the period.[3] The event, a trauma in search of signs, transforms into a text, written and circulated for the consumption of a wide audience. The event, thus mediated by the artifacts of inscription, becomes raw material for the work of historiography, the reconciliation "between the real and discourse" that makes history accessible to its reader.[4] In one of the images depicting the shower that circulated in W. A. Spicer's *Our Day in the Light of Prophecy,* the event is paired with a quotation from the book of Revelation (fig. 1). It reads: "The stars of heaven fell unto the earth, even as a fig tree casteth her untimely figs, when she is shaken of a mighty wind."[5] The stars, the pairing implies, feed the earth in their falling, planting the seed that would bear the American future. The sign, then, points not to the sky but to the earth, the final resting place of these heavenly bodies, these "untimely figs," that sow the future with their deaths.

That night in 1833, the stars fell over a camp of Mormon refugees on the banks of the Missouri River. The Saints came to Missouri by way of revelation, discovering through their prophet that the city and surrounds of Independence were the former and future site of Zion, origin of life and the "center place" of the second coming.[6] There, they were to build up the City of God, to prepare the way for Christ's return to earth at the place of man's beginning; Zion, the prophet had revealed, was also the site of the Garden of Eden.[7] But the Mormons in Zion lived among a hostile population of frontier settlers, where distrust was fomented by religious difference and aggravated by the political power of the Mormon voting bloc.[8] Smith's prophecy proclaimed that in Jackson the Saints should "obtain [land] for an everlasting inheritance" and the Gentile residents were made nervous by these declarations of an "inheritance" and resentful of claims to their land.[9] In the late fall of 1833, this strife erupted as mob violence against Mormon persons and property, and the Gentiles drove the Saints from city and county. The Mormons fled to the river, transforming the "wilderness" first into a "camp meeting" and then into "a village of wigwams,"[10] transformations that reflected the history of the Church itself, first as a part of evangelical revivalism and then as an indigenous movement.[11] It is at this encampment, on the edge of an apocalyptic city, that the Saints witnessed the stars fall from the sky. Parley Pratt writes:

> We were called up by the cry of signs in the heavens. We arose, and to our great astonishment all the firmament seemed enveloped in splendid fireworks, as if every star in the broad expanse had been hurled from its course and sent lawless through the wilds of ether. Thousands of bright meteors were shooting through space in every direction, with long trains of light

Fig. 1. "The Great Meteoric Shower November 13, 1833," printed in W. A. Spicer's *Our Day in the Light of Prophecy* (1917)

> following in their course. . . . Every heart was filled with joy at this majestic display of signs and wonders, showing the near approach of the coming of the Son of God.[12]

The Mormons, with their belief in the continued active presence of God in the material world, their literalist understanding of sacred texts, and doctrine of continued and personal revelation of the word of God, rejoice as the sky falls.[13] Pratt immediately understands the meteors as "signs," joyful signs in a troubling time. This "majestic display of signs and wonders" testifies to an encroaching deadline, an end that is in fact a return, as the Mormons themselves have returned to Zion. This is a future foretold, already inscribed in the sacred history of the world. It is this mixture of prophecy and history that has brought them to Missouri, back to Eden; their millenarian doctrine put them at the site of the beginning, which is also, as the falling stars confirm, the end.

One may be tempted to read the popular end-time fantasies attached to these "readings" by Mormon and Gentile alike as the "human instinct to purge by fire" the purifying narrative that clears away the past.[14] This period has been famously interpreted as a search for the American Adam, born into a new world cleared of the past. Critic R. W. B. Lewis argued that the past was a burden to the newly formed nation, one that impeded the "creative task at hand," that of cementing new national bonds and of transforming colonial communities into one independent nation state.[15] But as the Mormon position indicates, these millenarian scenarios may instead be understood as an embrace of this very past as it offers a more profound understanding of the current period and its fate through the projection of sacred history. Lewis juxtaposed those he called "believers in the future" with the burden of pre-Revolutionary history, but the Mormons were only one group among many in the Americas that found this history to be fecund raw material for narrating the future of their new communities. Their prophetic histories triangulated the contemporary position, lent it stability by its presentation of a past and a future; the chronology of a foretold, sacred history, a master sign, stabilized the uncertainties that could accompany the rupture implied by revolution. The Mormons, and many of their fellow Americans, were attempting to establish their position in respect to the biblical "fullness of time," the ultimate chronological marker. The failure of the secular historian, rebuked by a millennialist as one with the atheist and infidel, is that he simply fails to read history through the Text. When science, this same writer declares, addressing his antiquarian foes, "is relied on as a guide in our search of truth to the *exclusion* of REVELATION, [it] serves but to furnish evidence of the lamentable defectibility of *human reason.*"[16] This rejection of the disinterested nature of the antiquarian is also an argument for the given sacred text, the *divine* history, that has already been written, been *spoken through* and given *place* to man.

In his "Notes on Comparative American Literary History," John McCormick remarks that "the United States has been interpreted as a country without a pre-history," because the event of its creation occurred within "a given moment in *recorded* history."[17] The birth of the nation irrupted onto the already written page, suffering as a consequence a sense of destabilizing insecurity; "a society born in a certain moment of history comes to find itself outside history; . . . [it] lacks any deep rooted consciousness of history."[18] In this critical view, the new nations that emerged in North and South America were not only produced by print culture, as Benedict Anderson has claimed in *Imagined Communities*, but also victims of the same. These nations, McCormick's statement implies, faced strong challenges to the consolidation of their communities from their emergence under the documenting eye of print culture. They were new, and as colonizers-turned-citizens they held only tenuous historical claims to the land they inhabited. Americans needed to identify themselves as more than simply displaced Europeans, but the recorded history of their colonial experience stood in the way of this project.[19] While critics such as Lewis have read the answers to this challenge as a rejection or purgation of the past, it is my goal in this chapter to show how early national texts, and in particular *The Book of Mormon,* respond to this challenge by embracing and affectively writing over pre-Revolutionary history in a manner that subverted the dislocation implied by revolution, inscribing a genealogical heritage onto the landscape itself that could be read on and through the bodies of the citizenry. The American Adam, these authors argue, is not a *new* creation. The American Adam, as the Mormon revelation of Zion made known, has been here all along.

In this embrace of history and historiography, the revolutionary resistance to the past that one 1842 newspaper described as "a prolonged protest against the dominion of antiquity in every form whatsoever"[20] gives way to a search for origins, the sentimental education of history effected by the hereditary logic of a new family bond. If, in the revolutions of the eighteenth and nineteenth centuries, the colonial subjects divorced themselves from their parents, denying their filial loyalties, then those born into this postcolonial situation were tasked with discovering a history for this family romance that would encourage stability over rupture, that would allow for natural and nativist claims to the land that would strengthen the political identification of the state. The Mormon millennial view of the American landscape is indicative of this reconsideration of history, and the faithful Saints reading signs in the sky over Missouri are engaging not only with augurs of an end but with those of a restoration as well. In her study of this period in the United States, Joyce Appleby declares that because this generation of European Americans was "never forced, like their parents, to revoke an earlier loyalty to Great Britain . . . [they] were much freer to imagine what the United States might become."[21] But in order to understand who they might become, these second-generation Americans needed to uncover who they *were.* These early nationalists turned to the past to find stability for present condition and their vision of the future, finding there the "foundational fictions," as Doris Sommer termed them, that laid the groundwork for a distinct national culture. No longer faced with the need to justify the revolutions themselves, these citizens instead faced the task of establishing a national community that transcended the political identification of the independence period, one that gave foundation to the political community in an indigenous *feeling* for the state. This "emotional tie" is an affective assent prior to or distinct from the conscious solidarity described by theorists of nationalism. *Mourning the Nation to Come* traces this work, showing how during their respective periods of national development, North and South Americans accomplished this sentimental consolidation by writing history, more specifically by *romancing* history, creating an affective bond between the present community and an imagined past through the consuming, libidinal and identificatory excitement of the national romance. In this way, the historical romances of the early national period used the documentary and circulatory functions of print culture that threatened to expose their novelty (implicating not only their cultural newness but also their history as fictional) in order to create a new shared cultural heritage; the books themselves not only claimed to contain but also functioned *as* the material foundation for a new cultural history. Through the mediatory figure of the book, these readers attached themselves to the figures of their past. Through the identifying work of their sentimental journeys, the protagonists' loves, struggles, and, most importantly for the present study, their deaths, these novels interpellate their readers as the prophetic result of their narratives. In these narratives of the past, writers discovered a cultural and even familial inheritance that superseded, in large part because they anteceded, those recent political claims of revolution and independence. The reader's political existence is foretold in the social collectivity of the past. All that was needed was a sacred historian, the translator of God's word, a prophet to show them the way.

In the early morning of November 13, the Mormon faithful woke Joseph Smith, their prophet, so that he could interpret these signs in the sky. Just three years after organizing the Church of Christ (later the Church of Jesus Christ of Latter-day Saints), three years after publishing its central work, *The Book of Mormon,* Smith presided over a large congregation of Saints in Ohio, traveled frequently to groups of faithful in Canada and New York, and oversaw the settling of Zion from a distance. He was concerned about his followers in Jackson County, but had not heard of their most recent troubles when he witnessed the same meteor shower as the refugees in Missouri. He wrote in his journal: "I arrose and beheld to my great Joy the stars fall from heaven yea they fell like hail stones a litteral fullfillment of the word of God as recorded in the holy scriptures and a sure sign that the coming of Christ is clost at hand Oh how marvellous are thy works Oh Lord and I thank thee for thy me[r]cy unto me thy servent Oh Lord save me in thy kingdom for Christ sake Amen."[22] Like those faithful on the banks of the Missouri River, Smith does not see the event as a cause for panic but rather an occasion for joy, as the falling stars confirm the veracity of the text, offering "a litteral fulfillment of the word of God as recorded in the holy scriptures." What makes Smith's faith in the Text distinct from non-Mormon contemporaneous millenarian views is that these "holy scriptures" include his own productions, *The Book of Mormon, Doctrine and Covenants,* the texts later compiled as *The Pearl of Great Price,* and his inspired retranslation of the Bible. For Smith and his followers, the "holy scriptures" were distinctly American in their setting, preservation, discovery, translation, and reproduction. The fulfillment of the word of God and thus the true ability to understand these signs in the sky could only be done in the context of placing the Americas at the center of prophetic discourse, of understanding the land as unique in its ability to realize ancient prophecy. The Mormon scriptures transformed a universal Christian eschatology into a uniquely American phenomenon, bestowing upon the land a connection to a sacred history that preceded and therefore supplanted its secular history of conquest, colonialism, and political revolution. The Americas, in this structure, not only gained a stronghold within a recognizable "recorded history" but also resided at its center, rendering the Old World peripheral or perhaps even outside of this chronology. In this restructured filial heritage, the American citizen can imagine his or her heritage not as a direct line from Europe but rather, as one Mormon settler in Jackson County did, as an indigenous connection to the American landscape and "our first parents in the garden of Eden."[23]

A study of Mormon scriptures, and *The Book of Mormon* in particular, offers us an opportunity to better understand how narratives delimit a community in time and space. Read as an example of the historical narrative popular at the time, an artifact of social organization effected through its presentation as a shared sacred history, *The Book of Mormon* is useful for understanding community bonds because the text both participates in forming and responds to the ongoing needs of its community through its material medium. The circulation of the text (and the circulation of texts in its narrative) belies a mechanics of production and reproduction that influences its constitutive narrative strategies for creating and consolidating a community. If we put the extended historical narrative of *The Book of Mormon* in conversation with the contemporary rise of the national romance, we can better understand how both the novel and these religious writings contribute to a material culture whose consumption in kind by a dispersed readership functions as a strong affiliative bond. What makes the literary genre of the novel unique, as Walter Benjamin has pointed out, is its development *after* the invention of the press.[24] The circulation not only of narrative but also of its material bounds therefore inheres to the process of collective identity that these texts engender, and the modes of consumption and identification detailed in this study cannot be separated from the material exchange relations that gird the print market. Print-based communities in the Americas, those developed in plain view of an established print culture (its gaze already upon the land and its subjects), are helpful in understanding the materialism of community formation because they, by their scriptive nature, depended upon the rendering of traces of the past as material objects in the present. These textual artifacts cannot but work against the assumption that history and community are natural constructs, a procession of events external to the position of the observer, a gathering of *volk* exterior to the documentary process.[25] *The Book of Mormon,* like contemporaneous historical romances, transforms its reading community in the present by revising established historical narratives, attaching their readers to a new legacy through the effects, or rather affects, of the texts themselves. Reading, in this structure, is "a mass ceremony,"[26] a ritual of consumption that simultaneously and reciprocally establishes a national character and a national literature. The narrative strategies of the romances in this study are both effected and made manifest by the medium of their deployment and so the texts also function as insights into the mechanics that support the construction of the contemporary nation-state as well as the emotional and fetishistic structures that girds human social collectives in general.

The Book of Mormon is exemplary of what I will argue to be the materialist foundation of the psychic life of communities in the age of print. Benedict Anderson has famously argued for the foundational role of print culture in the formation of nations, defined in his terms as imagined communities. Shared cultural texts become the means of imagining the space of the nation, providing for the "rich legacy of memories" and producing the "present-day consent" that Ernest Renan famously argued to be the co-creation of nation and citizen.[27] Renan describes this consent as an expression of desire "to continue a common life," but by attending to the melancholic economy of *The Book of Mormon* we can rethink this voluntary work of consent as instead a structure of desire that stems from a pre-political primary desire that itself moves between pleasure and death, identity and disavowal. By shifting our attention to deep structure, we do not lose our connection to the material realities of lived experience. Instead, we can begin to think about how this structure of desire is mediated by the material of the text. National narratives, as the mode of communicating this "social capital," thus become part of a transformative material transaction. Here, print culture functions as a scryptural economy, one that transforms the book into a fetish object (both in terms of a figure of exchange and as access to the sacred), the material location of shared desires whose significance exceeds (and yet relies upon) its material bounds. This excess is manifested in the reader's libidinal cathexis of the text as an object of desire, shared with an unknown number of fellow readers. This libidinal and identificatory energy is in turn expressed through the affective and somatic transformations it effects. The reader sighs and sheds tears, loves and mourns, through the text. The recognition and consent described by Renan is not necessarily voluntaristic but, as I will argue, a somatic conscription, a *feeling with* the characters in the narrative. This interaction, between the body of the text and the body of the reader, form the affective bonds of citizenship that remains the goal of national literature.

Empty Tombs and Tabernacles of Clay

On a windy April day in 1844, in a grove just a short distance from the temple at Nauvoo, Illinois, Joseph Smith spoke to a congregation of Saints about a subject "of the greatest importance, and the most solemn of any that can occupy our attention." That is, Smith said, "the subject of the dead."[28] The sermon is widely known as the King Follett discourse, named after the fallen Saint whose death precipitated Smith's larger consideration of loss and those lost. In the sermon, considered "the Prophet's greatest" and "the very life-blood of Mormon theology,"[29] Smith outlines "the relation of man to God," a relation that requires us to better understand man's relation to the dead. "I will open your eyes in relation to the dead," Smith tells his followers; it is a relation marked by "responsibility," he says, "the awful responsibility, that rests upon us in relation to our dead."[30]

Smith's discourse preaches a doctrine of sealing, the work of binding mortal kinship as immortal relation, a practice that recent scholars like Douglas Davies and Samuel Morris Brown have used as central evidence of Mormonism's grappling with and ultimate rejection of death itself.[31] But while Davies and Brown focus on the theological conquest of death, I would draw your attention to the materialism of this supposed triumph over mortality. In order for the finality and dislocation of *death* to be conquered, the surviving community must embrace the *dead* through the material medium of their own flesh. In his sermon, Smith insists that the eternal quality of man, his soul, is not simply the disembodied spirit, freed from the mortal body, but rather a marriage of the spirit, which is always eternal, with the "tabernacle of clay" that is the human form, that which *will be* made eternal in the "fulness of the dispensation of times."[32] Because of their temporary absence from that "tabernacle," the dead rely on the living to fulfill their embodied religious practices in their place.[33] "The greatest responsibility in this world that God has laid upon us," Smith tells those gathered Saints, "is to seek after our dead. The apostle says, 'They without us cannot be made perfect.'"[34] Salvation, Smith says, can only be accomplished in *this* world, requiring precisely that space of the body, the material fact of the tabernacle.[35] When the conference continues the following day, Smith clarifies the *physical* practice of seeking after the dead: "For men to be baptized for their dead . . . every man who wishes to save his father, mother, brother, sisters and friends, must go through all the ordinances for each one of them separately, the same as for himself, from baptism to ordination, washings and anointings, and receive all the keys and powers of the Priesthood, the same as for himself."[36] In this structure, the dead call out to the living for their continued care, not in the lamentation of kinship ruptured, but in the physical rituals that affirm, solidify, *seal* that relation. In the repetition of religious practices as (or in the place of) the other, the baptism and anointing of the dead require the living to identify with—and as—the dead themselves, to act as (and in the interest of) an other. In other words, in "vanquishing death," as Brown describes it, the Saints have to be made responsible—to respond—to the dead by making their bodies a shared space, a space of community, a site of restoration and reconciliation.

The physical space of the body, then, is not the site of individuation, but rather a space for congregation, yoking together the past and the present in the service of a future that has already been written. But this "tabernacle of clay" also connects the living to the earth as the site of its origins, the raw material of its construction. In consoling the faithful on the "subject of the dead," Smith traces out this origin story, written on the body. At "the morn of creation,"[37] Smith reminds his listeners, "God made a tabernacle and put a spirit into it and it became a living soul. . . . God made man out of the earth and put into him Adam's spirit."[38] Over and over he insists on the material realities of creation, not as a way of dismissing the body as the other of the eternal spirit, the physical matter that must be sloughed off to enter eternity, but in sacralizing the material itself as inextricable to a doctrine of divine creation, salvation, and, ultimately, resurrection. But this spatializing effect isn't exhausted by the connection Smith draws between the mortal body and its material origins; the tabernacle of clay connects the living to their *historical* origins as well. The tabernacle was not constructed of clay gathered in some faraway place, but rather from the American landscape itself, the land of Zion, "the land which I will consecrate unto my people, which are a remnant of Jacob, and them who are heirs according to the covenant."[39] The consecrated space functions as the ligature that binds the contemporary community with the historical one; they are the "remnant" those who remain, who survive, who stand to inherit. Just as the living body becomes a site of communal expression in the repeated performance of ordinances, the land also functions as the site of restoration. This "land of promise" would be an "everlasting inheritance," for the community, a millennial space in which the fullness of time restores the community to the ur-clay of Eden itself. When Smith returns to his "subject of the dead" the following day, he emphasizes this connection between land, body, and community. Weakened by the exertion of the long sermon the day before, Smith defers to the Elders to guide the conference, but not before proclaiming "a great, grand, and glorious revelation"[40] regarding the place of this communion with the dead; "there must be," he says, "a particular spot for the salvation of our dead."[41] This place, he says, is Zion, which is no longer understood as restricted to the original revelation's location in Missouri, but rather coterminous with the country: "*The whole of America is Zion itself from north to south, and is described by the Prophets who declare that it is the Zion where the mountain of the Lord should be, and that it should be in the center of the land . . . I have received instructions from the Lord that from henceforth wherever the Elders of Israel shall build up churches and branches unto the Lord throughout the States, there shall be a stake of Zion.*"[42] The Promised Land, the land of our inheritance, is the whole of the United States.

If the Follett discourse effectively demonstrates a materialism that builds and sustains a community through a cathexis of bodies and land, the production and circulation of the sermon also serve as useful examples of the way in which the Latter-day Saints (LDS) community imagined itself through the text. Smith did not read from a prepared text that April, and there are no direct transcriptions of the sermon. Instead, what remains are recordings of the sermon by four trained secretaries, which demonstrate a span of textual variance. After Smith's death just a few months after the sermon, the records of the April discourse were compared and compiled in different combinations for church publications, first in the newspaper *Times and Seasons* (August 15, 1844), and later for official histories like the "Manuscript History of the Church."[43] The records of the sermon and their publication in various formats speak to the importance of creating and disseminating church documents for the early LDS community, a "documania" that characterized the community as one shaped by and through the press. When Fawn Brodie set out to write her famous biography of Smith, she finds no "lack of biographical data, for Joseph Smith dared to found a new religion in the age of printing. When he said 'Thus saith the Lord!' the words were copied down by secretaries and congealed forever into print."[44] Brodie nonetheless finds it difficult to map the structures of historiography and biography, that of linear narrative time in the former and individuation in the latter, onto her encounter with the sizable Smith corpus. Brodie details the variance and contradictory conclusions of Smith biographies as evidence that perhaps Smith's declaration "No man knows my history," a claim the Prophet makes at the conclusion of the Follett discourse, was more prophecy than description. "The reason for these disparate opinions," she writes, is in the form and purpose of his writing. "His story," she concludes, regarding his six-volume autobiography, "is the antithesis of confession," neither singular nor private. His autobiography is the official history of the church; it is not a personal document but a communal one. This official history of an institution is an "I" that is at the same time a "we." Even in its production (Smith rarely wrote for himself, choosing instead to dictate or defer to secretaries), the body of and behind the text is in fact multiple. Instead of revealing the object of its study, the individual, Smith's autobiography presents an individual identified completely with, and thus consumed by, the larger community of the church. The reverse also seems to be true. In the autobiography of its founder and most important prophet, the community of the LDS Church is contained within, consumed in its turn, by the "I" of Smith's writing. Brodie's introductory analysis indicates that Smith's church was not only a daring creation in the age of the (skeptical) press, but also that the publication and circulation of its own narratives actually formed the foundation for church identification. The community, moving between "I" and "we," was made possible or given form by this very "age of printing."

The identificatory strategies of Smith's "daring" work are easily compared to Benedict Anderson's argument regarding the centrality of localized print communities in the eighteenth- and nineteenth-century struggles for national recognition. The circulation of texts allowed readers to locate an idea of their community, constructing imagined borders of the nation, giving it a sense of enclosed space that is bounded both physically and temporally. Writing, in this structure, is "a practice, the endless production of an identity," as Michel de Certeau argues.[45] The practice of writing creates space, bordered space upon which a product (the text) is exchanged in the consuming act. This exchange, Certeau explains, is the essence of the scriptural economy that marks the modern sociality discussed by Anderson. The double isolation Certeau sees in this "scriptural apparatus," isolation from people and voice, is precisely the gap that creates the imaginary space upon which to project that modern community of the nation. There is no way to know fellow citizens through contact, Anderson argues, but print culture produces a space through which its scope can be imaginatively contained. The nation is *imagined* through the text "because the members of even the smallest nation will never know most of their fellow-members, meet them, or even hear of them, yet in the minds of each lives the image of their communion."[46]

Confronted with the challenge of creating a space for imagining community, the Mormons "dared" to write. Early Mormons were, and the LDS Church remains to this day, consummate record keepers. From documenting church activities, to publishing community newspapers tracking both local and global verifications of Mormon doctrine, to creating personal histories submitted to Books of Remembrance, the Mormon community in both its institutional and personal life produced and preserved great quantities of texts.[47] This profusion of textual production can be seen even in the daily journaling of its members. Many prominent early Mormons documented and published the stories of their daily lives (such as the work by Parley Pratt that introduced this chapter); this documentary mania carried over into the general populace as well. In his report on Mormon diaries and autobiographies, Davis Bitton writes that "it is hard to believe that any group of comparable size . . . has been so relentless as the Mormons in writing diaries and autobiographies," particularly in the nineteenth century.[48] One of the largest categories of autobiographical writing detailed by the Bitton report is the missionary diary.[49] These journals chronicled the experience of the Mormon missionaries and helped in part to understand and track communication between church branches, as missions were often structured as trips to other Mormon enclaves.[50] The church was spread out over a great deal of the country and these travels, and the diaries that documented them, functioned to undermine potentially divisive geographical distinctions by privileging a unified community. These texts, according to Certeau's economy, create a space, a page that "delimits a place of production for the subject."[51] The proselytizing "we" included these distant regions in their distinction from the Gentile or heathen "them," all while leaving, through the text, a trace upon the land. Publishing and circulating the diaries confirmed this inclusion and sense of community for the reader who was not necessarily herself one of these travelers.

The church did not rely solely on private writings to maintain its community across great distances but rather supplemented this journaling by publishing community newspapers that communicated the work of the church to its isolated enclaves. In England, Parley Pratt edited the *Millennial Star,* a Mormon newspaper that connected European adherents to the Saints in America by communicating, as the title page declares, "a great variety of useful information in regard to . . . the church of Jesus Christ of Latter-day Saints, and of the great work of God in these last days; with a faithful record of the signs and judgments which are beginning to be shown forth in the heavens and in the earth."[52] Its regular features included selections from *The Book of Mormon,* "News from the Saints in America," and "Signs of the Times," all articles that gathered the community under the aegis of shared texts and created for the diaspora the "existential experience" of community.[53] Reading, particularly for Anderson the reading of regional newspapers, is a shared private experience in which the reader is aware "that the ceremony he performs is being replicated simultaneously by . . . others of whose existence he is confident, yet of whose identity he has not the slightest notion."[54] Anderson argues that this new sense of community, based on the commodity culture that both includes and is encouraged by the growth of print, leads to the modern understanding of the nation as a limited sovereign community that conceives of itself as "a deep horizontal comradeship."[55] This "horizontal comradeship" depends, in Anderson's structure, upon the shared foundation of the "homogeneous, empty time" of "temporal coincidence . . . measured by clock and calendar."[56] This is marked in reading, he argues, by "the essential connection" among readers created by "the date at the top of the newspaper," the organizing medium that lends cohesion to its narrative, a shared location in time. This, Anderson is careful to point out, is not the "simultaneity of the past and future in an instantaneous present," the mark of prophecy or "Messianic time." Instead, this is the equalizing or democratizing "meanwhile" of the un-Event-ful secular or scientific experience of time.[57] But while Anderson juxtaposes this calendrical time to the "prefiguring and fulfilment" of Messianic time, this Mormon print community, and by extension the historical romances with which it shares its tropes, demonstrate the potential of a readership to consolidate through the shared consumption of revelation as well.

In early Mormon communities, their use of print to imagine a social relation was predicated upon the goal that this writing be "a faithful record of the signs," the shared material trace of a shared, prophetic history. Print culture was no afterthought in Mormon communities, but itself produced by the same prophecies that guided the faithful in their daily lives. Even the central narrative of *The Book of Mormon* itself could be described as the drama of inscription and circulation. From its opening description of the struggle to recover the plates of Laban (Nephi I) to Moroni's labor of recording and preserving the last words of his father, *The Book of Mormon* is preoccupied with the preservation and circulation of texts, populated by New World chroniclers whose holy work is to record the visions of their leaders and the events of their history in order to pass them down in written word. The early Mormon community mirrored this ancient script by connecting the holy work of the church with the work of the press. In Smith's Revelation 57, the same prophecy that reveals the original location of Zion and gives instructions for its settlement, the prophet declares that one of their members "be planted in this place, and be established as a printer unto the church," while another was to serve as his editor, "to copy, and to correct, and select, that all things may be right before me."[58] Even Eden, the beginning and the end, was to be settled in part by a visionary press.

These print communities come together not through the date on the page but rather by the apocalyptic "now" that marks their place as a point of fulfillment or realization. LDS foundational writings therefore demonstrate the continued deployment, rather than disappearance, of this proleptic or anticipatory narrative. They demonstrate that the modernity of social relations as defined by the constructive work of print culture need not also entail the wholesale disregard for the sacral discourse of prior social iterations. I see in the witnesses gathered by the river watching the sky fall, Smith's Follett sermon on the windy hilltop given just months before his death, and in Mormonism's central text *The Book of Mormon,* a way of challenging that narrative to better account for the pre-political *feeling* for community, one that draws together the affective work of mourning with the spatial practices of the national romance, the contemporaneous popular narratives that retold American history as a way to locate the nation. If we follow Anderson in neglecting the Messianic time of print culture, we risk misunderstanding those affective structures that sacralize the land and the bodies it contains as a means of consolidating the community *in* space by locating it *across* time.

By attending to the way these revelatory texts cultivate communities, this argument serves as a caution against the progressivist moves that Anderson sometimes makes in separating out this Messianic frame as itself lost to the past, a "dusk" in opposition to the "dawn" of print.[59] In doing so, we can attend more closely to the specter of that relationship between print communities and prophecy that haunts Anderson's study, a relationship that can be found in the grave signs that mark the opening and close of his book: the figure of death rendered legible upon the material marker of the tomb and the book. To "seek after our dead," as the citizen does when arrested by the tomb of the unknown soldier, as the historian does when exhuming narratives from the archive, as Smith urges his followers to do on that windy hilltop in Illinois, is to respond to the call of the dead, to be impressed into their service, and thus incorporated into their community. This venerative, mournful position is precisely that sacral prophetic simultaneity that Anderson marks as "wholly alien to our own."[60] It is, after all, the fear that "*even the dead* will not be safe from the enemy" that requires the Messianic vision of the historical materialist in Benjamin's theses. And it is to the past and its dead that we owe what remains in us of this "Messianic power."[61]

In *Dominion of the Dead,* Robert Pogue Harrison echoes this assertion of the foundational importance of the dead and the powerful hold of the dead over the living. "Whether we are conscious of it or not," he says, "we do the will of the ancestor." We are their creation, "authored always from the start by those that came before,"[62] and it is in our encounters with their memorials, those tombs and cenotaphs, that we are heralded by the text, the signs of their passing, and constituted by our consuming act of mourning. The community that gathers in and through *The Book of Mormon* and early Mormon writings not only evinces these humic foundations, but also attaches that necrogenic work to print culture itself. By attending to this corpus of church writings, we can better understand not just how a particular historical community consolidated through the production of texts, but also how print functions in this fetishistic economy of mourning at the heart of group psychology writ large. Harrison's acknowledgment of the authority of the dead, their constitutive hold over the living, offers us an opening onto Anderson's cenotaph, a way to expand the sociality of print culture to include the anticipatory voice of the dead who speak the living into being, precisely that Messianic voice that Anderson excludes when insisting on the secular modernity of national print culture. The dead have a "world-disclosive power," Harrison writes, an ecstatic power to gather and orient a community toward a future goal.[63] This is because the dead, as legible signs of death itself, are "the ultimate future possibility" of the subject. But this future possibility is also a return to the conditions that make possible the subject's birth as well. "As human beings," Harrison writes, "we are born of the dead—of the regional ground they occupy, of the languages they inhabited, of the worlds they brought into being, of the many institutional, legal, cultural, and psychological legacies that, through us, connect them to the unborn."[64] The dead do not pertain to the homogenous march of calendrical time precisely because they *perdure* in the "anachronic realm of the progenitors to whom the living remain beholden for their houses, their harvests, their laws, their customs, their patrimonies [and] their wisdom."[65] Mourning functions as a mode of confirming this heritage, of consuming the dead as a mode of affirming this very identification and indebtedness. The tomb incorporates the reader in its affective call, reminding her of a bond to her fellow readers, not through the simultaneity of the date on the page but rather as their shared location as the work of the dead upon the future, as the fulfillment of a foundational death that contains within it all such future iterations. Mourning, then, is necessarily prophetic in its narrative mode as the experience of loss or a passing produces the subject in the present. This is why, when Renan speaks of the sentimental side of nationalism, he produces the dead as evidence. "Of all the cults, that of the ancestors is most legitimate," he says, "for the ancestors have made us what we are."[66]

Voices Crying Out from the Dust

During the night of September 21, 1823, Joseph Smith was visited by a dead man who proceeded to map out his future. The visitant told the young man, then only seventeen years old, about a burial site in the hills near his home. There he would find redemption, for himself and the world, in the form of a book. Smith writes, "He said there was a book deposited . . . that the fullness of the everlasting Gospel was contained in it, as delivered by the Savior to the ancient inhabitants [of this continent]."[67] This event, which is recorded in Mormon Church history as Smith's Second Vision, was his first encounter with the angel Moroni, the celestial form of one of these ancient inhabitants, a prophet and chronicler of America who, "being dead and raised again therefrom,"[68] appeared to Joseph in order to incite this new prophet to exhume Moroni's writing from its resting place on the frontier.[69] Smith would not be able to retrieve the text, what would become known as *The Book of Mormon,* until the end of the decade, but it is this visitation, the announcement of all that will follow, that is laid out in official history as the foundational event for the Church of Jesus Christ of Latter-day Saints. It is here, in this Messianic moment, in which the past of Moroni, the present of Smith, and the future of the recovered text meet in "an instantaneous present,"[70] and it is to this moment that the Church-that-will-be returns to consume the narrative of its birth.

Smith's revelation is not the first vision that described the hills on the Western frontier as holding the redemptive remains of America's past. For several years prior to Smith's revelation, speculation regarding the earth mounds in Ohio and New York, as well as the Southern frontier in Virginia and the Carolinas, had become a popular topic among both professional and amateur antiquarians. In his *Notes on the State of Virginia,* Thomas Jefferson remarks on the "barrows" in which he discovers the bones of unknown people.[71] William Cullen Bryant wrote about these dead who "slumber" in the American landscape in his poetry.[72] And in 1820, just a few years before Moroni appears to Smith, the American Antiquarian Society's inaugural publication contained the first comprehensive survey of the mounds to date.[73] These mounds, most often understood as both burial places and fortifications, held the American historical imagination in thrall, offering, as remnants of the past, a connection between the new and ancient worlds. "Here," as critic Curtis Dahl points out, "were mighty ruins comparable to those of Egypt or Greece";[74] the land itself thus became "an emblem of antique grandeur."[75] This vision of American history transformed the earth itself into a tomb. Ohio, one writer declared, was "nothing but one vast cemetery of the beings of past ages,"[76] and the attendant excavations and exhumations were done in the hope that hidden in the land was evidence of a civilized legacy that would "rival" the European ruin and lay to rest those skeptical of the possibility of building a civilized nation in an uncivilized world.[77] The mounds offered unprecedented historical depth for the American landscape and so offered the newly established nation a chance at cultural redemption.

It is not surprising, then, that those Euramericans interested in the mounds discovered in them a melancholy narrative, not of a "savage" otherness, but of a "slain white race."[78] Accounts of the burial mounds insisted that they were evidence that ancient America was not the untamed, unkempt wilderness now before them but rather traces of a developed polity consisting of large cities and a burgeoning population.[79] And while the great mound builder civilization was a *n*ative American history, it was *not* an Indian history. Dahl notes that most studies of the structures agreed that "Mound-Builders were not Indians at all but men of a different and now extinct race."[80] In fact, when the Indian did find his way into this narrative, it was frequently as the exterminating force, the violent usurpers that wiped this civilized people from the earth. The poet Bryant, for instance, implied in his work that these builders "were not red men, for it was the red men who massacred them."[81] The mound builder narrative thus accomplishes the dual task of establishing America's claim to historical grandeur, and thus its potential to house a grand civilization again, while at the same time denying the viability of the Native American's claim to that civilization by divorcing him from its legacy, even blaming him for its disappearance, a doubled confirmation of his supposed barbarity. Veneration, in this historical narrative, was thus accompanied by erasure or condemnation. In the Indian's place, the white American, whose civilized and civilizing potential was seen as self-evident, rose to claim this heritage as his own, confirming his right to the land as his society expanded westward.[82] "The mounds," as Gordon Sayre writes, "made possible an imperial historiography in which western frontiersmen became the heirs to a classical civilization destroyed by invaders who were not truly *native* Americans."[83] These burial mounds thus became the scene of writing, not only a new past for America but a new present and future as well.

When Moroni appears to Joseph in 1823, he tells him that it is precisely this history of the ancient mound builders that the buried text will reveal. Smith's *History of the Church* records the announcement as "there was a book deposited, written upon gold plates, giving an account of the former inhabitants of this continent, and the sources from whence they sprang."[84] When Smith published his translation of the plates in 1830, the text contained a head note reminiscent of this announcement, saying that the text that followed was "an abridgement of the Record," or rather record*s* of the Peoples of Jared, Nephi and Laman; it offers "a Record" of the past, "*the* Record" of the people that came before.[85] The book is the "cornerstone" of the Mormon faith, and so it is often read by secular critics in the context of religious texts, but I would draw attention to how the text embraces the character of the chronicle and history, a narrative that *accounts* for or makes a *record* of America's past. While studies of *The Book of Mormon* frequently focus their analysis of the text and its production on the context of competing Evangelicalisms after the period called the Second Great Awakening,[86] I want to shift that focus here to this other, perhaps similarly devout discourse taking place at the same time: the question of an American history and how it would be written. *The Book of Mormon* offers a new way to read the latter issue precisely because of its engagement with the first. As Paul Gutjahr explains, *The Book of Mormon* "appeared at a time when religiously bent American readers were immersed in a print culture with two basic, overarching characteristics: the culture was saturated both with the Bible and with an interest in historical writing."[87] The popularity of the Bible is understandable in a period of revivalisms so strong they "burn over" New York, but it is the rising popularity of a particular fictional genre that both explains and aggravates the interest in history. This is the conquering historical romance, an incredibly popular genre that gave rise to the first proliferation of national literature in the New World.[88] It is a genre developed around the model of Sir Walter Scott's fiction that through close imitation developed as a domestic literary product with the help of American readers' hunger for Scott's texts. In James David Hart's study of popular fiction in North America during this period, the author states "from 1814, when Waverly appeared anonymously, to 1832, when the last of the Tales of My Landlord was issued, [Scott's] novels were the most popular of all American pleasure reading."[89] The author and politician Samuel Goodrich (1793–1860) said of the Scott model: "Everybody read these works; everybody—the refined and the simple—shared in the delightful trances which seemed to transport them to remote ages,"[90] and author Catharine Maria Sedgwick (1789–1867) said of one of Scott's novels: "I salute it with as much enthusiasm as a Catholic would a holy relic."[91] Scott's romances thus created a shared reading experience, a consumption in kind that allowed one to imagine her fellow readers as part of a particular community.[92] The popularity of Scott also provided American writers with a useful model for narrating their own past, supplanting his Highland history with an American heritage. This desire on the part of the reading public to consume historical narratives led to a dramatic increase in national production of the genre, peaking during the 1820s when "almost a third of the novels written by Americans dealt with the colonial period or the Revolution."[93] The devout readers of historical romance, taking in a text in the sacrosanct manner of a "holy relic," thus formed the basis of a national readership and the texts that responded to their call transformed the Scottish medieval landscape into a more familiar one.

While *The Book of Mormon* does not take as its object colonization or revolution in the traditional sense, its layered narrative does circulate around a people's journey to the New World and their schisms and struggles and deaths there. This structure is instantly recognizable by the American reader as that of her own family, her own nation in its journey west to the New World and its struggle to establish a thriving, independent society. The "Golden Bible," as it was called by contemporaneous critics, thus explicitly engaged with this interest in national history and, as a textual artifact, participated in the material scene of the book. For Mormons, history was not a distinct interest apart from scripture; for these Americans, as Harold Bloom argues, "their history *is* sacred."[94] The righteous Nephites, the last of whom will visit Joseph in 1823, were not a people of the Book, but a people of the book*s*. When Lehi receives his revelation of the Promised Land, it is a vision of a book that guides him, his divine knowledge the product of reading.[95] Before his family can leave for this new land, Lehi sends his sons to retrieve another book, the brass plates that contain "the record of the Jews and also a genealogy of my forefathers" (1 Nephi 3:3), in order for the family to "preserve unto our children the language of our fathers; and also that we may preserve unto them the words which have been spoken by the mouth of all the holy prophets" (1 Nephi 3:19–20). If *The Book of Mormon* can be characterized as a foundational text, both as the "cornerstone" of a religion and an explanation of New World origins, then it is one that rests in its turn on the foundation *of* the text, or rather, two texts: the brass plates of history and the visionary book of revelation. Even when the presence of a prior civilization is announced, it appears *as a text,* the book of Ether, which tells the story of the Jaredites that preceded Lehi and his family in settling in this Promised Land and is itself absorbed into Moroni's record ("And now I Moroni proceed to give an account of those ancient inhabitants which were destroyed by the hand of the Lord. . . . And I take mine account from the twenty and four plates which were found by the people of Limhi," Ether 1:1–2). The American past in *The Book of Mormon* addresses itself to its future in the form of its present reader. The past creates, in advance of its coming, a space for the present, incorporating the present reader into its heritage through its prophetic voice.

In her introduction to the Penguin edition of *The Book of Mormon,* religious studies scholar Laura Maffly Kipp notes that "The Book of Mormon does not dictate lifestyle traits or health codes, nor does it educate readers about priesthood hierarchy, ordinances for the dead, esoteric rites, or eternal marriages. The Book of Mormon is, first of all, a story of ancient peoples."[96] The text, as Smith himself directed, was to be understood as a history, and the "curious book" was received by many as yet another iteration of the popular historical romance.[97] The text itself foregrounds history and historiography, the chroniclers often speaking of this purpose and process in their record. Nephi, for example, frequently reflects on his motivations, both in his past, within the narrative he records, and in the present of his writing. After describing his family's flight to the "land of promise" (1 Nephi 18:25), Nephi turns to consider again the work of writing. "I did make plates of ore that I might engraven upon them the record of my people," he notes, "and upon the plates which I made I did engraven the record of my father" (1 Nephi 19:1). He then quickly moves to a consideration of reception and the work of reading the history he records, writing, "Now it came to pass that I Nephi did teach my brethren these things. And it came to pass that I did read many things to them which were engraven upon the plates of brass, that they might know concerning the doings of the Lord in other lands among people of old" (1 Nephi 19:22). Nephi here marks the reading of history as not only instructive but also restorative; he reads these historical writings to his community in order to recall them to their proper heritage: "Hear ye the words of the prophet, ye which are a remnant of the house of Israel, a branch which have been broken off... that ye may have hope as well as your brethren from whom ye have been broken off" (1 Nephi 19:24). And directly before this remonstrance to read and remember, Nephi is careful to remember his own readership, which has yet to come. He writes, "I, Nephi, have written these things unto my people, *that perhaps I might persuade them that they would remember* the Lord their Redeemer" (1 Nephi 19:18, emphasis added). Just as reading functions as a restorative remembrance, here he reflects his own writing as a memorial act, its goal the future performance of memory. Nephi's sense for posterity, as this pairing demonstrates, is not limited to the history that he and his brethren have inherited, but includes those who *will have inherited,* the present reader who is enfolded into this community by the text.

Emphasizing its work as a chronicle, the text is marked by an aggressive chronological structure that foregrounds the passage of time. The phrase "and it came to pass" overwhelms the opening of the text; seven of the first fourteen verses contain versions of the phrase that Fawn Brodie claims appears at least two thousand times in the text.[98] This repeated structure announces the progress of time in the text, what will become history as it comes "to pass," marking that history itself as sacred, and transforming the present community of readers into a realization of a pre-scribed destiny.[99] As Robert Flanders argues, Smith saw his work and himself "as a kind of prime agent in inaugurating the new premillennial history . . . a hinge between the old profane history and a new sanctified one."[100] The book published by Smith in 1830 is a history composed of several chronicles, a single tome but multiple texts. Together, these texts tell the story of two Jewish immigrant groups from the Middle East: the Jaredites, who came to America at the fall of Babel, grew into a society that numbered in the millions and self-destructed, leaving a lone survivor to record their history; and the Lehites who came to America around 600 BC, split into two fraternal factions, one following the righteous prophet Nephi and the other his jealous brother Laman, whose descendents eventually exterminate those of the former, again leaving one survivor to record the events of the end.[101] The Lamanites, debased by their neglect of both religion and civil society, physically darkened to mark their fallen state ("that they might not be enticing . . . the Lord God did cause a skin of blackness to come upon them," 2 Nephi 5:21), survive in their contemporary descendants, American Indians.

The narrative is thus remarkably similar to the structure of popular mound builder theories. It describes an advanced, exterminated race while condemning the Native American for its death. Like the burial mound narratives, *The Book of Mormon* presents its reader with familiar bodies but pushes this identification even further by making these bodies not only *not* Indian but *white* and not only advanced but *Christian.* The Nephite race is "white and exceeding fair" (2 Nephi 5:21), marked in contrast to their dark brethren and, while they began their New World venture as part of the Jewish diaspora, they receive the ministry of Christ in America and so become Christians, distinct from the Lamanites, who "have rejected the gospel of Christ" (Ether 4:3). The Nephites had, through the prophecies of Nephi and Jacob, already heard of "this Jesus Christ" (3 Nephi 11:2), but Christ realizes this work of prophecy himself by appearing in the text, revealing himself to the inhabitants of the New World. "Behold, I am Jesus Christ—of which the prophets testified—that should come into the world," he tells them, inviting all to investigate his mortal wounds, confirming his identity through the signs of his death and asking them to *remember* the (historic) prophecy of his coming (3 Nephi 11:10–15). He ministers to all, and in doing so brings about a period of peace between the two groups, but only the fair Nephites retain their faith and finally only Moroni remains to beseech his reader to remember. He concludes the text by saying: "I exhort you to remember these things, for the time speedily cometh that ye shall know that I lie not, for ye shall see me at the bar of God. And the Lord God will say unto you: did I not declare my words unto you, which was written by this man like as one crying from the dead, yea, even as one speaking out of the dust?" (Moroni 10:27). This prophetic cry is structured as a mournful wail from the dead and so the text draws the ear of the reader near the earth to listen to the grave narrate its destiny. The text's frequent invocation of the reader gives him material space on the page ("you . . . ye . . . ye . . . you . . . you"), and inscribes upon him a future accounting, not only with the figure of history ("ye shall see me at the bar of God") but also with the figure of historiography, the "words . . . which [were] written by this man." If the living hold the "awful responsibility," as Smith named it, of "seeking after our dead," then this includes the dead letter, the text itself.

Moroni's is not the only grave that speaks, either. Nephi concludes his books in the same sepulchral voice. Acknowledging his impending death, he says, "I speak unto you as the voice of one crying from the dust" (2 Nephi 33:13). Here the dust, that material connection between the bodies of the present and those of the past, echoes with the voice of one who bids two farewells, one to the reader who heeds—who *responds to*—his words ("farewell until that great day shall come") and another to those who will not hear his cry. "Behold," Nephi says to those unresponsive readers, "I bid you an everlasting farewell, for these words shall condemn you at the last day. For what I seal on earth shall be brought against you at the judgment bar" (2 Nephi 33:14–15). *The Book of Mormon* thus opens and closes with writers calling out from the grave, these sepulchral voices requiring response from the living by reminding them simultaneously of a shared past and a future reconciliation. The text also posits a foundational vacancy for the Americas, a primary emptiness marked by the stories of immigration, stories that all occur within the frame of documented history. There are no shadowy, mythical beginnings for a native race. First there is nothing, and, as the texts mark upon it, the land is filled; the book thus clears the ground of any claim to immemorial nativity and leaves only the voice of these familiar dead. All here are immigrants and it is only through the word of God that this promised land is made available for settlement.[102] It is only through the work of the prophet, the figure who mediates between mankind and the Word, that their land can become "the land of their inheritance" (1 Nephi 13:30), and it is only through the book that one can access this prophetic voice. It is into this blank page, this primary vacancy, that the dead prophets are interred; if these prophets speak from the grave, as both Moroni and Nephi assert, that grave is at the same time the earth, body, and book, and so the text functions as a memorial not only to the past but also to those who have passed.

The reader is thus hailed by the dead who speak from this grave, called by bodies so familiar in their social identifications that they function as an anticipation of the reader herself. If I were there that would be me, she says, and, as he goes so will I. But even as the reader volunteers identification by mourning this familiar form, she has *already* been spoken into the text by its prophets. In his study of the text, Monte Nyman says that "The Book of Mormon is unique because it was written hundreds of years ago but is addressed to and for a people hundreds of years in the future."[103] The arrival of the Gentile in the Promised Land, the revelation of *The Book of Mormon,* and the absorption of the faithful Gentile into the New World heritage has already been revealed by the text (1 Nephi 13). Nephi writes:

> And it came to pass that I beheld many multitudes of the Gentiles upon the land of promise. And I beheld the wrath of God, that it was upon the seed of my brethren [the Lamanites]. And they were scattered before the Gentiles and they were smitten. And I beheld the Spirit of the Lord, that it was upon the Gentiles, that they did prosper and obtain the land for their inheritance. And I beheld that they were white and exceeding fair and beautiful, like unto my people before that they were slain. (1 Nephi 13: 14–15)

Here the ancient prophet sees the Gentile lay claim to the land, removing the Indian with the blessing of divine order. Nephi also describes the Revolution, during which the Gentile was "delivered by the power of God" (1 Nephi 13:19) from "their mother Gentiles" (1 Nephi 13:17), and finally the coming of a book that will restore truth to the land, the adherents of which "shall be numbered among the seed of [Nephi's] father. . . . And they shall be a blessed people upon the promised land forever" (1 Nephi 14:2). The reader is already inscribed in the book, already impressed into its service, and so the prophetic history marks upon the present subject, interpolating her into this new narrative of history. Through Smith's later restoration of the Aaronic priesthood, this prophetic incorporation becomes a corporeal one as well. While the future Saints were "cultural Gentiles," their true heritage, Smith revealed, pertained to the same family as that of these ancient people, and therefore they were "lawful heirs, according to the flesh" as well.[104]

The incorporating work of these prophecies is supported by the structure in which they are spoken in *The Book of Mormon.* The experience of revelation in the book of Nephi repeats the event of witnessing by pairing the injunction to "Look!" with the responses "and I looked" and "and I beheld" (1 Nephi 11–14). "Look! And I looked," Nephi writes over and over:

> "And it came to pass that the Spirit saith unto me: Look! And I looked and beheld a tree. . . . And it came to pass that [the spirit] said unto me: Look! And I looked as if to look upon him and I saw him not, for he had gone from before my presence. . . . And the angel said unto me again: Look and behold the condescension of God! And I looked and beheld the Redeemer of the world. . . . And it came to pass that the angel spake unto me, saying: Look! And I looked and I beheld the heavens open again. . . . And he spake unto

> me again, saying: Look! And I looked and beheld the Lamb of God going forth among the children of men. . . . And it came to pass that the angel spake unto me again, saying: Look! And I looked and beheld the Lamb of God, that he was taken by the people. . . . And it came to pass that the angel said unto me: Look and behold thy seed and also the seed of thy brethren. And I looked and beheld the land of promise." (1 Nephi 11:8–12:1)

Here, Nephi describes the work of a spirit, an angel, upon him, but in his repetition of the imperative paired with the first-person assent to the required action, he also hails the reader by pairing the command with the descriptive text. Nephi is told to look, and he does, but in doing so he reflects the position of his reader, who is also enjoined also to "look." Like Smith's "anti-confessional" writings, which enfold multiple subject positions within the assertion of an "I," this first-person observation point "and I looked" becomes the "I"/eye of the reader as she witnesses the revelation as well. But the reader is not limited to the "I" of Nephi's witnessing. This first-person incorporation is echoed in the structure of testimony carried throughout the text. *The Book of Mormon* opens with the words "I, Nephi," an identification that he repeats over and over in the hundreds of pages filled by his chronicle. When others interrupt the text, they present themselves in the same manner. "I, Jacob," his brother's speech begins; "I, Jacob. . . . I, Jacob" it repeats until it returns to "I, Nephi," then "I, Mormon," and finally to Moroni, who begins the last chapter of the text "Now I, Moroni" (Moroni 10:1). The proliferation of authors laying claim to that "I" means that these declarations do not function as assertions of autonomy or individuality but rather become through their repetition a corporate "I" of testimony. As the reader identifies with this prophetic heritage, the "I," jumbled among the numerous narrators, becomes her eye/"I" as well, her own witnessing of and testimony to the past.

The Book of Mormon, as a collection of records, thus functions as a memorial akin to Anderson's tomb, one that arrests the subject, that requires from the living an acknowledgment of their connection to those who have passed. The Mormon historical revelation bequeaths to the Americas not only a locatable native heritage, but also what Renan described as "the will to perpetuate the value of that heritage," the responsibility of the present to pass on this legacy. In this way the consent of the community is founded on an absence that presses upon the subject and directs her actions toward a future. This is what Robert Pogue Harrison describes as the *humic* foundation of community, the foundational burial that renders the land habitable for human society. The dead retain ownership of a legacy inherited by the living and, whether or not this is the Lamanites' suffering due to the iniquity of their fathers or the Nephites' compulsion to record and thus preserve the words of the past, the dead mark upon the living and hold sway over the future. While it may be easy, then, to place *The Book of Mormon* in conversation with the larger contemporaneous national concern for the past, that which emerges in both the mound builder writings and the lineages outlined in the popular historical romance, we shouldn't do so without considering the revelatory or Messianic time in which such narratives structure the reader's relationship to the text, and through the text, to those historical communities that ground (or rather give ground) to her sense of self. Like *The Book of Mormon,* all of these texts revisit their national histories in order to discover traces of a shared heritage. The heritage they trace, though, does not proceed in the homogenous empty time of Anderson's newspaper, but rather in the proleptic, anticipatory time of revelation, the coincidence of past and future in the present that marks Messianic time, in which both the dead of the past and the unborn of the future come to bear upon the present. In attempting to retell a history that *foretells* the present, these texts—including *The Book of Mormon*—demonstrate how mourning becomes a way to inscribe prophecy into history. The *perdurance* of the voice of the dead, manifest in the material of the text, imagines the space of the reader for her, and her responsibility to that voice requires her to fulfill that promise laid out for her in advance by the text, the land, her body.

2

Sovereign Tears, or, The Indian Is History

"Fathers! Sons!" said Mohegan with firmness—"all gone—all gone! I have no son but the Young Eagle, and he has the blood of a white man."

—Cooper, *The Pioneers*

The worst feature in the history of those years, is, that no man spake for the Indian.

—Emerson, "At Concord"

Vengaréis la América

In 1826, the historical romance *Jicoténcal* was published anonymously in Philadelphia. The novel's subject is Mexican, focusing on the eponymous Tlascaltecan general, and for years it was considered by scholars to be the first historical romance written in Spanish, an honor it has since conceded to *Ramiro, conde de Lucena* (1823).[1] But *Jicoténcal*'s early appearance is notable in that the genre, while popular in the United States at the time, did not become so in Spanish-language literature and in particular the publishing markets of Latin America until the middle and latter half of the century. The romance was the first in Spanish to take as its subject the era of conquest in the New World and so, as Mercedes Baquero Arribas argues, "nos coloca en una situación privilegiada para observar el nacimiento de la interpretación de la conquista de América en el romanticismo [gives us a privileged vantage point from which to observe the birth of the interpretation of the conquest of America in Romanticism],"[2] an important vantage point because considerations of conquest would become a prominent setting for the national novel that, in its search for patriotic origins, displaced the rupture of revolution onto a more distant historical scene.[3]

Shortly after its publication, William Bryant offered a review and lengthy translated sample from the romance in the *United States Review and Literary Gazette*.[4] The review noted that the journal had been "principally induced to notice this book on account of its belonging to the Spanish literature of America," an exceptionalism that identified the novel as both an exotic artifact and an area of growing interest for English-speaking Americans.[5] The review focused primarily on the historical romance's presentist political arguments, "enlightened notions on political government and other important subjects" designed to introduce political philosophy to readers of fiction, those described by the reviewer as seeking only amusement, "who look upon books as a quiet and innocent expedient to get rid of their time."[6] Comparing this work to that giant of the genre Sir Walter Scott and his efforts at "political conversion" through historical plotting, the reviewer credits the author of *Jicoténcal* with effectively sneaking something more substantial into the amusements of fiction: "By frequent references to important principles scattered throughout the works which naturally come into the hands of this class of readers . . . the rudiments of an opinion are sometimes communicated to those who never expected to trouble themselves with reflection on such subjects."[7] The reviewer thus identifies the novel as broadening the appeal of modern *liberales* by transforming their contemporary political arguments into historical complaints against conquest, a move that places the novel in a continuum with the already-popular Indianist rhetoric of creole nationalism that pervaded contemporary political debates, patriotic displays, and even Spanish American poetry. Translating the contingencies of political identification into the patrimony of New World nationalism, this popular troping of the nation identified the emerging postcolonial states with tragic Indian predecessors, figures like Jicoténcal who were "crushed in the ruin of that country's liberties" even as they traced an indigenous "degradation" that made possible this original loss of sovereignty. "Such," the reviewer notes, "is the political tendency of the tale; it has also a love-plot for the youths and maidens."[8]

In tracing the political work of the historical setting and in disregarding as secondary the "love plot" of the novel, the reviewer elides the emotional logic connecting the tragedy of conquest to the triumph of early national romances in the Americas, overlooking how readers who "get rid of their time" by reading such historical romances engage in what Achille Mbembe calls the "chronophagy" that creates the state, the work of "consuming the past" as a way to free itself from its constitutive violence.[9] In theorizing the archive as an "instituting imaginary" of the state, both as an edifice and in its identification of documents worthy of preservation, Mbembe calls the mass consumption of popular historical narratives a "talisman" that protects the state,[10] one that "[removes] any subversive factor in memory" by making the public into a "community of time, the feeling according to which we would all be heirs to a time over which we might exercise the rights of collective ownership."[11] Mbembe writes that "in giving those who carry it (in this case those who consume it) a feeling of being protected or of being co-owner of a time or a co-actor in an event, even if in the past, the talisman softens the anger, shame, guilt, or resentment which the archive tends, if not to incite, then at least to maintain, because of its function of recall."[12] This ownership of the past that institutes a community is made possible by the archive's relationship to death. Mbembe describes the collective historical memory (produced by the collection of artifacts in the archive) as "rooted in death as an architectural event. A death has to occur to give rise to a time characterised by not belonging to a private individual, precisely because this time, from that moment on, founds or institutes something."[13] Attending to this foundational work of death gives us a new way of understanding both the seductive love plot of the historical romance and the work of popular historiography, seeing these as an extension of what Mbembe calls the necropolitics that characterizes state power.[14] By expanding this power over the death of the other to include the cultural imaginary of national feeling, we can see how literary narratives make space for the nation, calling their readers into a community of time as do *The Book of Mormon* and early LDS church writings. These texts institute and repeat a foundational loss for the nation, offering a structuring death to the reader and so becoming sites of mourning through which the creole present lays claim to the past.

Recuperating this "love plot" as central rather than supplementary to the "political tendency of the tale," we can see how *Jicoténcal* cultivates a devotion not between a living couple but rather between the living and the dead, the affective investment of a reader who mourns a seminal loss. The inscription of foundational deaths into the national heritage is, after all, central to *Jicoténcal,* which chronicles disintegration instead of union. In an extratextual gloss of the historical setting, Bryant's review notes that Jicoténcal's execution is witnessed and mourned by "his countrymen, by whom he was beloved and venerated" and who, afterward, "cut his garments in pieces, and carried them away as sacred relics," identifying a contemporaneous polis consolidated through the common consumption of Jicoténcal's remains.[15] But while the death of the hero remains an important touchstone in the text itself, the performance of mourning in the novel is quite different. As the presentist framing of Bryant's review indicates, the novel celebrates the fervent patriotism, proto-Christianity, and republican values of Jicoténcal and his noble wife, Teutila, by isolating them from their historical community, and nowhere is this alienation more clearly expressed than in their death scenes, twinned losses that conclude the narrative. In considering his own imminent death, Jicoténcal imagines it as a sacrifice that will awaken his people and inspire resistance. "La horrorosa muerte que me espera, los tormentos que sufro, van a despertar tu antiguo valor . . . vengaréis la América [The horrifying death that awaits me, the torments that I suffer, they will awaken your ancient valor . . . you will avenge America]."[16] Alone, he addresses his thoughts to his native Tlascala, but the reader is the sole witness to this call to action. At the execution, the hero is first gagged and then drugged so that he can neither resist nor call for resistance, and so Jicoténcal's death is doubly muted, his own silence mirrored in the response of the gathered crowd that the narrator describes as "una quietud estúpida," a stillness "que demuestra su envilecimiento y que evidencia que dobló para siempre la cerviz al yugo que le tiene preparado la tiranía [that demonstrates their debasement and shows that they had bent their necks forever to the yoke that tyranny had prepared for them]."[17] Privy to Jicoténcal's eloquent vision of sacrifice, the reader is here distanced from those who cannot hear his words and are therefore unable to mourn, an inability that becomes evidence of a passive, permissive, and forever-colonized people.

This contrast between those who do mourn and who do not, and the connection between this lament and sovereignty, is further emphasized in Teutila's response to Jicoténcal's execution. At the conclusion and emotional climax of the romance, that portion of the text translated in the English-language review and offered as exemplary of the author's work, Teutila becomes herself an agent of death. Deciding to avenge her husband's death by killing his murderer and escaping retribution by poisoning her own body, Teutila transforms herself into a martyr whose self-sacrifice both claims power over another through annihilation and reclaims sovereignty over her own body, even as it is reduced to the raw material for inscribing the subject who will have emerged through death. She drinks the poison and sends for Cortés, but the Conquistador is fatefully delayed. Arriving too late to be consumed himself, Cortés and the reader instead bear witness to Teutila's torturous final moments. Overcome by the spectacle of death, Cortés waivers on the edge of repentance and retreat, only to finally recommit himself fully to conquest. "Esta dolorosa escena es ya demasiado larga," Cortés declares, "El camino que conduce al templo de la fama tiene grandes tropiezos y, por lo mismo, es tan glorioso vencerlos . . . Mañana salimos para Méjico [This painful scene is already too long.

The road that leads to the temple of fame has great impediments and, by the same measure, it is so glorious to defeat them . . . Tomorrow we leave for Mexico]."[18] Witnessing the death of the other, Cortés experiences his survival as an exceptional state, a confirmation of his own sovereignty expressed as colonial occupation. But Cortés is not the only witness who remains. The heroine's rumination on loss and the spectacle of her tragic death scene draw the reader into a community of feeling with the dying figure whose struggle to avenge the tyranny of Cortés recalls in advance a rallying cry of Spanish American independence. Through their deaths, Jicoténcal and Teutila emerge from the romance as a prefigurative polis. Their values and struggles are echoes of the present-day creole, the anticipation in the indigenous past of a *criollo* future. The pair's dying proclamations of a vengeance yet to come mark their deaths as "laboring under the sign of the future,"[19] translating their struggle to end European occupation into an as-yet unfulfilled promise inscribed into the prehistory of the nation.

In consuming the narrative, contemporary readers lament these losses and so prepare for their own independence as a continuation of that struggle, a substitution (fighting as or on behalf of) that is predicated upon a primary assertion of vacancy (there is no one left to fight for themselves). "Vengaréis la América," the reader hears Jicoténcal declare to the empty room. The novel thus participates in the work of disentangling the creole reader from Spanish filiation and legitimizing his claims to a native sovereignty, translating creole nationalism as an indigenous patriotism, a birthright claimed through the sighs and tears of the romance's reader that evoke simultaneously a feeling in common and the exceptional position of the survivor, the one who remains to mourn the loss. In this way, the romance's historical displacement also demonstrates an anxiety regarding the consuming forces of identification, maintaining an important site of difference from the exceptional Indigenous figures that it lauds. This distance is granted by its mournful position that celebrates the lost Indigenous figure even as it disavows a contemporary identification with the *indio* who is marked by the inability to mourn and so divorced from those who have fallen, never to return. In his essay "Reflections on Exile," Edward Said writes that nationalism, an "assertion of belonging in and to a place, a people, a heritage," retains an "essential association" with exile, a dis-locative or negative space of *un*belonging that is "like death, but without death's ultimate mercy."[20] This displacement marks the narrative structure of the subject-as-exile as a mournful one, a commemorative invocation of a loss that can never be repaired even if the subject himself is repatriated. But in the narrative of creole nativism authorized by the early national discourses in the United States and Spanish America, writers not only curate a sense of national belonging by affective investments in "a place, a people, a heritage," but also appropriate the exilic lament as its narrative voice, foreclosing its use by any antagonistic site of Otherness, ensuring that there are no other survivors. This doubled disavowal of New World nationalism produces what Jodi Byrd describes as the unfixed "non-recuperative category" of Indianness that can then be deployed by the state as a figuration of otherness barred from the experience of melancholy and grief, the "distances and sutures of recognitions and belongings."[21] By cathecting these tragic figures, the national novel draws on the commemorative work of mourning in order to gather a community of readers into a community of time marked by their shared foundational loss while at the same time insisting upon the temporal displacement of that loss to which mourning responds. Jicoténcal and Teutila are not lost in the present, but in the past, and through their deaths they become foundational figures by creating a space, an original loss, upon which the creole can trace his connection to the land and its history.

Sovereignty: A Vanishing Act

The first edition of Catherine Maria Sedgwick's historical romance *Hope Leslie; or Early Times in Massachusetts* (1827) opens with a poem on the title page, a preview of (or perhaps a warning about) the narrative inside. The two stanzas, attributed only to "E." read as follows:

> Here stood the Indian chieftain, rejoicing in his glory!
> How deep the shade of sadness that rests upon his story:
> For the white man came with power—like brethren they met—
>
> But the Indian fires went out, and the Indian sun has set!
> And the chieftain has departed—gone is his hunting ground,
> And the twanging of his bow-string is a forgotten sound:—
> Where dwelleth yesterday? and where is Echo's cell?
> Where has the rainbow vanished?—there does the Indian dwell.[22]

The stanzas, selected from the poem "Sachem's Hill" by Eliza Lee Cabot Follen, describe the former inhabitant of the eponymous hill located outside

Boston.[23] It was in this place, Follen notes in her preface to the complete poem, that a group of friendly Native Americans lived until their demise at the hand of an unnamed epidemic that occurs *after* the colonists appear but is not, in Follen's preface, causally linked to the Europeans. "In a short time," she writes, "nothing was left of them," except "the name of this little hill, which some suppose . . . was given to this state."[24] The material upon which she inscribes her poem, then, is only a vague reminder of a long-gone community, gesturing to a lost figure who, even in the verses dedicated to him, remains unspecified, unnamed. He is only "the chieftain," the "sachem," whose removal made space for and, through "a light alteration," gave title to the new colony in her genealogical tracing. The shadowy, passive structure of this last gift ("the name . . . was given to this state") removes the state in question from the active stance of *taking* the land or name. The giver is, like the Sachem himself, mysteriously removed.[25]

This missing actor also fails to appear in the poem itself. The first stanza, not included in Sedgwick's novel, describes the Sachem gazing out from his hill, actively and possessively *taking in* the landscape: "His were the pathless forests, and his the hills so blue; / And on the restless ocean danced only his canoe."[26] The "eagle eye" of the Sachem gazes down from his seat of power, seeing all and seeing all of it as *his.* The repetition of the possessive pronoun reinforces not only his stature but his very existence as well. The forests, the hills, the canoe are all material signs of *his* world, the objects that serve to establish his identity. But these physical objects are, like the Sachem himself, supplanted by "yesterday," an "echo" and a "rainbow," the immaterial and ultimately unlocatable Native life that concludes Sedgwick's selection. When the poet imagines the possible return of the departed and the opportunity for a new gaze, the powerful and possessive Sachem of the first stanza is presented as a passive, captive audience. "Should his free-born spirit descend again to earth," the poet writes, ". . . Would not his altered nature rejoice with rapture high/ at the changed and glorious prospect that now would meet his eye?" By using "eye" at the end of the line, as conclusion to the rhyme scheme, the voice recalls the only other such ending, the second line of the opening stanza, "Glanced over hill and valley the Sachem's eagle eye." In this return, though, the voice rewrites the Sachem's possessive eye/I as a passive receptor. In the revision, the "changed and glorious prospect" acts *upon* the Sachem's eye, his "altered nature" no longer able to summon the sense of entitlement with which he had previously viewed the land. In this new prospect, the material signs of white life, the "stately domes . . . happy homes . . . village bells . . . and many a gleaming spire, of faith in Jesus tells,"[27] overwhelms the Sachem, allowing him to overcome his feelings of loss and revenge with a holy calm,[28] a calm sanctified by death. In this imagined return, the Sachem becomes a passive object through which to project white postcolonial gratification for the accomplishments of their colonial predecessors. The Native American, once spectator, becomes the speculum through which the author can reveal her own origins.

Mediating between the "Here . . . glanced" of the first stanza and the "has departed" of the remainder of the poem is the moment of contact, "like brethren they met." But missing between the Indian's material and active existence and immaterial and passive afterlife is the event of removal itself. Instead, the verse describing contact moves directly to an extinguished Native population: "But the Indian fires went out, and the Indian sun has set." The active potential of "went out" is limited by the intransitive verb; the object here does not receive the action but rather itself functions as the subject of the verb, excluding the possibility of an external actor and maintaining a silence about the conditions that made this extinguishment possible. This gap is reinforced by the transformation of the departure into a sunset, a movement that remains external to, even in defiance of, human action. Just as the poet is silent in her preface regarding the origins of the epidemic that wiped the tribe from the pages of history, so the poem itself describes the Natives' departure while refusing to acknowledge its cause. The poem's structure thus makes removal simultaneous with but not causally connected to white settlement, removing, along with the transitive verbs, the assignation of responsibility for this "shade of sadness." Nothing is permitted to act upon and therefore no actor can be held responsible. The poet then goes on to make the departed Indian into a symbol for an immaterial afterlife, but she gives the Native "the land of deathless glories" without giving him death itself. The parting of the Indian is a *non*-event: "in the land of spirits," the poet writes, "the Indian has a place," but behind him he leaves no remains; he has death with no actual dead. In contrast to the insistent physicality of the gaze in the first stanza, "*Here,* from this hillock," the Sachem is now "*there,* midst saints and angels" (emphasis added), a spirit in the unlocatable beyond. "Where?" the third stanza asks, "Where? . . . Where?" but the answer, the "there," is *no* place. The removal is a complete one, tinged with an amnesia compelled by the mystery of this disappearance. The Native American's absence is one with no memorial, making him, like the "forgotten sound," outside of memory. Instead, the Native becomes a way to imagine other, more recognizable deaths, like those of the "friends we love so dearly" that conclude the poem. The Sachem's death, a death that remains inscrutable, is in the end a way to understand the mortal inheritance of the present community. By revealing the Native American as a presence barred from our understanding and physical reality, the poet can recognize by contrast the continued presence of these more familiar dead in "all the treasures of their souls [that] shall be with us forever."[29]

Following the poem, Sedgwick's romance reinforces the removal of Native and narration. Her novel tells the story of one Indian maiden's sacrifices, both social and corporeal, that made possible the survival of a white colonial man and later the reunion of his future bride and her captive sister. Magawisca's heroic action is selfless, as Nina Baym notes, saving Everell Fletcher not for herself "but for white culture and the white heroine Hope Leslie,"[30] but it is also self-effacing. Instead of a hero's reward, Magawisca is banished from the scene of the novel in a voluntary exile that erases her claim to land, heart, and page. For much of the novel, Magawisca's active and affecting presence dominates the narrative as she struggles between loyalties to her family and her white friends. But she ultimately fades, ceding her place to the title character in the last two-thirds of the text, and the reader, perhaps confused by the focus of the novel thus far, is reminded by this concession that this is indeed the story of *Hope Leslie.* Magawisca's early heroic work, including her spectacular Pocahontas-like intervention on behalf of Everell Fletcher that costs her an arm, is supplanted by the eponymous Hope, who becomes "*our* heroine" (emphasis added),[31] even as Magawisca "disappeared forever."[32] This triumph of the white colonial subject over her Native rival (both in love and as an alternative focus for the affections of the reader) also necessitates the departure of other Indians that remain. Both women are restored to their families, but while Hope joins the Fletchers in their foundational efforts in Connecticut, Magawisca and the Pequots "began their pilgrimage to the far western forests." "That which remains untold of their story," the narrator says, "is lost in the deep, voiceless obscurity of those unknown regions."[33] Sedgwick concludes the historical contest between white settler and Native Americans in the language of removal, but a removal that seems to resist comparisons to contemporaneous political debates surrounding Indian Removal policy in the United States by framing the migration not only as voluntary but, more precisely, as a "pilgrimage." Envisioning it as a pilgrimage, Sedgwick transforms removal into a devotional act, its sacred destination "unknown," remaining beyond the veil, reserved from white understanding. The Native Americans' story is, through this pilgrimage, "lost in the deep, voiceless obscurity" of this no-place and so their geographical displacement becomes a temporal one as well. Their (hi)story ends with removal, the rest, including their possible survival, is illegible: "voiceless" as a "forgotten sound," "unknown" and "lost" as the "yesterday," "echo," and "rainbow" in Follen's verse. The exile's dislocation is not only a physical absence of the subject but a supplementary material loss as well. What lingers in Follen's verse and Sedgwick's prose is only the recognition of passing; the recovery of the subject himself remains impossible because he remains *undocumented,* an exile "without a tellable history."[34] This persistence of *lost* memory reinforces the connection between the material documents of memory and the possibility of a narratable subject, maintaining the undocumented subject *exterior to* the figure of the citizen.[35]

To turn the reader's mind from what she cannot know (or rather what she is kept from knowing), the novel returns to the colonial marriage plot and, emphasizing the continuing histories of the white population, moves quickly forward in time through condensed biographical notes on the lives (and deaths) of those that remain. The reader sees Governor Winthrop on his deathbed, refusing to sign orders of banishment; Master Craddock spending his final years being doted upon by Hope; and the recovery of wayward Jennet's body, whose sins in life caused severe grief for our heroine, but through death is restored to a community of mourners. Emphasizing the importance of her mortal state in this recovery, the narrator writes, "Even Jennet, *dead,* was wrapped in the mantle of charity." It is Hope herself who pleads for her mortal rites/rights, and "tears, of humility and pity, were shed over her grave; a fit tribute, from virtuous and tender woman, to a fallen, unhappy sister."[36] These brief histories reinforce what is lost by the Pequot "pilgrimage," and so the novel, like the poem, only *gives death* to the Indian in the form of removal, itself a voluntary exile, the banishment to a nonlocation that, while marked by an "essential sadness,"[37] cannot be restored through the affective work of mourning. There are no bodies to recover, no gravesites over which to shed tears. Through such displacements, these texts extend exile as a double-edged necropolitics, one that denies the inscriptive possibilities of death for the Native American as a way to clear the ground for more recognizable, more formative deaths: those pertaining to the white colonial community.

These national romances foreclose the possibility of an Indian present in consigning Indigenous peoples to the past. History and progress, time itself, becomes the actor in the drama of Indian removal: the historian is merely an impartial and innocent observer of a *translatio imperii* that at times becomes, as I explore in chapter 4, actual acts of translation. The history she writes is offered as mere transcription, carrying a mantle of passivity that denies its own creative work even as it offers Indigenous voices only as echoes of an unreachable past. There are, by its own account, no Other visions. Sedgwick herself admits as much when she claims that the Indian population "could not submit, and live."[38] Defining herself as an "impartial observer," Sedgwick assures the reader that she views the situation of the Native American "in a light very different from that in which they were regarded by our ancestors." She says, "In our histories, it was perhaps natural that they should be represented as 'surly dogs,' who preferred to die rather than live. . . . Their own historians or poets, if they had such, would as naturally, and with more justice, have extolled their high-souled courage and patriotism."[39] The author's parenthetical "if they had such" denies the opportunity for alternative voices in the historical tradition; "our" histories are written and remain as cultural legacy while "their" histories can only be imagined in the conditional tense of her "would . . . have," their inscriptive possibilities unrealized. If the relationship with historical figures is cultivated through documentary "traces," as Charles-Victor Langlois and Charles Seignobos forwarded, then the silent exodus of the Native American and the refusal of Indigenous historiography mean that the community has disappeared *without a trace,* leaving an insurmountable gap between present and historical subjects.[40] Instead, all that can be recovered are the marks made by the white historian who writes upon the Native body, whose writing reconstitutes the Indian as the inscriptive space for American history even as she writes the Native American herself out of the scene of history. In this scryptural economy, the book functions as the replacement for the relic, the substitute trace object and therefore the only material through which to develop knowledge of the past, rendered here as the figure of the Indian. Sedgwick's concluding wish, then, that her book "so far from being intended as a substitute for genuine history," should encourage "our young countrymen . . . to investigate the early history of their native land"[41] depends on a chain of consumption that can only be fulfilled by the sources she describes, and so the "young countrymen" is constituted in his turn by creole historiography, the history written by white Americans of European descent.

By historicizing removal, this orthodox history overwrites Indigenous presence and so participates in what Patrick Wolfe has called the "elimination logic" of settler colonialism through which the violence of displacement, while required by the territorial demands of the emergent state, is revised through later expressions of regret and deferrals to the "tide of history." "The tide of history," Wolfe writes, "canonizes the fait accompli,"[42] and so the writing of this history shares with the poem and novel a trope that critics commonly refer to as the "Vanishing American" or the "Cult of the Dying Indian." Amid the rush of Indian-themed works in early national literature, authors overwhelmingly concentrated on the idea of the Native American's disappearance.[43] Once the Indian was proclaimed the most proper subject for the national romance, "it was quickly discovered," George Orians argues, "that the most romantic feature of the Indians was their decline."[44] These authors posited that Native Americans, if not already an extinct race, were on the verge of being so; they believed, as Washington Irving did, that the Indian would soon "vanish like a vapor from the face of the earth; their very history will be lost in forgetfulness."[45] The "Vanishing" texts argued that the Indian's community had shrunk, and continued to shrink, before the growth of civilization, rendering his existence contradictory to the condition of modernity. "Society," Irving wrote, "has advanced upon [the Indian] like one of those withering airs that will sometimes breathe desolation over a whole region of fertility"[46] In this deferment to an intractable conflict between civilization and barbarity, these writers express what critic Joshua David Bellin describes as the "quietism so characteristic of nineteenth-century thought on the Indians,"[47] a quietism that removes Native American extinction from the realm of human action. Convers Francis, brother of Lydia Maria Child, whose own Indianist romance *Hobomok* was published just a few years prior to Sedgwick's, articulated this view in his biography of John Eliot, the Puritan "apostle to the Indians." "I do not say that blame is necessarily to be attached to those by whom [the Indians] were crowded out," Francis writes, "For, the world over, it is, and has been, generally a law of human progress, that civilized man must overtop and displace uncivilized man."[48] Francis's "quietism" is expressed as a dampening of guilt, a removal of responsibility for or possible action to avoid Indian extinction. Instead, Francis echoes his contemporaries who see Native disappearance as "natural" or an "unavoidable operation of natural causes."[49] This recourse to a "law," shared throughout the world, "unavoidable" and therefore unchangeable, effects the same active gap witnessed in Follen's poem. No one *makes* the Indian disappear. He disappears because it is in his nature to do so. Because of this, its speakers often "summed up Indian fate in images drawn from nature," painting Indian's disappearance variously as a sunset, snow, morning dew, leaves before the wind, and the sand washed away by the sea.[50] "One could deplore the fact that the Indian was earmarked for extinction," historian Brian Dippie says of this rhetoric, "but one could not alter it."[51] This was, in Leslie Fiedler's words, "the pathos of the lost cause."[52] Displaced as an idealized triumph of civilization and development over barbarism and primitive life, the disappearance of Indigenous peoples was naturalized as a progressivist fantasy of chronological inevitability. The trope of the Vanishing American thus served not only to elide the violence of conquest and naturalize claims for removal, but it also functioned as a historical foundation for narrating the American historical romance.

The Vanishing American appeared in verse, drama, romance, and history through what Jean M. O'Brien has called "lasting," an extinction fantasy that allowed authors to write Native peoples out of existence.[53] In *The Last of the Mohicans* (1826), the most famous example of the genre, James Fenimore Cooper prefaces the novel with his own discourse on the Vanishing American:

> The Mohicans were the possessors of the country first occupied by the Europeans in this portion of the continent. They were, consequently, the first dispossessed; and the seemingly inevitable fate of all these people, who disappear before the advances, or it might be termed the inroads of civilization, as the verdure of their native forests falls before the nipping frost, is represented as having already befallen them. There is sufficient historical truth in the picture to justify the use that has been made of it. . . . The Red Man has entirely deserted this part of the state. Of all the tribes named in these pages, there exist only a few half-civilised beings of the Oneidas. . . . The rest have disappeared, either from the regions in which their fathers dwelt, or altogether from the earth.[54]

Like his predecessors and the multitude he would inspire, Cooper strives to record the dark fate he sees hanging over the Native American history. While he gestures toward the culpability of colonial displacement, blame fades before his concession to the progress of civilization. He groups together its necessary victims, "all these people," as those who remain forever excluded from its realm. The true Indian, in this logic, is never civilized. The "seemingly" that implies that this "inevitable fate" is subject to the error of perception, becomes a weaker and weaker qualification as he moves through the comparison with nature to the "historical truth" of disappearance. In his reference to history,

Cooper clarifies that he himself is not the author of this prophecy, merely the messenger of its realization. The Mohicans, "historical truth" reveals, are already gone. Indeed, marked by the progress of Cooper's own novels, the extinction he offers has already occurred. Early on in the novel, Chingachgook recalls the title by declaring that "my boy is the last of the Mohicans."[55] Uncas does not survive the text, though, passing the burden of the "last" back onto his father. But by the time these words were published in 1826, Chingachgook had been dead himself for three years, having died during the forest fire at the conclusion of Cooper's first Leatherstocking novel, *The Pioneers* (1823). In that first novel, Chingachgook is left to sing his own death song and lament that, as he goes off to join his ancestors, there is no one left to mourn for him. Just as he outlined in his preface, Cooper's "Last of" novel performs a lament for a passing that has *already happened* and the reader, having arrived on the scene too late, is left to shed a tear for a man she has known only as a figure in (and of) history.

The trope thus cultivates sympathy for an ultimately irreconcilable figure, one that remains always at a distance temporally and, because of his flight before the advances of civilization, physically as well. In another famous "vanishing" text, Henry Wadsworth Longfellow's epic poem *Hiawatha* (1855), the Indian hero is not only displaced as colonial prehistory but his departure moves him beyond physical reach entirely. Like Follen's Sachem, who transforms from material possessor to spiritual receptor at the moment of contact, Hiawatha translates the event as a self-imposed exile, removing himself from his home and going "On a long and distant journey, / To the portals of the Sunset."[56] Those whose coming he had prophesied in a vision ("Painted white were all their faces / And with hair their chins were covered")[57] have at last arrived and, as they sleep as guests in his home, Hiawatha leaves, whispering a brief goodbye to his community. As in Follen's verse, Hiawatha's sudden departure leaves a causal gap in the narrative. There is no reason given for his journey; perhaps it seemed "natural" for him to go. In this dark caesura the Vanishing act encourages an amnesia regarding conflict. It, in Lora Romero's words, "expunge[s] imperialist conflict from Jacksonian cultural memory."[58] These men have come from the East, "From the land of light and morning," but Hiawatha sets off "Westward! westward!" driven forward in advance of these new men.[59] Hiawatha's removal is notably voluntary and optimistic, though, not mournful or nostalgic; he urges his people to listen to the proselytizing message of his guests, proclaiming its truth up to the moment he pushes his canoe from shore. The Indian does not mourn his departure but moves willingly toward it, toward "the glory of the sunset . . . the Land of the Hereafter!"[60] Hiawatha, like Follen's Sachem, is removed from the realm of material recoverability and exiled to a noncorporeal, idealized realm, out of history itself. From his place of banishment, the Indian maintains a utopian distance, the *un*-place of the *u*-topos; Hiawatha's sunset is unreachable for those that would pursue him, "a horizon that keeps pace with the traveler."[61]

While posturing as a mournful recollection, this trope works to confirm the *no place* of the Native subject and so clears the ground for white habitation, the growth of which, as the "natural" progress of civilization, the speaker is also unable to staunch. In this way, the lament for the Vanishing American, its impossibility of a present Indian subject, contributes to the contemporaneous political arguments regarding the government's Indian Removal policy. In her study of the spectral Native American, Renée Bergland says of this trope, "By focusing almost exclusively on those who perished, early American writing enacted a literary Indian removal that reinforced and at times even helped to construct the political Indian Removal."[62] This is because the nostalgic performance, while nominally celebrating the lost object, works to confirm that the object is indeed lost. Renato Rosaldo called this posture "imperial nostalgia," tracing a pattern in which "agents of change experience transformations of other cultures as if they were personal losses."[63] The loss is doubled here because the object upon which it fixates is an impossible or fictive condition, an idyll of primitive conditions that exists only as a product of modernity. This vanishing discourse is therefore not merely a nostalgic celebration of the Indian as lost object but, more importantly, a celebration of loss itself. The Native American becomes, as we see in Follen, Sedgwick, Cooper, and Longfellow, a naturalized symbol of loss and so the denial of a possibility of material presence for the Native American inheres in the structure of the trope. The Vanishing American discourse aggressively excludes the Native American from contemporary participation in the national community even as, at the same time, this figuration, circulated in history, poetry and prose, is elevated as the legitimizing claim to a national culture.

It is not surprising, then, to see this trope, frequently the provenance of New England reformers, being deployed in defense of Andrew Jackson's Indian Removal Act. In Jackson's 1830 Annual Message to Congress, the President grafts this romantic language onto his defense of the Removal Act, describing his "liberal" removal treaties with the Choctaw and Chickasaw as the same natural, generational shift that his critics claimed for their regional "lost" tribes:

> Humanity has often wept over the fate of the aborigines of this country; and philanthropy has been long busily employed in devising means to avert it. But its progress has never for a moment been arrested; and one by one have many powerful tribes disappeared from the earth. To follow to the tomb the last of his race, and to tread on the graves of extinct nations, excites melancholy reflections. But true philanthropy reconciles the mind to these vicissitudes, as it does to the extinction of one generation to make room for another.[64]

The contentious removal of Native Americans from Georgia and Alabama is framed here as an iteration of the same natural movement that New Englanders claimed for the Pequot and the Narragansetts. "The present policy of the Government," he concludes, "is but a continuation of the same progressive change by milder process," changes that, despite the attempts at intervention made by "philanthropy," remain outside the realm of human intervention. Instead, all that remains is the trope itself, the possibility of mourning, the "melancholy reflections" that constitute the discourse. These melancholy reflections are the province of the sovereign body of the survivor, the one who is left to mourn. The sentimental performance, the weeping over an already lost cause functions as an assertion of this powerful position. Mourning in this discourse is not the identificatory act of melancholic adoration but rather an exorcism of the other, the lost object, beyond the incorporative realm of available material. The Native American here is *au-delà,* beyond reach, an other who remains in the Other world. Through the deployment of this trope, the Native is circulated among the community as an object to share and speak through but never incorporate. The possibility for a shared identification, encouraged by the cooptation of Native history as national history, is ultimately disallowed by the insurmountable gap between subject and object. The reader can consume the narrative of the Vanishing Indian but the Indian himself remains extrinsic, evading the consuming affection of the ego even as it grants the terms of its assertion. The loss of the Native is doubled and he transforms into a figure of pure longing. It is not, then, ultimately contradictory that the Native is simultaneously asserted as the most authentic, most romantic subject for national literature and done away with, over and over again, in its pages. The repetition of his extinction, being made present only to be erased, functions as a ritual of consumption that perpetuates a desire for this national form as pure figuration, for the nation as it presents itself on the page and yet is everywhere evasive.

Mourning the Vanishing American thus becomes a way to confirm the presence and sovereignty of the nation while at the same time excluding Native American presence. The melancholic meditation upon the inevitable extinction of the barbarous Amerindian functions as a survivor logic for the creole community that circulates it. Andrew Jackson's claim that the grand sentiment of philanthropy will be appeased by the extinction of one civilization insofar as it makes room for another resonates with Follen's poem in which the "changed and glorious prospect" of a civilized land full of churches would cause the imagined Sachem to "rejoice with rapture high."[65] Speakers on both sides of the Removal Act debate laid claim to the Vanishing American in a manner that highlighted not only the Indian's disappearance but more importantly the *fact of white survival.* By engaging with the logic of survival, these speakers implicate white sovereignty as the double of the Indian disappearance.[66] Achille Mbembe, following Elias Canetti, describes survivor logic as how "one's horror at the sight of death turns into satisfaction that it is someone else who is dead. It is the death of the other, his or her physical presence as a corpse, that makes the survivor feel unique. And each enemy killed makes the survivor feel more secure." Survival thus opens up a state of exception, one in which the survivor surpasses death in that he or she "having stood in the path of death, knowing of many deaths and standing in the midst of the fallen, is still alive."[67] The survivor is the one left to mourn and so the spectacle of mourning for the Other is an assertion of difference from and sovereignty over that Other. The Native American community is, in funerary language, *survived by* the white American population; at the center of this spectacle is not the suffering object but those who follow the advice of Bancroft's *History of the United States* and, in looking backward, "drop a tear."[68] In the land of the fallen, tears confirm simultaneously that those for whom you mourn are dead and that you yourself are still alive.[69]

"Ha de Venir": The Fatal Book of Destiny

While in the United States, and in particular New England, the Vanishing American discourse imagined the Native American disappearing without a trace in order to make way for the white American population, the creole elites who were preparing for and stabilizing the independence movements in Spanish America were finding traces of a heroic Indigenous past everywhere and prophesying its return. Creole patriotism, as critics commonly name this attachment to the past, prepared the way for these new nations by laying claim to historical identities, first as the heirs of conquest and then as an assertion of continuity with antique Indigenous claims to land. In its earlier iteration, the creoles' genealogical claims to colonial occupation and the Conquistadors themselves grounded their complaints regarding the "unjust secondary role the Creole played within the colonial Spanish system."[70] As the heirs of conquest, they argued, they were due preference in governmental appointments as their families made colonization possible through conquest. "Behind this return to history," D. A. Brading argues, "lay the bitter grievance that the creole had been deprived of his rightful inheritance—the government of a kingdom conquered by his ancestors."[71] Even before the nativist moves of the independence era, creole identity was produced as a concern about the past and the artificial rupture of family lines, a concern for "the origins of a sociocultural group in a given territory" that yoked identity to the landscape by laying claim to its history and its dead.[72] As the movement for independence grew stronger after the Napoleonic invasion of 1808, this rhetoric turned back on itself and discovered a new and yet more ancient political inheritance in pre-Columbian empires. In Mexico, where creole patriotism found its earliest and most lasting iteration, this new vocabulary allowed creoles to articulate "an identification with the Indian past,"[73] what Rebecca Earle has called a regional "logic and coherence separate from Spain," an "autochthonous patriotism" that made space for the emergence of Spanish American nationalism in the nineteenth century.[74]

Instead of being sons of Cortés, the creole patriots now proclaimed themselves to be the sons of "Moctezuma, Cacamatzin, Cuahtimotzin, de Xicotencalt y de Catzonzi." In the opening speech of the 1813 Congreso de Chilpancingo, where revolutionaries in Mexico proclaimed their independence, General José María Morelos delivered a speech written by Carlos Maria de Bustamante, a speech that translates this newfound paternity into claims of inheritance. In it, the patriot calls upon the Indigenous fathers listed above and links their historical struggle to the contemporary one:

> Celebrad, como celebrásteis el mitote en que fuísteis acometidos por la pérfida espada de Alvarado, este dichoso instante en que vuestros hijos se han

> reunido para vengar vuestros desafueros y ultrajes, y librarse de las garras de la tiranía y fanatismo que los iba á sorber para siempre! Al 12 de Agosto de 1521 sucedió el 14 de Setiembre de 1813. En aquel se apretaron las cadenas de nuestra servidumbre en Méjico Tenoxtitlan; en este se rompen para siempre en el venturoso pueblo de Chilpantzinco.[75]
>
> [Celebrate, as you celebrated the mitote[76] in which you were taken by the treacherous sword of Alvarado, this happy moment in which your sons have come together to avenge your wrongs and outrages, and to liberate themselves from the clutches of tyranny and fanaticism that were going to swallow them forever. From August 12, 1521 follows September 14, 1813. On that [day] the chains of our slavery were fastened in Mexico Tenochtitlan; on this one they broke forever in the happy town of Chilpantzinco.]

Bustamante, the son of a Spaniard, declares not simply independence but restoration, finding in his contemporary scene an ancient power struggling against a foreign invader. The experience of colonization (and consequently the origins of the creole elite) disappear in the unspoken years between 1521 and 1813 and this ellipse allows "vuestros" [your] outrages to become "nuestra" [our] slavery. The body that vanishes here is that of the *español americano,* as the nineteenth century becomes a reiteration of the sixteenth and the contest for independence is recalled as the familiar struggle between *indio* and *conquistador.* The creole patriot declares himself an avenging son and so acts *in place of* the Indian and, through this mediation of revenge, assumes the Indian's claim to the land and its attendant sovereignty, the object of contestation. Unlike in Anglo-American writings, where claims to land and sovereignty were predicated on vacancy, the Spanish American situation here relies on the (re)affirmation of precolonial Native states.[77]

Several scholars have argued that the creole patriotism described above is limited to areas like Mexico and Peru, areas with extensive and documented Indian pasts, witnessed by the *conquistadores* in their chronicles and present in the text of their grand ruins. But there is evidence that other areas with strong independence movements but limited Indian histories, such as Argentina, also shared in this patriotic nativism.[78] A prominent example is the "Marcha Patriotica," adopted as the Argentine national anthem in 1813. Its author, Vicente López y Planes, who would later become president if only for a month in 1827,[79] opens the anthem with the sound of breaking chains, "el ruido de rotas cadenas," metaphorically displacing the creole's oppression as yet another iteration of the actual slavery endured by Amerindians at the hands of the Spaniards, as Bustamante did in Mexico. He then connects Argentina explicitly to areas more closely associated with a heroic Indian past by invoking the suffering of Mexico, Quito, Potosí, Cochabamba and La Paz,[80] setting up this comparison by introducing the figure of the ancient Inca into the contemporary struggle. In the second verse, López moves quickly from classical allusion, "De los nuevos campeones los rostros/Marte mismo parece animar [The faces of the new champions seem to be animated by Mars himself]" to the resurrection of the lost Native.[81] "Se conmueven," he writes, "del Inca las tumbas/Y en sus huecos revive el ardor, / Lo que ve renovando a sus hijos/De la Patria el antiguo esplendor [The tombs of the Inca rumble/and in their depths revive the ardor, / which renews their children/of the *Patria* the ancient splendor]."[82] Like Bustamante in Mexico, López y Planes places the creole patriot in a filial relationship with the ancient Indian, shifting his inheritance from European conquest to the "ancient splendor" of the land itself, the *Patria* that is now quite literally his *father's land.* But the renaissance, the rebirth of Native sovereignty, recalls the death, the dwelling in tombs, of the sovereign himself. As in Bustamante's speech, this filial connection requires a unique relationship with time, one that forgets to remember difference and so eases the identification across a long chronological gap. Here, the creoles, the "hijos de la Patria," are renewed by ancient splendor, an action that is both a return and a pressing forward, an appearance, again, of what once was that allows the subject to break from his current condition. Just as Bustamante's ellipse recreates the creole's struggle in the figure of the exemplary *indio,* the past and the future work together in a way that represses the present and thus the revolutionary rupture of independence.

The move toward independence was not imagined in these texts as a violent break with tradition but rather the result of a long struggle against always-foreign powers and the return of states whose own origins seemed *immemorial.*[83] Such collapsing of temporal and racial distinction accomplishes two crucial tasks for the creole: it legitimizes the claim to an independent state by providing it with a pre-Columbian foundation and it separates the creole from the Spaniard, who is exorcised as a foreigner and usurper of power. If, as Nicolas Shumway has argued, "the Spanish colonies were carefully designed to extend the Spanish Empire . . . they were not intended to develop a unique and independent sense of nationhood, but to be extensions of Spain,"[84] then this rhetoric creates a "sense of separateness" for the creole, the space in which to assert his difference.[85] In Spanish America, then, romantic *indianismo* also flourished as the means by which to assert creole claims to a homeland, but seemed, superficially at least, to resurrect what those in the United States would banish, to reanimate those who, in texts such as Follen's poem, remain mute in face of their own removal.[86] These patriots did not deny death to the Amerindian, but rather denied the finality of death. Mortality was frustrated by the survivors, themselves postured as the *traces* of the Indian past. Through the creole, the Indian lived again.

Emphasizing this resurrection, the Inca that rumbles in his grave in López y Planes' verse finds his voice in José Joaquín de Olmedo's poem "Victoria de Junín: Canto a Bolívar" (1825). Olmedo, a fervent patriot who also served briefly as president of Ecuador (from March to December, 1845), wrote the poem to commemorate the eponymous victory and to rally the sometimes ambivalent Peruvian elite behind Bolívar and the fight for independence.[87] But while the efforts of the creole leader are the nominal focus of the poem, the majority of the work is consumed by the appearance and prophetic address of Huaina-Capac, an Inca king who ruled from 1485 to 1525. The Inca's appearance in the poem marks a stark change from the dark, chaotic opening that depicts the battle itself. The poem begins with the rumbling sounds of thunder, "El trueno horrendo que en fragor revienta / Y sordo retumbando se dilata / Por la inflamada esfera [The horrible thunder that in crashing bursts / And deafening rumbling swells through the inflamed realm]."[88] This aural "shock and awe" is reinforced by the "r"-based consonant clusters and alveolar trill of trueno, horrendo, fragor, revienta, and retumbando. When, in the opening of the second stanza, the reader locates herself on the battlefield with "el *rayo* que en Junín *rompe* y ahuyenta/ La hispana muchedumbre" (emphasis added), the cacophonous rumble has already set the stage for the chaotic, unstable scenes of war. In contrast to the swelling, rumbling, and deafening crashes of this opening scene, the Inca appears when "Ya cesa el mal y el llanto de la tierra [now ends the evil and the cries of the earth]," during the brief respite provided by victory.[89] Against the dark chaos of the battle, the skies take on a markedly different appearance, an "éter / Allá lejos purísimo aparece, / Y en rósea luz bañado resplandece. / Cuando improviso, veneranda sombra / En faz serena y ademan augusto / entre cándidas nubes se levanta."[90] The rumbling sky becomes a pure ether (éter), and in the glow of a rosy light (en rósea luz) the venerable shade (veneranda sombra), serene and august, is lifted by light clouds. This shadow, before he can introduce himself to the gathered troops as Huaina-Capac, already appears as a stable, peaceful figure and so by his influence over the environment brings with him the hope of balance and harmony disrupted by the "hispana muchedumbre [Spanish crowd]." This is not the figure of conflict; the Inca is not "Marte [Mars]," the god of war referenced earlier in the poem.[91] Instead, Huaina-Capac is the promise of peace found in victory, the peace for which the troops had clamored ("Victoria, paz, clamaban, / Paz para siempre").[92] In his notes that accompany the poem, Olmedo remarks that he chose Huaina-Capac specifically because he reigned during a period of stability and unity, saying, "los demás reinaron en un reino dividido, agitados siempre de guerras civiles o encadenados por los españoles [the rest reigned over a divided realm, continuously agitated by civil wars or chained by the Spanish]."[93] If, then, Huaina-Capac is the vision of a future harmony for the creole, the use of a historical figure to presage this signifies not so much a revolutionary break with colonial disorder but rather a return of a precolonial edenic state.

Huaina-Capac makes this connection between the past and future explicit as he hails those on the field at Junín as his sons: "Hijos, decía, / Jeneración del Sol afortunada, / que con placer yo puedo llamar mía [Sons, he said, / Generation of the fortunate Sun / That with pleasure I can call my own]."[94] Not only are these men declared to be the sons of the Inca, but Huaina-Capac's possessive emphasizes his role in their creation. Instead of the creole harkening back to an Indigenous father, here we have the Inca answering back and confirming their relationship. Here, the Inca king is quite literally the seminal figure for independence. Huaina-Capac also marks a clear distinction between the creoles and their Spanish opponents. Promptly after addressing these men as his "hijos," the Inca laments "tres centurias / de maldición," condemning the Spanish as both usurpers and blasphemers.[95] In contrast to these charges, the victorious at Junín are his avengers, those who bring justice and glory to his people ("la vengaza y gloria de mi pueblo").[96] The Inca thus bookends his introduction onto the scene with an identification with the creole population, interrupting these filiative assertions with the supporting insistence on his, and consequently *their*, difference from the Spanish. Civically, the Inca argues, the Spanish have no legitimate claim as they are the "usurpador," gaining power by murdering Native monarchs. "Los asesinos" (the murderers), as Huaina-Capac calls the Spanish, committed countless horrific acts during those three hundred years, and all for material gain ("¡Tantos horrores y maldades tantas / Por el oro que hollaban nuestras plantas!").[97] Even Spanish claims to legitimacy through their religious mission are undermined by the Inca as he asks "¿Qué relijion? ¿la de Jesús? . . . ¡Blasfemos! / Sangre, plomo veloz, cadenas fueron / Los sacramentos santos que trajeron [What religion? That of Jesus? . . . Blasphemers! / Blood, flying shot (fleet lead), chains were / The holy sacraments that they brought]."[98] In this rejection of Spanish colonial justifications, Huaina-Capac also bars any easy identification between the Spaniard and the creole. Even a shared religious identification is denied here as the Inca reveals that the Spaniard's Christianity was not a pure faith but one tainted by greed, violence, and superstition. The Inca thus stands *between* the Spaniard and the creole, illuminating their differences and claiming the latter as his own. This interpolation of the creole troop into his own family ("todos sois mis hijos!"),[99] its victory into his own historical struggle, indicates that it is the Inca, not Bolívar, at the head of this patriot army. His leadership role is confirmed by the advice he gives to the soldiers and the prophecies he makes concerning their future. He exhorts the troops to courage and urges them not to rest on this victory but to continue the fight.[100] His words of advice approach the rallying speeches of a military leader, and while he has praise for Bolívar, his rhetorical position seems to supplant that of the general. The famous leader is included in his address and not given a voice of his own. Instead, in the "Canto a Bolívar," it is Huaina-Capac who orates for almost half its length. In Olmedo's poem, the voice of the Inca simply dominates the other figures. He speaks to the creole but also in his place, reversing the silencing moves of the Vanishing trope in use in the United States at the same time.

Finally, the Inca king's role as prophet concretizes his privilege as speaker. As a prophet, the Inca king stands between confusion and knowledge, the creole and his future. While Huaina-Capac tarries for verse after verse, condemning the Spanish while praising and spurring on the creoles, the reason for his appearance is the prophecy of *other* victories that await them, "nueva lid, mayor victoria [a new struggle, a greater victory]."[101] He depicts this future battle in detail for his audience and tells them it is at *that* battle at Ayacucho that their freedom will finally be won. Olmedo says in his notes to the poem, "En el campo de Ayacucho fue la célebre victoria que predice el Inca, y que fijó los destinos de la América. En el mismo lugar, al principio de la conquista, se disputaron los Almagros y Pizarros el dominio del Perú [On the field at Ayacucho was the celebrated victory that the Inca predicts, and that fixed the destinies of America. At the same location at the beginning of the Conquest, the Almagros and Pizarros (two factions of the Spanish conquering force) fought over who was to rule Peru]."[102] The Inca's prophecy (already realized—*fue*—and part of shared history for Olmedo's audience in 1825) is notably a return to colonial beginnings, a revision of battles fought on the same ground and a restoration of sovereignty wrested from its Indigenous inhabitants over three hundred years previously. The Inca and his kingdom may have passed away centuries ago, but in his creole counterparts he lives again. While some critics see the recollection of conquest as a parallel for the disruption of revolution,[103] this recourse to an immemorial history can also be seen as a stabilizing force for the claims of independence, one that lends historical precedent so that revolution reads more like restoration. The victory at Junín and the prophesied victory at Ayacucho are *already* presided over by the ruler/prophet who gives them form. The power ceded to the figure of the prophet is mirrored by the material space consumed by his lengthy address. This prophecy of return is the "objeto de su aparición [the object of his appearance]," according to Olmedo's notes, and the poet goes on to ask for his readers' forgiveness for his character, who despite his brief and direct task perhaps allowed his "vaticinio . . . demasiada extensión [prophecy . . . too much space]."[104] Acknowledging that the Inca had carried on for quite a long period of time, the poet declares this to be the Inca's *right to speak:*

> Pero ¿no se perdonará a un INCA que ántes de pronunciar el grande oráculo, objeto de su aparicion, exhale algunas quejas al ver por la primera vez los lugares que fueron el teatro de los horrores de la conquista? ¿No se perdonará a un buen padre y a un buen rei lamentar ántes de todo la suerte de sus hijos y de su pueblo? ¿No se perdonará a un guerrero alentar el valor de las tropas con el recuerdo de agravios pasados, aunque sean sucesos mui conocidos de la historia de su país? ¿No se perdonará a un anciano el ser prolijo en sus discursos, y a un sabio de edad el no perder la ocasion de dar consejos a los hombres? ¿No se perdonará, en fin, a un sacerdote prolongar un tanto la espectacion del pueblo al anunciar los oráculos del cielo?[105]

> [But will one not forgive an Inca who before pronouncing the great prophecy, the object of his appearance, heaves some complaints on seeing for the first time the places that were the Conquest's theater of horrors? Will one not forgive a good father and a good king for mourning above all the fate of his sons and his people? Will one not forgive a warrior stoking the courage of the troops with the memory of past wrongs, even if they were well-known events in the history of his country? Will one not forgive an old man being

verbose in his speeches, and a man wise with age not to lose the opportunity to give advice to mankind? Will one not forgive, after all, a priest prolonging a bit the peoples' expectation at announcing the oracles of heaven?]

The poet's lengthy defense of his ancient speaker is based on the repetition of the question "No se perdonará," a structure that echoes Follen's verse in its open questioning ("Where?") but differentiates itself significantly in that it addresses not a missing *elsewhere* but a present audience. It is the creole reader to whom the questions are directed and it is this imagined reader's impatience at the length of the Inca's address that must be ameliorated. This figure, Olmedo's questioning insists, has the right to speak, and the right to speak at length. Making space on the page for this work, the physical expanse of the poem itself stands in for the figure of the Inca, a figure who must make himself known, whose redress requires address, the *presence* of a voice. His physicality thus becomes irrepressible for the reader, who must forgive, must welcome him into his space. Because of his prominence, the Inca here seems not simply to stand between the creole and the Spaniard, but to supplant the *criollo* altogether. The Inca's dominance leads to Bolívar's response to the poem: "El Inca . . . parece que es el asunto del poema: él es el genio, él es la sabiduría, él es el héroe, en fin [The Inca seems to be the subject of the poem; he is the genius, he is the sage, he is, in the end, the hero]."[106] Bolívar's complaint is marked by a persistent "he is," "he is," "he is," a concern that in making space for the Inca speaker Olmedo has left no room for the assertion of a separate creole identity.

But while Spanish American independence claims are postured here as a restoration of fallen Amerindian empires, they were, in reality, the province of the elite creole class, the product of Spanish colonization. Hans-Joachim König writes that "la dedicación al pasado indio fue un deseo criollo de los españoles americanos, es decir, de aquellos que si bien pertenecían, con los españoles europeos, a una misma clase alta blanca [The dedication to the Indian past was a creole desire on the part of the Spanish Americans, that is, of those that belonged, along with the peninsular Spaniards, to the same white upper class]."[107] Thus while these creoles sought to establish new independent governments, they also sought to maintain the same social structure as their colonial counterparts. In this regard, the formation of newly independent states sought to conserve much of the economic and social disparity established by Spanish colonial power, a power that their own rhetoric declared as foreign and corrupt. Bolívar, it seems, understood this irreconcilable tension between rhetoric and realities when he protested the prominence of the Amerindian king. While contemporaneous reviewers like writer and statesman Andrés Bello considered the Inca's appearance to be "la parte más espléndida y animada de su canto [the most splendid and animated part of the song],"[108] Bolívar cautioned against an over-reliance on such tropes. Olmedo, Bolívar insisted, had made of the Inca "un coloso," a colossus that "cubre con su sombra a los demás personajes [overshadows the other characters]."[109] Bolívar's protest, that the Indian covers everyone with his shadow, indicates the threat to the subject posed by identification. Freud details this power of the lost object in his essay "Of Mourning and Melancholia." The melancholic relationship is described as an incorporative one in which an identification is produced between the subject's ego and the lost object. "The shadow of the object," Freud says, falls upon the ego, becomes part of the subject's self-identification.[110] The Inca, Bolívar protests, threatens to consume the creole completely and exposes the subject to other dangerous identifications with contemporary subaltern Indian communities. It doesn't seem appropriate, El Libertador complained, that the Inca gives preference to the *criollos,* to the "extranjeros intrusos, que, aunque vengadores de su sangre, siempre son descendientes de los que aniquilaron su imperio [foreign invaders, which, despite being avengers of his blood, are always descendants of those who annihilated his empire]."[111] Bolívar thus refuses the amnesia required by the identification of creole with Inca; against the oppressive "he is" that threatens his own annihilation, Bolívar resists by articulating filial ties to the Spanish. We are—we *always* are—descendants of the Conquistador, he says, not the Inca; we are—*siempre*—the "extranjeros intrusos."

But perhaps Bolívar's rejection of the Inca prophet is a bit too hasty. If we look beyond Olmedo's overt attempts to identify the struggle for independence with the resistance to conquest, we can see how this anxiety regarding identification with Indigenous communities is already contained within the text itself. Beyond the dreamscape of his appearance, Olmedo's Inca also displaces his relationship to the "hijos" he addresses by lamenting the fate of his *actual* sons, the unfortunate Atahualpa and Huáscar for whom he mourns,[112] for whom, Olmedo's lengthy justification implies, he *must* mourn or must be allowed to mourn. Against the image of the creole as "vengador," then, rises the specter of the son and the rupture of inheritance or filial continuity. Simultaneous with the Inca's assertion of patriarchy is the tacit acknowledgment of the end of his line. This can be seen in the assertion, made by both the Inca himself and the poet in his explanatory notes, that Huaina-Capac is the last of his kind. "Yo soi Huaina Capac," the Inca tells his audience, "soi el postrero / Del vástago sagrado [I am Huaina-Capac, I am the last / of the sacred line],"[113] the poet seconding his assertion by calling him "el último."[114] Olmedo's poem thus participates in the "lasting" described in the Vanishing American trope. Here, as in the US American texts, the assertion of his last-ness is a legible sign of his sterility, his inescapable and profound loss (both of his own material body and of any remaining signs of self), and his inability to identify with the surviving community. As the Inca works to consume the creole and thus annihilate the difference between them, the reader is also reminded that the bodies on the field of victory are *not* his, not of his blood, of which no trace remains. This spectralization of the father emphasizes the illusory nature of their relationship, as figural rather than formal, thereby rendering it tenuous, unable to withstand any rigorous interrogation.

This sterility also distances the historical Huaina-Capac from the contemporary Indian population, barring any easy translation of the *criollo*-Inca identification into a *criollo-indio* one. The vengeance Huaina-Capac requests is for the blood of his own ancient family of rulers, not for the sufferings of the contemporaneous Indigenous population, about which he remains silent.[115] This "quietism" evinces a common distinction exploited by the rhetoric of creole nationalism between the historical community they lauded and the contemporary one that remained by and large unincorporated into the independent states. Historian Rebecca Earle calls this exclusion of present Amerindians from the creole celebration of an Indigenous past the "double discourse on the Indian."[116] In contrast to the ancient glory of the Incas or Aztecs, Earle argues, "contemporary Indians . . . were dirty, degraded and, infinitely worse, just as likely to support the royalists as they were to support their metaphorical cousins, the insurgents." This double standard was provided for, not by the rhetoric of exile and disappearance, as in Anglo-American writings, but by the assertions of a conditional degeneration that severed present Indigenous populations from the past. Contemporary *indios,* the creole patriot argued indignantly, were irreparably cut off from their noble heritage by the intervening period of colonial slavery and corruption. What results from this doubled discourse is a similarly doubled concept of time. At the same time the colonial period was banished from memory in order to facilitate creole identification with a pre-Columbian indigenous past, it also was forwarded as an irreversible and lengthy period of corruption for the surviving Amerindian population. "The degradation of the Indian to the state in which we see him today," Colombian patriot José Francisco de Caldas (1768–1816) argued, "is the work of the oppressor government that has brutalized us for three consecutive centuries."[117] The creole patriot also relied on this reminder/remainder of colonial violence in order to bolster his claims to independence and erase the present *indio.* This trope is often summed up in complaints such as Caldas's that the American had suffered for three hundred years. While the colonial period is forgotten in the assertion of a direct inheritance from the Amerindian "fathers," it is memorialized as the immense span of traumatic time, the endurance of which marks the creole, not the Indian, as the survivor and so the claimant of the survivor's rights/rites to the deceased. As historian Cecilia Méndez argues, "El indio es, pues, aceptado en tanto paisaje y gloria lejana. . . . Apelar a la memoria de los Incas para despreciar y segregar el indio [The Indian is, then, accepted as long as he is a distant glory and landscape. . . . Appealing to the memory of the Incas was a way to despise and segregate the Indian]."[118] This "double discourse" reconciles somewhat the two nationalist projects of the Vanishing American and creole patriotism. Despite the laudatory tendencies of the latter, its connection to an ancient Amerindian civilization is predicated upon the impossibility of recovery, and thus the assertion of mourning in both discourses functions as a confirmation and celebration of loss itself and so a vacancy on which the creole can craft his own claims to sovereignty. "Las culturas indígenas fueron reconocidas," critic Raul Ianes writes, "sólo en calidad de un sustrato históricamente cancelado [Indigenous cultures were recognized only as a historically canceled substrate]."[119] This renders early national nativism a type of "patriotismo arqueológico" (archaeological patriotism) in which the national character is predicated upon, not Indian realities but the narratives invented for the traces that the creole resurrects and perpetuates as textual artifacts.[120] The Indian thus becomes an artifact of history, an object of knowledge whose value is produced by the loss of a living original.

One can see this diminishment in Olmedo's poem, as the urging by the Inca for restoration exists in tension with the Inca's own self-negation and erasure. Despite his overwhelming presence, and despite his own prophetic framing of independence as the return of indigenous sovereignty, Huaina-Capac insists that the creole *not* reestablish an indigenous state. After insisting that here begins the new age promised to the Inca, "Esta es la hora feliz. Desde aquí empieza / La nueva edad al INCA prometida," the Native prophet asks that this new age *not* renew his reign. "No quisiera/" the Inca says, "Que el cetro de los INCAS renaciera [I would not want the Incan scepter to be reborn]." After condemning the Spanish for cruelty in conquest and corruption in their Christianity, the Inca chooses to indict his own state, and, because he was king, himself as well, when advising the creole on achieving independence. "Ya se vió algún INCA," he says, "que teniendo / El terrible poder todo en su mano / Comenzó padre, y acabó tirano. / Yo fuí conquistador, ya me avergüenzo / Del glorioso y sangriento ministerio [Already one has seen an Inca that having / The terrible power in his hand / Began as father and ended as tyrant. / I was a conqueror, now I am ashamed / Of the glorious and bloody ministry]."[121] Not only is the tyranny against which the creoles fight the province of the Spanish but it is also that of their venerable Indigenous fathers. In the confessional moment of "Yo fui conquistador," the colossus that speaks is severed from his audience by explicitly identifying with the culpable and representatively *Spanish* figure. In a perverse echo of the original creole patriotism, it is the *Inca* who declares his identification with the *conquistador.* In cautioning these *independentistas* against tyrannical possibilities of their own, the Inca indicates the limitations of the identifications they would foster between the living and the dead.

This limitation is emphasized by the Indigenous prophet's corporeal exclusion, his confinement to the realm of spirits. The Inca appears on a battlefield and in his revelations he sees more, prophesying future violent contests. These are scenes of action and their requirements upon the subject (to battle or be lost) emphasizes the Inca's own inability to act. The Inca, consigned to the realm of spirits, can only foresee the work done by others, even if imagined done on his behalf. When the Inca sees the sacrifice of lives Ayacucho will require, he laments his own inability to stop it. After witnessing to the blood sacrifice, the Inca calls out, "Yo me estremeciera, / Si mi ser inmortal no lo impidiera! [I shudder / That my immortal being cannot stop it]."[122] The power of the seer is thus revealed to be a passive one; barred from participating in the struggle, the Inca is confined to the role of spectator. The Inca, present as a spirit, still remains exiled from active realization and so speaks from a distance, removed much like Follen's Sachem from the present/presence of the contemporary white community. The insistence on the Indian as *historical* here works to privilege the corporeal present that acts on his behalf. The creole here dies for the Inca because the Inca, being already dead, cannot fight for himself. The passivity of his state requires him to take on the debt of the creole's sacrifice and so, reversing the mournful posture of the patriot toward the historical Indian community, the imagined future death of the creole becomes itself a mournful wail.

The removal of the Indian from the realm of action facilitates the transition of the creole from mediatory figure working on behalf of Native sovereignty to sovereign himself. As he progresses in his speech, the Inca indicates this switch as he begins to address Simón Bolívar specifically. After communicating his vision of victory, the Inca emphasizes that he does not own or is not responsible for this glory. Instead, the Inca proclaims, "Tuya será, BOLIVAR, esta gloria: / Tuya romper el yugo de los reyes [Yours will be, Bolívar, this glory, / Yours to break the yoke of kings]."[123] The second-person possessive is emphasized here not only by word choice (*tuya*), but also by the repetition and placement of the emphatic possessive at the beginning of successive lines. Bolívar, here, is not in the shadow of the Inca, but has himself consumed the Indigenous patrimony. When the Inca proclaims to Bolívar that "Tú la salud y honor de nuestro pueblo / serás viviendo [You the health and honor of our people / will be living]," he gives corporeal form to independence, ceding "nuestro pueblo" to the body of El Libertador.[124]

Jicoténcal effects much the same definitional work as Bustamante's speeches and Olmedo's flowery verse, translating the contingencies of political identification into the patrimony of New World nationalism. In mourning the tragic couple, the novel builds on its work of separating out the nineteenth-century reader from a Spanish heritage and instead identifying him with the long-dead Tlascaltecans. Like Olmedo's ethereal Inca, *Jicoténcal*'s narrator and characters pay careful attention to the uniquely American landscape in a way that simultaneously asserts a filial familiarity and an exotic estrangement. The land is rough, marked by canyons and mountains, a landscape that overwhelms the foreigner, besieging them with storms that ask the reader to compare the vulnerable displaced European and the capable control of the *americano.* It is in one of these storms that the soldier Diego de Ordaz and Fray Bartolomé de Olmedo meet Teutila, the woman who will marry Jicoténcal and emerge as the romance's heroine. The two had been discussing the former's reservations regarding their mission when the environment rebels against them. Suddenly, they are assaulted by a great storm and forced to seek shelter from the swelling rivers. The narrator describes a threatening scene: "Las nubes casi sobre su cabeza oscurecen enteramente el horizonte, el agua cae a torrentes, y, a los pocos pasos, un caobo tan antiguo como el mundo estalla y se incendia por el fuego de un rayo [The clouds almost over their heads darkened the entire horizon, the water fell in torrents, and, a few feet away, a mahogany tree as old as the world exploded, bursting into flames from a lightning strike]." The thunder, lightning, torrential rain and surrounding fire are all signs of hostility from the sky and mark the New World as dangerous and inhospitable to these men; it attempts to expel them and they answer by running away. The two men are discovered by Teutila, who shelters them from the storm, saying, "Vuestro temor manifiesta vuestra flaqueza, y ésta os hace dignos de compasión. Entrad [Your fear makes visible your weakness and that makes you worthy of compassion. Enter]."[125] In contrast to their fear, Teutila demonstrates "serenidad"; in the midst of their chaotic and dangerous expulsion, they find her comfortably at home. When Teutila offers to guide the pair back to their camp, for fear of them getting lost, she again emphasizes her familiarity with the landscape and its potential to overpower these strangers. She says, "Os conduciré hasta cerca de Jacacingo, porque temo que os extravíes estando tan próxima la noche [I will guide you almost to Jacacingo because I fear that you will go astray, the night being so close]."[126] The effect of this encounter is to establish the identificatory terms that will continue throughout the novel. The Spaniards, as Teutila addresses them, are "extranjeros," or strangers, foreigners, while she herself is "la americana," the American.[127] These definitional terms consolidate both the Spanish and indigenous divisions, secular and clerical, tribal and geographical, into a simple opposition based on the idea of nativity and homeland.

The religious distinction between the creole present and the historical indigenous community is also elided by the main characters' assertions of a natural monotheism that maintains Christian values while highlighting the hypocrisies of Spanish Catholics. When Teutila saves the pair from the storm, the Priest, impressed by her generosity, decries the fact that she, as a pagan, does not know the source of these virtues. Teutila, taken aback by the presumption of her guest, answers "vivamente [animatedly]" by demanding "Y quién te ha dicho, extranjero . . . que yo no adoro al autor de todo cuanto existe [And who has told you, stranger . . . that I don't adore the author of all that exists]."[128] She declares that her ignorance of the Western world and its technologies does not mean that she has no knowledge of or respect for God. "Para conocer la existencia de un Ser que ha ordenado el sol y las estrellas y que preside a toda la naturaleza," she tells them, "basta no cerrar los ojos a lo que ésta nos dice continuamente [In order to know the existence of a Being who has arranged the sun and stars and that presides over all of nature, it is enough not to close your eyes to that which [nature] continually tells us]."[129] Teutila's monotheism, a knowledge of God garnered from the natural world, is echoed by other virtuous indigenous characters (such as Jicoténcal, the elder, in his invocation of the first cause that governs the world).[130] This offers a stark contrast not only to the polytheism of corrupt Amerindians like Magiscatzin but also to the hypocrisies demonstrated by the Spanish troops and clergy. When Fray Bartolomé de Olmedo tells the elder Jicoténcal "somos hijos de un mismo Dios . . . debemos amar . . . a nuestros hermanos, que son todos hombres [we are all sons of the same God . . . we should love . . . our brothers that are all men]," the wise Tlascalan answers in surprise that while these words echo the feelings of his heart, "vuestras acciones son tan contrarias a estas mismas máximas [your actions are so contrary to these same maxims]."[131] Like Olmedo's Inca, the *americanos* of *Jicoténcal* find Spanish Catholicism blasphemous, "la monstruosa mezcla de las máximas más justas y más dulces con los hechos más atroces y más inicuos y de los discursos más profundos y delicados con los absurdos más necios y despreciables [the monstrous mixture of the most just and sweet maxims with the most atrocious and wicked deeds, of the most profound and delicate discourses with the most absurd and contemptible fools]."[132] This dark contrast to their innocent spirituality furthers the identification of Native with creole reader, denying, as did Olmedo's poem, the religious justification for colonial violence by relocating Christian values to the historical Amerindian population.

Finally, the present-day creole is linked with the Indigenous past through the Tlascalan state, a political organization that is insistently referred to in the novel as a republic. Rather than portraying the monarchical heritage of the Incan or Aztec communities, *Jicoténcal* focuses on Tlascala as a way to highlight Indigenous resistance to absolutist power. The narrator speaks of "la igualdad que formaba el espíritu público del país [the equality that formed the public spirit of the country]" and the selfless patriotism and dedication to independence demonstrated by its people.[133] "El espíritu nacional de los tlascaltecas," the narrator says, "era tan decidido que, careciendo éstos de sal, preferían vivir privados de este condimento a disfrutar de él abriendo relaciones comerciales con sus enemigos los vasallos de Montezuma [The national spirit of the Tlascaltecans was so strong that, having no salt, they preferred to live deprived of this condiment rather than have it by opening commercial relations with their enemies, the vassals of Montezuma]."[134] This self-deprivation is a sacrifice made for the health of their political state, keeping them from the reaches of their imperial (and here, by the use of the term "vassals," feudal) neighbors. These are a people dedicated to their freedom, not individually but as a political community. Our eponymous hero represents this political idea and is surrounded in the text by overwhelming reminders of his patriotism. He is described by the narrator as a man of "puro y desinteresado patriotismo [pure and disinterested patriotism]," and his speeches are peppered with reminders of this devotion. In his opening address to the Tlascalan *senado,* Jicoténcal says he is "conducido por mi ardiente amor a la patria [driven by my ardent love for the homeland],"[135] and when he calls out in longing for Teutila, he first calls out for his home: "¡oh patria mía!, tú, ¡mi adorada Teutila!, caros objectos de mi corazón [both objects of my heart]."[136] The construction of Tlascala as an egalitarian republic is, according to critic D.W. McPheeters, "una ficción novelesca," an understanding of Indigenous society that has less to do with historical realities than it does with the deformed mirror of creole nationalist historiography.[137] The *senado* described in Tlascala, though, serves to highlight the corruption and irrationality of the Spanish political state. Its members marvel at the Spaniard's monarchical system, which they understand as concession to a distant tyrant. Even Cortés, in his local power, established in contrast to the Tlascalan representative and deliberative political bodies, is portrayed as illegitimate and possibly even disloyal. "Cortés tenía la fuerza de su parte, y sin ésta el gobierno no es más que un fantasma impotente y ridículo [Cortés had force on his side and without this the government is no more than an impotent and ridiculous ghost]."[138]

But even as the novel celebrates the familiar love of land, God, and *patria,* fostering affiliative bonds between creole reader and Tlascalan community, there is a persistent caution against a hospitable exposure to the other, as contact becomes darkened by violent consumption and erasure. Teutila's hospitality, while virtuous, initiates the actions that lead to her captivity and Cortés's pursuit of Jicoténcal. Reacting to her offer to meet Cortés and mediate between the Spaniard and Jicoténcal, the narrator declares that "la inocente americana corre a su pérdida con el mismo entusiasmo que si fuera a hacer feliz al mundo entero [the innocent American ran to her doom with the same enthusiasm as if she were to make the entire world happy]."[139] Marina, the Amerindian slave who serves Cortés, laments her exposure to Catholicism as her conversion isolates her from her family and community and perverts her natural sense of right and wrong. "Cuando yo seguía mi culto sencillo y puro, pues que salía de mi corazón,"she tells Father Olmedo, "cuando yo era una idólatra, segun tú me llamabas, yo fui una mujer virtuosa [When I followed my simple and pure religion, it flowed from my heart; when I was an idolatress, as you would call me, I was a virtuous woman]."[140] These women, in the liminal positions of ambassador and translator, are figures of contact between the two communities who each come under the influence of the Other to the detriment of their personal sovereignty. But even the Tlascalan state is vulnerable to this contamination through its hospitality and confederate structure. Against the physical walls that separate the state from its neighbors, "la gran muralla de piedra . . . señalando y fortificando los límites de la república de Tlascala [the great stone wall . . . marking and fortifying the limits of the Tlascalan republic]," its confederacy with the neighboring Cempoalans allows Cortés to contaminate them by sending their allies as his spokesmen to the Tlascalan *senado.*[141] The Cempoalan ambassadors ask that the *senado* consider the Europeans "bienhechores," and, already allies of their allies, they ask the Republic to accept the Europeans as part of their confederation. Through these native speakers, the Europeans ask for the considerations of hospitality, but, as "aliados de vuestros aliados," they have already become part of the confederate community. Speaking through the Native body, the Spanish plea takes on a familiar form, or more precisely four familiar forms. This infection of a familiar body with a foreign presence, already *in* Tlascala and in that way prior to (and thus not subject to) the approval of the Tlascaltecan assembly, reveals the exposure of their confederate community, the many ways their borders can be violated. Finally, by offering to represent the Tlascaltecan concerns in the European stand against Montezuma and his empire ("tomar por suya vuestra causa"), Cortés moves to transform the representative body from the Indian ambassador to the European soldier.[142] In taking the Native cause as their own, the Europeans in turn become the *indio*'s ambassador. The imported figure consumes the indigenous concern, adopting it as his own and thus forging a bond of identification that is both prior to assent and ultimately spoken by the European. The romance, then, repeats in these various forms the anxiety surrounding the vulnerability of ego and community identifications through the very values and institutions that it deploys to protect them, through the definitions of difference based on home, religion, and state. Modes of distinction, the novel tells us, also function as sites of exposure and so even as it encourages identification it admonishes the reader to fortify herself against this site of vulnerability.

The resulting degeneration of Tlascalan society takes the form of an infection or sickness from which the Indigenous republic cannot recover. The exposure to and identification with the Spanish robs the Native of sovereignty, consuming him as it corrupts him, and this is made explicit in the twinned death scenes of Magiscatzin and the elder Jicoténcal. The former, the strongest ally of Córtes, foresakes land, religion, and country and so dies in an "espectáculo horroroso [horrific spectacle]" in which the criminal "muerde sus cadenas atado a un poste, y que rechina los dientes y se despedaza con sus propias uñas [chews at his chains tied to a post and grinds his teeth and tears at himself with his own nails]."[143] The author departs from his historical sources in depicting this spectacle of suffering, choosing not to depict Magiscatzin's death with the "olor de santidad" as did Antonio de Solís.[144] Instead, Magiscatzin suffers and suffers terribly; in dying he leaves no one to mourn for him except Cortés himself, who does so only in farce.[145] Directly following this terrifying scene is the beatific deathbed of Jicoténcal's father, the only Tlascalan governor to resist incorporation into the new Spanish rule. The serenity and joy of his death is a stark contrast to the chaos and fear at Magiscatzin's house, as is the overwhelming procession of mourners against the "farsa." The consuming force of the Spanish, its colonial contamination, this juxtaposition seems to argue, takes over death as much as life.[146]

This Spanish power over the lives and deaths of the Amerindian people inscribes upon them a structure of servitude that annuls their claims to home, religion, and political sovereignty. But the Amerindian is not merely the victim, the narrator declares, but rather is himself culpable in his refusal to resist. When he first heard Cortés's ambassadors present the Spaniard's offer of friendship to the Tlascalan *senado,* the elder Jicoténcal understood the message to be: "Yo vengo a esclavizaros a vosotros vuestro pensamiento, vuestros hijos y vuestra descendencia; vengo a destruir vuestro culto y a haceros apostatar de vuestra religión [I come to enslave you, your thinking, your children and your descendants; I come to destroy your culture and make you renounce your religion]."[147] But despite this revelation of their future, the community ceded to Cortés's demands, welcomed the foreign power, and, when the results turned grim, still refused to act against it. Because of this the narrator displaces the responsibility for conquest and colonial submission onto the Native population, saying that "ese pueblo sufre justamente sus cadenas [that people justly suffered their chains]." Moving away from the vilification of the Spanish forces, the narrator turns against the Native population, declaring that Liberty herself "vuelve la espalda al país que no sabe vengar sus insultos, y abandona la generación presente y las futuras a la orfandad y la escalvitud [turns her back on the country that doesn't know to avenge its insults, and abandons the present and future generations to orphanhood and slavery]."[148] The consequences of conquest are thus laid at the feet of the Indian, blame for the three hundred years of suffering protested by the creole patriot here lies with the Native himself.

These consequences are increasingly a mortal concern in the novel, as the contamination of envoys and ambassadors leads to the unspeakable violence and horror of Cholula, now no more than "un desierto sembrado de cadáveres [a desert sown with cadavers],"[149] to the imposition of Spanish necropolitical rule. After gaining control of the indigenous population, Cortés "se imponía la pena de muerte por los delitos más leves [imposed the death penalty for the mildest of crimes],"[150] grounding his authority in his ability to "give death" to his subjects. It is against this overt exercise of sovereignty as necropolitics that Jicoténcal and Teutila resist by reclaiming the very commodities upon which the Spanish power relies. In Olmedo's text, the Inca stands between not only the creole and the Spanish but also the creole and the *indio*. In *Jicoténcal,* the Indigenous republicans separate out the *extranjero* from the *americano,* but it is the deaths of the noble *republicanos,* Jicoténcal, elder and younger, and Teutila, that distinguishes them from the degenerated masses. This alienation of the heroic indigenous past from a possible indigenous present is emphasized in the text when, in the moments before her death, Teutila takes shelter with another widow, a mirror of Teutila herself except that this woman is surrounded by her children. Here, Teutila's chastity is emphasized as sterility, her inability to bestow an inheritance of her own made clear through the knowledge that she will die and leave nothing, no one, behind and so is completely divorced from the contemporary indigenous community. With no children, the only central character who is entirely fictional, having no "existencia (histórica) previa a la ficción [(historical) existence outside of the novel],"[151] leaves no trace for posterity. No trace, that is, except for the textual artifact of the historical romance itself. Those left to consume their deaths and mourn for them in their turn are the creoles, absent from the romance entirely and so freed from responsibility for the destruction of conquest. These readers, through mourning Jicoténcal and Teutila, become the affective descendants of the Native heroes, replacing the contemporary Indian population from which the two are filially divorced through their sterility and affiliatively distinguished by their resistance to the Spanish. The reader bears witness to these events and so Jicoténcal's wish that his death may move the patriotism of a population retains the possibility of success in the sentimental extension of the romance's reader. His audience at Texcoco responded "stupidly" to the mute, drowsy death, but to the reader of the romance such cruel mechanisms, "bajos and viles [base and vile]," heighten the sentimental effect of the scene.[152] It is thus the nineteenth-century reader who, through mourning the fallen hero, lays claim to his heritage of "antiguo valor," grafting herself onto his prophecy so that her reading of it, in the end, is self-revelatory.

Following the anxiety regarding exposure and identification in the novel, the reader is guarded from the contaminative possibilities of such affective connections by the barriers offered by the novel itself. By cathecting *historical* figures, the novel reassures its reader with the distance of the past, engaging her with a shared desire for an irremediable loss. Like Follen's Sachem, the remnant of this heroic Indian is vacancy itself; both Jicoténcal's and Teutila's only lasting memorial is the book and, in the novel, even this conduit to an-Other land is mediated by other texts. Much of the Indian's direct speech is recorded as lengthy citations of popular history itself, specifically Antonio de Solís's seventeenth-century chronicle *Historia de la conquista de Méjico,* an extremely popular text that had by 1826 gone through forty editions.[153] The author cites extensive speeches from Solís's *Historia,* creating a palimpsest out of his novel that locates his romance within the realm of a verifiable, referential discourse, in much the same way that recourse to footnotes and found manuscripts support the historical work done by his generic peers. But the layers here also make the work self-referential, a network of texts from which the reader cannot escape. Solís's history is itself largely based on Bernal Diaz's account of conquest and so the historical subject is actually mediated by several levels of white, European authorship. By incorporating Solís's work seamlessly into his novel, the author effectively re-places the need for a blank page by writing his romance onto the text of history, crafting a historical romance of historiography. The effect of this layering is to call attention to the textuality of the romance and so to its subjects, the Indian empires, as historical themselves. In a rare direct address to Jicoténcal himself, the narrator cries out "¡Generoso Jicoténcal! Tu noble franqueza va a perderte [your noble honesty will be your downfall]," a cry that betrays the narrator's historical perspective and a cry that the young general cannot hear because it comes three centuries too late.[154] These Amerindians, like Huaina-Capac, are exiled from the present action, their chronological displacement an assurance that the space now occupied by the creole is indeed vacant, and so an elision as well of any present, living Amerindian community.[155]

This barrier to identification and responsibility is supported by a final supplanting of Native authorship by a much greater text. As Bolívar's response to Olmedo's Inca indicates, ceding the power of the prophet to the indigenous past could be dangerous for the creole, whose inheritance is still traceable to the Spanish and whose post-independence social and economic structures still relied on the unequal distribution of resources and, in some areas, the continuance of Native tribute. The power of Native prophecy over independence threatens to make the creole responsible to the Indian, who, through his death, offers to legitimate the rejection of Spanish rule three hundred years later. Jicoténcal's prophecy, as a call from the dead, serves as an unnerving reminder that "we are not self-authored, that we follow in the footsteps of the dead";[156] the Native as prophet of my present/presence threatens to overwrite my *I* with the *he, he, he* of Bolívar's complaint. The threat of the colossus is attenuated in *Jicoténcal* by the intervention of a much greater Other, the presence of another book that takes from the Indian the possibility of authorship and instead inscribes him into "el libro fatal del destino." The romance opens with a debate about signs in the sky, their meaning and their influence, as prophecy, over action taken on earth. While the reader's alliance with Jicoténcal may lead her to reject Magiscatzin's passive response to this celestial text in favor of the young general's active resistance, both of these readings follow the introduction of and are limited by the contents of the Other book. The first sentence of the novel reads: "Estaba escrita en el libro fatal del destino la caída del grande imperio de Motezuma, bajo cuyas ruinas debían sepultarse la república de Tlascala [It was written in the fatal book of destiny the fall of the great empire of Motezuma, underneath whose ruins lies buried the Republic of Tlascala]."[157] This romance, the author warns, is a book about the Book, a realm of action that has already been dictated. The hermeneutical debate in the *senado* is thus restricted by the interpretive possibilities of the text in which it takes place. As the plot moves forward, the active, resistant heroes make frequent reference to this book that is as fatal in its inevitable terms as it is in its deathly effect on Indigenous life. Jicoténcal ruminates on the "cadena de sucesos que la fatalidad había dispuesto contra su república [chain of events that fate has disposed against his republic],"[158] Teutila laments the "poder fatal e irresistible de los hados [the fatal and irresistible power of the fates]" that prevents her from succeeding in killing Cortés,[159] and the narrator consigns himself to be merely the chronicler of this destiny already written upon the bodies of the Indian, the "destino fatal que había decidido la pérdida de América."[160] Beyond the historians that have chronicled its fall, the collapse of the American Indigenous states has already been authored, has already been written in (sacred) History itself. As Jicoténcal and the narrator indicate, the outcome of the Tlascalan struggle has already been decided—*ya había decidido*—circumscribing their actions within the limits of this "libro fatal," constraining any inheritance they would bequeath to that which the text allows them. The creoles' responsibility to the death of the Indian, the death that makes their existence possible in both its failure to eradicate the Spanish and its prophecy of an independent state, is thus displaced as a responsibility to a greater Other. Even Olmedo's Inca is constrained by this text, in which he also functions as a character. The vengeance he calls for on behalf of the "pueblo americano" is not his to invoke; it is already "en el gran libro del destino escrito [in the great book of destiny written]."[161] The Inca thus moves from prophet to character, or, in his moment of revelation, to reader. Prefacing his vision of the future independent America, Huaina-Capac says, "La página fatal ante mis ojos desenvolvió el destino [the fatal page before my eyes unwrapped the destiny]."[162] Creole independence in the poem is thus already written, an event that will occur despite the intervention of the Indian past. In *Jicoténcal,* Magiscatzin's exposition of the signs in the sky is a direct citation of Solís, a history of the future that becomes revelation when spoken in the past. This prophecy declares that the Spanish "ha de venir," an indication not only of a future event (one that will come) but a structure that *requires* it (it has—*ha*—to come).[163] All of this, including the sacrificial deaths of the Amerindians, was written before and by another, not by the Indian who, even in death, remains exiled from the documentary assurances of subjectivity in the new states.

The creole patriot thus celebrates and at the same time exorcises a *lost* Native heritage, a mourning that bars creole identification with present Amerindians even as it works affectively to distinguish a creole cultural heritage that is distinct from the Spanish, whose cruelty caused this loss to take place. This distinction between historical and contemporary indigenous populations makes it possible for a nativist sovereignty, articulated as a sentimental attachment to a foreclosed Native identity, to provide impetus for revolution and to stabilize emergent political forms, and yet achieves this "without radically altering relations between the state and the indigenous population."[164] "All nationalisms," Said writes, "develop from a condition of estrangement. . . .

Triumphant, achieved nationalism then justifies, retrospectively as well as prospectively, a history selectively strung together in a narrative form."[165] What we see in putting the discourses of creole patriotism together with that of the Vanishing American is precisely this work of producing history among early national writers, and doing so by addressing the estrangement of shifting political definition not simply in the dislocation of contending claims to land, to heritage, but in appropriating the lament attendant to that estrangement as precisely the heritage to be claimed. That is, the exilic position that Said imagines produced exterior to the nation is here positioned as a condition for interiority, a national feeling curated as an extension of this recognition of irremediable loss. In outlining his theory of necropolitics, Achille Mbembe frames the basic limits of sovereignty as a power over death, "the capacity to dictate who may live and who must die . . . to kill or to allow to live."[166] The dead, those whom we have lost, assume cultural significance for living structures because they mark the boundaries of this power. But unlike cultural analysis of sentimental writings of or about death, Mbembe does not ascribe power to those who, in death, recall us sentimentally toward identification,[167] but rather to those who take up the work of death as a legitimate and legitimizing space upon which to inscribe their own (sovereign) position. By incorporating the Indigenous past into the prehistory of the nation, a memorial crafted out of the pages of their writings, these writers create simultaneously a national feeling for their creole readers and a radical discontinuity between that past and the possibility of an Indigenous present.

3

The Shadow of the (m)Other

You have every reason to exult in your descent, for, surely, if any man may claim to be a citizen and a proprietor in the Union, it is one, that, like yourself, can point to a line of ancestors, whose origins is lost in the obscurity of time. You are truly an American.

—Rev. J. R. C., preface to Cooper's *The Wept of Wish-ton-Wish*

Born all of the same mother, our fathers [are] of different origins and blood.

—Bolívar

On the Frontier, a Gravestone

At the conclusion of *Jicoténcal,* Teutila seeks redress for the death of her husband, the eponymous general who, drugged and gagged, died among "dumb" strangers, far from home.[1] Traveling to Texcoco for her own act of destruction, Teutila realizes that she *may* be treading over the location of her husband's execution. "Tal vez estoy pisando—exclama llena de horror—la sangre de mi Jicoténcal!—y diciendo así hace esfuerzos por arrojarse a besar la tierra [Perhaps I am treading over—she exclaimed full of horror—the blood of my Jicoténcal! —and saying so threw herself down to kiss the earth]."[2] No sign marks Jicoténcal's death, no memorial remains to commemorate his work, and so his lover (both Teutila in the text and the reader through the affective extension of the romance) can only commemorate a vague possibility, an act of devotion that is attached to *no* place. In the dislocations that accompany the vanishing discourses of North and South America, such assured and yet imprecise deaths accorded Indigenous figures function to separate the Amerindians from the landscape, containing them instead in narratives passed among a surviving creole readership, their remains unmarked except by the body of the mourning citizen, who incorporates the disavowed figure as one of memory but not memorial. In this chapter, we turn from the creation of an originary vacancy to the material attachments of the memorial, the venerative material spaces of the grave and page that ground the creole community, making locatable a shared identity predicated upon (instead of riven by) the experience of loss. In contrast to the uncertainties of Teutila's "tal vez" and Follen's "where," we move to consider the cultural work of the memorial marker forwarded by writers who discover in that cleared ground the remnants of more recognizable figures.

One can trace this distinction clearly in the Leatherstocking novels of James Fenimore Cooper. Focusing on the early novels (1823–27), we see Cooper using deaths and burials as a means of concluding each tale, culminating with that of Natty Bumppo himself in the vast unincorporated space of *The Prairie* (1827). But before he lights out for the territories, Natty is marked indelibly on the New York landscape and in the process recalled to a particular community and heritage while his Native companion, Chingachgook (also called John Mohegan or Indian John), remains excluded from the incorporative work of the memorial. In separating out the frontiersman, Bumppo, from his Lenape intimate, Cooper distinguishes between the containment of an always-historical memory and the perduring work of the memorial. A full five chapters before the reader is ever introduced to the person of Chingachgook, she is admonished several times to remember him. On departing from his injured young friend in the first chapter of *The Pioneers* (1823), Leatherstocking advises him to look for Indian John, a man invoked previously only as witness to memory ("In the old war . . . I travelled . . . with a rifle bullet in my thigh, and then cut it out with my own jack-knife. Old Indian John knows the time well").[3] Sending off his friend, he calls for Indian John and his ancient knowledge again, this time of herbal remedies to aid the town's doctor. "Remember old Indian John," he reminds the young hunter, and, again, "remember Indian John" before the boy departs.[4] John, a Christian Indian living among the settlers at Templeton, is the baptismal name for Chingachgook, a Delaware chief and Natty's only human companion to appear in more than one of the novels. His invocation in the opening of the series makes of the man a figure of and in memory, a representation cemented when the reader is finally given his story and an explanation of his name. He is the last of his line, determined to die in the land of his ancestors. "He stood alone," the narrator says. "The last of his family, and his particular tribe, the few Delawares, who yet continued about the head-waters of the river, gave him the mournful appellation of Mohegan." The name Mohegan "recalled the idea of his nation in ruins" and so the title, together with his conversion, becomes a sign not only of loss but also of erasure. "The settlers had united," the narrator continues, "according to the Christian custom, his baptismal with his national name, and to them, he was generally known as John Mohegan, or, more familiarly, as Indian John."[5] Chingachgook, the reader discovers, is a character who is already lost to us.

The violence of erasure that may be implied in renaming the Indian chief seems to be ameliorated by the Native American's own grave perspective; he understands himself to be a remnant who lingers only "with a determination of laying his bones in that country, where his fathers had so long lived and governed."[6] When the time comes at the conclusion of the novel to accomplish this task, amid a forest fire and a rescue adventure definitive of the genre, Indian John merely sits down and waits to die. Chingachgook does not fall in a grand battle, like those Indian deaths that mark the other Leatherstocking novels, or even amid the minor violence of *The Pioneers* itself, as in Judge Temple's siege on Natty's home. Instead, Chingachgook simply gives himself up to death on the mountain as it is consumed by fire. Natty urges his friend to preserve himself and flee the fire, but Chingachgook replies: "Why should Mohegan go? . . . He has seen the days of an eagle, and his eye grows dim. He looks on the valley; he looks on the water; he looks in the hunting-grounds—but he sees no Delawares. Every one has a white skin. My fathers say, from the far-off land, come. My women, my young warriors, my tribe, say, come. The Great Spirit says, come. Let Mohegan die."[7] The Delaware chief sees his death as an answer to a call, a request made not by the displacing white population but by his own ancestors, the community from which the simple fact of survival has isolated him. First the fathers, then the women and youth, and finally God herald Chingachgook from "the far-off land," a call that he answers with a passive resistance to life. He doesn't kill himself; he simply refuses to live. If romance, and historical romance in particular, can be defined as a version of questing fiction, then refusing to "shake off your apathy,"[8] merely refusing to rescue or work toward salvation, is a fundamental transgression of its heroic logic. This resignation is implied even in the very act of self-naming. In this response, the reader witnesses Chingachgook embrace "the mournful appellation of Mohegan" that he had previously refused to acknowledge "excepting on the most solemn occasions."[9] The name is a tribute to the destruction of his larger community, and labels John as a man not only out of place but also out of time. The nation it names is already gone. Waiting to die on the burning hill, the Indian's eyes fix on "distant hills" but also on "the womb of futurity." The imagined future place, gestational and therefore maternal in its description, is also a return to the former glory and kinship of his tribe, and John understands his death, "the happiest moment of his life," to be the only way to fulfill this revelation.[10] It is at this moment that Chingachgook throws off the mantle of his Christian name and the English language as well. "It's hard to keep them from going back to their native ways," Natty tells the distraught clergyman,[11] reminding the onlookers that "flesh isn't iron, that a man can live for ever, and see his kith and kin driven to a far country, and he left to mourn, with none to keep him company."[12] Neglecting to consider the crowd of white spectators or even his own friendship suitable for the definition of "company," Natty sees the event of Chingachgook's death as isolated and untouchable, a man returning to his community before or outside the boundaries of white, Christian culture. In death, Chingachgook finds the world he once knew, a world that had long since abandoned him. In death, he says, "the eyes of Mohegan grow young. I look—but I see no white-skins; there are none to be seen but just and brave Indians. Farewell, Hawk-eye—you shall go . . . to the white man's heaven; but I go after my fathers."[13]

This declaration of an insurmountable separation, one that continues even after death, is confirmed by the legible spaces of the memorial markers that conclude the novel. Investigating the monuments that mark the graves of his friends Chingachgook and Major Effingham, Natty has his young companions read the inscriptions only to find himself included in the latter's epitaph. On Major Effingham's stone, "a rich monument, decorated with an urn, and ornamented with the chisel," the inscription, consecrated to the memory of the once rich and mighty landowner, details the man's titles, bravery, religion, and personal history. The memorial concludes by remarking on Natty, saying of him that the old man's cares "were alleviated only by the tender care of his old, faithful, and upright friend and attendant, Nathaniel Bumppo. His descendants rear this stone to the virtues of the master, and to the enduring gratitude of the servant."[14] Leatherstocking, joyful at his inclusion on the monument, has his friends point out his name and, feeling the shape of the letters on the stone, remarks that "'tis a gin'rous gift to a man who leaves none of his name and family behind him in a country, where he has tarried so long."[15] His friends, inscribing Natty's name on the headstone, have given the itinerant frontiersman a permanent space through which he can be remembered and thus, despite his lack of actual heirs, a way to bequeath a heritage, to continue on in the country. Even after he has passed (or even after he is past) there is a material connection that remains. In memorializing Natty on Effingham's stone, the marker offers Natty an enduring material connection to a community that is emphatically white, not Native. Although Effingham hardly appears in the novel, and Natty's personal reminiscences usually carry an invocation of Chingachgook as witness or friend, Leatherstocking is permanently inscribed as a white man's companion, a relationship witnessed by those who will continue to read or consume the text, a love that is transferred from master to servant.

On the smaller, plainer stone next to this marker, Natty's friendship is neglected in memorializing the Indian. Unlike Effingham's stone, Chingachgook's grave bears no mention of friends or family; instead the stone insists that he was all that remained, saying, "He was the last of his people." The inclusion of Chingachgook in the community graveyard seems to bring him into relation with those who gather to remember the dead, but a comparison between his simple marker and the grand stone next to it undermines this project and instead emphasizes the erasure and exclusion of the Indian's death from the project of mourning. "It may be said of him that his faults were those of an Indian, and his virtues those of a man," the stone reads. While the latter addition attempts to incorporate the Native figure into a larger group, defined by the white Christian norm, the juxtaposition between Indian and man implied in the faults/virtues attribution imposes upon the Native a humanism from which he is also already excluded. Not only is Natty's companionship disavowed, but the statement puts in doubt the possibility of any shared relationship between Native and "man." The structural changes and orthographical errors also emphasize the difference and distance of the Native in death. In opposition to Effingham's memorial, which contains his one name and several titles (both specific, like Esquire and Major, and general, like Christian and master), the Native's stone has one title (Chief) and several names. The deceased, the stone reads, "was known by the several names of John Mohegan; Mohican . . . and Chingagook," the last two of which Natty has to correct, the former on pronunciation and the latter on a much deeper error, one that is literally carved in stone. "'Gach, boy," Natty says, "—'gach-gook; Chingachgook."[16] The order of names moves from baptismal appellation to Native American and as it does its errors and misunderstandings become more evident and more grievous. If Chingachgook was rendered inaccessible through a Christian renaming in life, in death he remains similarly removed from the process of mourning. The misspelling changes the meaning of the name, the only Native and singular name (particular to the man) offered by the memorial. "The name should be set down right," Natty tells his friends, "for an

Indian's name has always some meaning in it." In changing the spelling, the inscription divorces the name from its meaning and, because it was bestowed on him as a descriptor of his own actions in the world, its deformation marks a loss of Chingachgook's history from the broader memorial narrative. Chingachgook is a *mournful* subject, in that he is a representation of a general loss, but he is also removed from the realm of the mourn-able through both his self-effacement in death and the acts of erasure that mar his memorial. If Natty's affiliation is written in stone, Chingachgook fails to leave a legible mark.

Natty's own death and memorial marker reaffirm his affective relationship to a white community bound off from Native influence. In *The Prairie,* his companionship with Chingachgook seems to live on, despite his friend's death, through the figure of Hard-Heart, a Pawnee warrior whom Bumppo "adopts" and of whom he speaks in a paternal manner. But as the trapper prepares to die, the event of death and the communal act of mourning convince Natty of the impossibility of such relationships. We can see this in Natty's rejection of an Indian funeral and tribute in favor of the durable inscription of a gravestone. When his "son" offers him traditional heralds and ceremonies, Natty answers, "Pawnee, I die, as I have lived, a christian man.... [God] knows my colour."[17] Death here, as with Chingachgook's in *The Pioneers,* is a moment of cultural affiliation, an act (continued through the repetition and return of mourning) that is culturally and, here, racially distinct. When Natty says of the Pawnee that a white man's death is simply not "among the gifts of their colour," he is practicing death as a form of identification and consequently one that disavows his previous Native practices and affiliations. He dies as he has lived, and he dies a white, Christian man. Because of the shared, communal work of mourning, Natty's end is riddled with familial anxieties, a concern that he too dies alone, "an end of my race,"[18] a lament that recalls Chingachgook's "lasting." But taking up the mantle of kinship is Captain Middleton, the grandson of a couple united by Natty's heroism in *Last of the Mohicans.* Middleton argues that he owes his life to Natty, not just because of the adventure the two had on the eponymous prairie but as a primordial debt as well. Without Natty's intervention, Middleton would not exist and so the Captain "inherits a heavy debt of gratitude from his ancestors." This structure of indebtedness incorporates Middleton into the body of Natty's community. He offers to act as Natty's kin and make him a stone of his own, work that assuages the old man's mortal anxiety. He instructs the Captain: "Put no boastful words on the same; but just the name, the age, and the time of the death, with something from the holy book. . . . My name will then not be altogether lost on 'arth; I need no more."[19] His enduring name saves Natty from the loss suffered by his friend and in consequence his grave becomes a marker to traveler and trader, a reminder of civilization ("a just white-man"), of a common heritage on the threshold, in 1804, of the new frontier.[20]

By reading the stones together, we see how the memorial inscription distinguishes the work of death as a mode of erasure, as detailed in chapter 2's investigation of the twinned discourses of the Vanishing American and creole patriotism, from those deaths that serve as a *generative* structure for community, which will be the focus of the chapter at hand. Natty Bumppo, in his confirmed bachelorhood and sexual sterility, may be a strange location for an argument about generation or reproduction, but through his death Natty takes on the procreative role of the lingering memorial. We can see Chingachgook's illegible marker as an erasure worked upon the Native community, one that effectively clears the land of prior claims, but a society cannot be founded on a vacancy, it cannot be established in a *no* place, so death must work upon the dominant community as well in order for them to inhabit the land seemingly abandoned by their Native precursors, reminding them of these claims through the headstones that begin to dot the landscape. Death thus *gives place* to community through the *hic jacet* or "here lies" of the memorial inscription. In *Dominion of the Dead,* Robert Pogue Harrison describes the *hic jacet* of the gravestone as a mechanics of place, grounding a shared identity. "The surest way to take possession of a place and secure it as one's own," he writes, "is to bury one's dead in it."[21] Burial of the dead is an appropriation of land that, through the affective ties between the living and the dead, grounds a community's claim to a specific location. This work, Harrison argues, is akin to building, "the domestication of space" effected by the establishment of a horizon or containment, a containment that is simultaneously the establishment of physical locatability, the "here" of "here lies," as well as a historical understanding implied in the temporal *hic* as the "now" of "here."[22] To read a gravestone is to recall simultaneously a historical event and its perdurance, its continued presence across time, yoking the past, present, and future. This signifying force depends on the inscriptive work of the cenotaph that distinguishes this cultivated land from the chaos of unmarked space. "It does not suffice," Harrison says, "to place the dead in the ground . . . it is also necessary to mark that burial."[23] If interment allows for a space upon which to write, the memorial gives *place* to a social relation by inscribing space with "here" and "now."

In thinking through this marking of space, Harrison connects the social signification of the *hic jacet* to the *sema:*

> It is not for nothing that the Greek word for "sign," *sema,* is also the word for "grave." For the Greeks the grave marker was not just one sign among others. It was a sign that signified the source of signification itself, since it "stood for" what it "stood in"—the ground of burial as such. In its pointing to itself, or to its own mark in the ground, the *sema* effectively opens up the place of the "here," giving it that human foundation without which there would be no places in nature. (21)

Harrison's argument makes clear the relationship between writing and death that inheres in our assertions of identity, and therefore our understanding of community or relation in general. Death and burial cultivates a *textual* relationship between a subject, his home, and fellow mourners. Natty's grave marker, a simple stone with his name, age, and scripture, speaks to, and so serves as a foundation for, a community, while Chingachgook's error-filled marker signifies nothing, can speak to no one. Natty's foundational act on the frontier is death itself, a death that tames and claims the prairie, his grave the place where "it is in the earth itself that it is 'written' that we have our 'place here.'"[24] The signifying work of the memorial is therefore a "grounding" of space, a containment through which it can become possess-able and therefore a boundary between the *mine* and *yours* of identificatory objects. The land—constructed as empty through cultural narratives such as the "Vanishing American" trope—is possessed by the dead and, through our memorial rites we lay claim to these dead and the land in its turn.

Despite his sterility, then, Natty is a generative figure for the expanding American state, going forth onto the frontier in order to make a place for those who follow. The Leatherstocking novels have and continue to be read by critics as masculine rejections of domestic structures of control: Natty rejects marriage for himself and flees before the advances of civilization, finding refuge in the expansive, unmarked land of the frontier. Standing at the head of this field of criticism is Leslie Fiedler, who, in his *Love and Death in the American Novel,* declares Cooper's hero to be "always opposed . . . to the 'stickier' and more sentimental kinds of relationships."[25] Bumppo, Fiedler declares, is a "protest against the gentle tyranny of home and woman."[26] But while Natty himself has no children, his adventures do circulate around the (re)establishment of order and the (re)uniting of white, socially dominant couples whose reproductive capabilities are in turn assured by Natty's intervention. This makes *their* legacy, or rather their ability to create a legacy, *his* legacy. In his adventures, Natty guides and defends, rescues and restores troubled couples, finding for them the domestic happiness and reproductive capabilities that he seems to reject. This community-building work is fully articulated by his death and burial. Captain Middleton is evidence of a community of mourners that Natty has, despite his sterility, generated as his descendants, he their ancestor. The "debt of gratitude from his ancestors" writes over the fact that Middleton is "not of my kin" and so the Captain can assume the responsibility of familial tribute.[27] Despite the famous and persistent criticism that places Natty in a rebellious flight from domesticity, the reproductive work of the dead frontiersman means that the *late* Natty can be understood as a *maternal* figure, giving birth to a community that expands with his travels, each adventure westward leaving sentimental remainders in the couples he rescued. Death and the presence of Middleton-as-mourner marks Natty as a sentimental medium, a shared love object that binds together a diverse community of which Middleton is metonymically representative. The continued reading of his *sema,* the sign that indicates "where a just white-man sleeps,"[28] places Natty as an object of desire and ritual consumption, a sentimental commodity for imperial American culture that echoes the work done by the suffering yet sacred mothers of the domestic romance. Through death the wayward hero is incorporated back into the domestic structure of the nation; through his *sema* the hero reproduces that structure on the previously unmarked land of the frontier.

If Natty, or at least a dead Natty, can be reincorporated into the national romance, then, because his life and death occur on and impact the racialized borderlands of the nation, Natty can be placed in a clear relationship with those domestic novels that take as their subject these issues of contact and contest, the miscegenist romances that seem to imagine American history as a commingling of racial groups.[29] In particular, I would like to compare the cultural work accomplished by Cooper's hero with that done by the heroine (or, as I will argue, heroines) in a novel that was offered as a direct response to Cooper's conquering *Pioneers,* Lydia Maria Child's *Hobomok.* By comparing Leatherstocking with the interracial sexual coupling of Child's novel, I do not mean to argue that Natty does not represent, in the words of Leslie Fiedler, a "dread of miscegenation."[30] Rather, I will argue that the supposed egalitarian or intermediate work that the interracial romance accomplishes is undone or *overwritten* by the work of death in the novel. By cathecting dead white mothers, Child's novel reinforces racial barriers that its interracial marriage would transgress. I will conclude by comparing the work of these dead "mothers" in US national romances with a nineteenth-century Brazilian historical romance that takes as its focus the Other mother, the Indigenous mother, in order to understand how the rituals of redress represented by these maternal deaths might function differently according to the cultural location and definition they offer to the present community.

In That Grave, My Mother

In a country marked by "a steadily hardening definition of racial categories,"[31] a young Lydia Maria Child published the novel *Hobomok* (1824), the tale of a Puritan settler who marries and has a child with an Indian chief. The author, who would later rise to prominence as a social reformer and abolitionist, recounted the origins of her first novel by insisting that that book was her answer to the call, made by the *North American Review,* for a national literature that would exploit "the unequalled fitness of our early history for the purposes of a work of fiction."[32] New England history, the magazine declared, was populated by "prominent and high-toned" men who abandoned "all that belongs to the recollections of infancy" and invented themselves anew upon the "outside of the world."[33] These men, therefore, were the perfect foundation for establishing claims to national character and literature. A consciously historical literature, populated as it would be with these epic men in their epic struggle, could demonstrate to European doubters that the United States did not achieve independence at the cost of its cultural life.[34] Citing this as her inspiration, Child explicitly posits *Hobomok* as an attempt to define a national historical character, displacing the divorce from European heritage made explicit by the Revolution onto a colonial precedent. It was to this end that Child, upon reading the article, "siezed [*sic*] a pen, and before the bell rang for the afternoon meeting I had written the first chapter, exactly as it now stands."[35]

Hobomok therefore participates in the project to resurrect the historical body in order to define a present citizen and so it also, as indicated in the novel's preface, is in dialogue with the popular historical romances of Sir Walter Scott and James Fenimore Cooper, which were trying to do the same. The narrator sees the works of these authors "galloping over hill and dale, fast and more successful than Alexander's conquering sword"; they are an imperial force, conquering both the literary market and its readers, whose "mind is every where supplied" with *Pioneers, The Spy* lurking in their closets, and *The Pilot* in the deep.[36] The popular genre is here imagined as an all-consuming one, one that invades the reader's physical space, including her very body, and so the demands of the reader upon the book market are matched by the demands made by the book itself upon the reader. The narrator does not conjure the image of the historical romance as consuming martial force in order to protest its work of occupation upon the American land ("Even American ground is occupied"),[37] but rather to make space for New England in its conquering discourse, to "rouse the dormant energies" by resurrecting New England's past.[38] Child's narrator here relies on the affective power of these sentimental histories to effect a change in their reader, not just in expanding her knowledge about the past, but more importantly making her *feel differently* in and about the present.

While this affective power of the romance was shared with other fictional texts, the historical romance maintained a moral superiority over its fanciful counterparts. Because of their seductive or romantic themes, novels were vilified as dangerous, contaminative influences, particularly for their female readership, who, isolated from public education in both official and unofficial forms, relied on reading to provide them with information about the world.[39] Early American novels picked up on this anxiety; works such as William Hill Brown's *The Power of Sympathy* (1789), Hannah Webster Foster's *The Coquette* (1797), and Tabitha Tenney's *Female Quixotism* (1801) warned against the exposure to romance by pairing the act of reading novels with the perils of seduction. Reading novels, these texts implied, led to irrational and immoral behavior because, exposed thus to fiction the reader no longer understood reality as it presented itself outside the written page. Nina Baym asserts that these protests were founded on the belief that reading novels encouraged a type of social passivity; "Saturating women's interior worlds with fantasy," Baym says, "novels ruptured their connections with, loyalty to, interest in, and usefulness for, the everyday republican world."[40] Seven years after publishing her first historical romance, Child herself articulates this fear of novels in her domestic manual *The Mother's Book*. There, the author decries the pernicious influence of novels, joining her voice to the common discourse that posited them as false prophets, frivolous and even dangerous means of distraction. Instead of novels, Child promoted "serious" literature, encouraging mothers to foster a love for "History, Voyages, Travels [and] Biography" in their children in order "to prevent an exclusive and injurious taste for fiction.[41] If novels were dangerous because they threatened to break down a sense of continuity with and responsibility to one's community, history, as a referential discourse, was to be praised because it grounded its reader in the realities of her world. History, Baym argues, was promoted "in rhetorical contrast to the evils of novel reading."[42] If the Radcliffean romance could be charged with isolating its reader, carrying her away from "the everyday republican world," then the study of history grounded the subject in her own reality, allowing her a connection to the polity and a sense of participation in the community. The advent of the historical novel, then, changed the terms of the literary debate and allowed fiction to escape its negative stigma. "Hostility to the novel per se," Baym argues, "began to evaporate only with the success of Walter Scott's historical novel *Waverly* in 1814. This suggests that the novel, demonized as history's other, escaped its pariah status by becoming historical itself."[43]

To illustrate this redemption Baym cites Child's assertion that the novels based on Scott's model could be read "in connexion with history to great advantage." Their influence, Child says, "is never in opposition to good; and to the thinking mind they afford abundant food for reflection."[44] This favorable effect derives from the cultural work of the historical study; instead of disabling its audience with escapist fantasies, the historical novel encourages active participation in "the patriotic work of establishing and affirming national origins, characters, and values."[45] The (re)presentation of the past not only illustrates a foundational community but also serves as a positive act of construction in that it ties the present to that past, linking the contemporary national subject to a protonational community. The historical romance has a distinct advantage over other forms of history in effecting this cultural work. As Ernest Renan states, "A community of interest is assuredly a powerful bond between men . . . but nationality has a sentimental side to it."[46] By its appropriation of the sentimental tropes of the domestic novel (love, marriage, suffering, death, and dying) the historical romance produces an intimate, affective foundation for community and in so doing makes a corporeal appeal to the reader. The sentimental nature of the historical romance forces its reader literally to *feel for* the protagonists in their loves, losses, and redemptions. The reader's sighs and tears are corporeal signs of a textual possession, both of the text by the reader and of the reader by the text. The text incorporates the reader through the protagonists' corporeal excitation and so she becomes physically involved with the community at/in hand. This is her "abundant food for reflection," as Child states, a distinctly national and nationalist consideration that rests on the author's ability to produce and reproduce community.[47]

It is notable that this cultural work is couched in the language of the table. Novels were considered light and airy "confectionary" for the reader,[48] satisfying a selfish indulgence, a luxurious desire that exceeds material necessity. They were, as one concerned female reader complained, not "solid works";[49] they neglected to give the subject anything to take in, any substance with which to commune or create community. The profane "infectious fantasy," the "exclusive and injurious taste for fiction," separates the reader from the sacred practices of the citizen, their productive (or rather reproductive) burden of the "everyday republican world." These are self-contained, onanistic fantasies that isolate the reader from her social responsibility. The America "occupied" by the "solid works" of Scott and Cooper is one in which, as Steven Mailloux has argued, reading itself formed "part of the specific disciplinary targeting of the body."[50] These historical romances grounded the subject in the material world. By embracing the historiographical posture, a referential discourse, these novels exorcised fantasy, becoming themselves substantial and the reader well-fed. The readers of these novels, their defenders argued, did not feed on the imaginary figures of romance, but on their own dead, the material of their own cultural past. As an iteration of history, therefore, the historical romance is not only a necrophilic but also a necrophagic discourse. Reading as a consumptive act (as both eating up the reader, bringing her into a structural system, and a using up of the written resource as a productive cultural chain) ties the subject to the mode of production, her body to the body of the text and to the bodies in the text. The deviant seduction of the novel is displaced by the chivalric mode of Scott's romances and further removed by the austere sexual attitudes of the chaste hero and the hesitating, aristocratic lovers in Cooper's novels, making solid promises about what was and is and not airy threats about what could be.

Child's recourse to the interracial sexual coupling in her novel was, accordingly, the focus of the strongest criticism, even from her source of inspiration. Child's critics in the *North American Review* focused their attention almost entirely on the issue of miscegenation. In an 1824 brief note about the book, the reviewer declared her depiction of a "high born and delicate female" wedding an Indian "not only unnatural, but revolting."[51] A subsequent extended review ruled that "there can be . . . but one opinion respecting this story; it is in very bad taste, to say the least, and leaves upon the mind a disagreeable impression."[52] But despite the clamor regarding sexual coupling, the interracial marriage is displaced in the novel by other, mortal concerns. While the mixed-race union produces a new native subject that could speaks to hybrid possibilities for the national character, the community that is actually (re)born in and through the novel is a familiar, and, to these reviewers, a better-tasting one. Both reviews make brief positive remarks regarding Child's depiction of the Puritan family, and the later review calls out one scene in particular that it has found worthy, despite the novel's "bad taste," of eager consumption: "The death bed scenes of the Ladies, Mary Conant and Arabella Johnson," the reviewer informs us, just before the magazine's reproduction of that very scene, "are described with feeling and pathos, and varied with considerable skill."[53] The interracial eroticism is overwritten by a new gestational location for New World identity; the American is born from the grave of the sacred mother. By looking at how Child deploys death and mourning in her text, we can see how, despite the notoriety of its interracial romance, the novel's central concern remains community—and racial—fidelity. This foundational narrative produces a sentimental attachment to the white colonial community within the novel, and this work is mirrored in the act of writing the history itself.

This community is the effect of both a sentimental and a historiographical relationship with the dead body, a key trope in sentimental literature, an act (dying) that Jane Tompkins defines as "the supreme form of heroism."[54] Describing perhaps the most famous death scene in nineteenth-century literature, that belonging to Little Eva in *Uncle Tom's Cabin,* Tompkins declares that death "brings an access to power, not a loss of it."[55] She argues, following Stowe, that death and the dead minister to the living and so hold redemptive or salvific power over them. Through confronting death and mourning the dead, the lost are brought back into the fold of their sacred communities. Along with the departed child, Tompkins argues that it is mothers who are "uniquely capable" of laying claim to the spiritual power of this deathly work.[56] But while the child often represents innocence, or the innocent victim, why does the mother retain a privileged place in this grave discourse? Tompkins and other critics have argued that this is because of the mother's important role in the moral or sentimental education of the child, particularly for the child-as-future-citizen under the aegis of "republican motherhood," but I would trace the mother's formative role to a much earlier intervention. As the site of original partition, of birth itself, the mother's body is linked inextricably with dissolution and death. As the site of physical and later egoic separation that makes space for identity and identification, the mother's body is indelibly marked by the loss by which living is made possible. At birth, the child becomes separated physically from the mother's body; the child's somatic continuity with the mother is at that moment severed. As the mother's body becomes psychically disentangled from the child's imaginary space, a lack opens up through which the child begins to consider its own limits and identity. The mother's body, then, presents itself as a somatic remainder and thus a reminder of the division and dissolution that occur biologically and psychically in order for the subject to begin to be, and even "to be," the definition of a subject position that conjugates an ontological position in language (i.e., "I am"). In the Americas, this knowledge of dissolution was historically pressing, as the newly independent nations articulated their distinction from mother lands and mother tongues. But surely they could not afford to allot those European mothers the power of death in their separation. Instead, the new nations chose to imagine their family otherwise.

Freud described this reinvention of one's parents as "the family romance," an imaginative fantasy in which the subject rejects the authority of his parents by latching onto the idea that those he has always known as his parents are not his *real* parents. The presence of *other* parents signals to the child the possibility of his own parents' insufficiency, introducing with them the idea "that other parents are in some respects preferable."[57] Freud remarks that after the child becomes conscious of the role sex plays in procreation, the fantasy is emended to no longer question the role of the mother but to focus its narrative upon the father. The author of the fantasy imagines infidelity on the part of his mother, inventing a new, exalted paternity that articulates the understanding that *pater semper incertus est* [the father is always uncertain].[58] The mother, who by contrast is always *certissima,* "remains firmly and certainly planted in reality, excluded from the process of 'fictionalization.'"[59] But while she is excluded from the fictional schema, the mother remains necessary for this narrative process as this fiction is *inscribed upon her body;* the mother becomes the blank page upon which the child projects this generative fantasy. Even more pertinent for the application of this structure to national discourse is the *narrative* power that Freud ascribes to this fantasy. The original title of his essay, Peter Gay points out, is "Der Familien*roman* der Neurotiker" (emphasis added), "roman" translating more specifically to "novel," a translation that complicates the idea of authorship and inscription implied by Freud's analysis.

The "authority" under scrutiny in the fantasy is connected to the author-ity of the fictional text, the narrative alternatives invented by the child, what Freud himself calls "these works of fiction."[60] Freud also declares that the child's new position of author-ity is simultaneous with a growing nostalgia, "an expression of the child's longing for the happy, vanished days when his father seemed to him the noblest and strongest of men and his mother was the dearest and loveliest of women."[61] The child's narrative invention, his claim to authorship, is therefore a mournful act, one that attempts, over and over, to recover what has been lost to him. But while the father is restored in the fantasy (Freud reassures anxious parents that "the child is not getting rid of the father but exalting him"),[62] the child's narrative space is opened up by, and thus relies upon, the mother's defilement, her fall from an original grace or preoedipal wholeness. The mother's loss must therefore remain irremediable if "the novel instinct" that grasps the subject is to remain.[63] The narrator's mother is thus forever lost, or, if she remains, only does so incompletely, as an enduring reminder of lack that the fantasy can only exploit and never resolve. The powerful death of the mother, imagined by Tompkins, can therefore be understood as the opening up of an inscriptive space that is at the same time an affective commodity. This "heroic" sacrifice makes of the mother a text whose circulation becomes a mode of communion, or, in Anderson's terms, a shared imaginary, whose affective power consolidates a reading public, consumers bound by their shared object choice.

If dying is akin to heroism, then, in Child's sentimental historiography, death is the hero. It is death that allows the historical community to become geographically located, it creates and maintains sentimental ties above and beyond those "of interest," and it permits the story its historiographical posture from which the cultivated relationship to the past effects cultural work in the present. Death is literally central to *Hobomok.* Despite his eponymous presence, Hobomok remains only a titular subject, the relationship between the Indian chief and Mary consigned to a few chapters in the last third of the work. The majority of the work instead focuses on the personalities and conflicts within the white settlement, particularly the religious debates that threaten the stability of the group. But at the physical and narrative center of the novel, the narrative of the community changes from a focus on dogmatic conflict to various confrontations with loss. From Sally's marriage and subsequent move to Plymouth to Charles's social death at the hands of the Puritan elders, consequent exile, and supposed watery grave, a feeling of separation and mourning builds throughout the heart of the romance, culminating in the melodramatic death scenes of Lady Arabella and Mary's mother. These two deaths function as the sentimental spectacle that raises the novel's central question of community, of how to build and sustain a community in the harsh new world. The interracial romance, the focus of the reviewers' disgust, functions as only part of the denouement of this central scene. It is what leads the heroine away from her social role, her "wayward fate," that which temporarily impedes her from accessing what these deaths would accomplish.[64] The pair's theatrical demise reflects the "painful power of tragic representation" that the narrator signals as a mode of confederation, a coming together through the emotional excitation of the spectacle.[65] This "tragic representation" preys upon what the narrator sees as a "fundamental principle in the human mind,"[66] the "love of excitement" that finds its release in these sad spectacles that constitute and reconstitute, that establish and affirm, a community. At the heart of Child's narrative we find exactly this generative tragedy; it is through the deaths of the two white mothers that the community consolidates as both a sentimental affiliation and a geographical location.

Before the mothers' deaths, the settlement already suffered from a high mortality rate, evinced not only in the climbing body count at the center of the novel but also in continual references made to those nameless settlers already lost during the crisis described in the novel's opening chapters. But notable figures like the pious Reverend Higginson do not become notable in their deaths; Higginson slips by without the excitement of "tragic representation" afforded to the dead mothers. The Reverend is a divisive figure, holding a hard line against dissenters with his insistence that "the threshold of hell is paved with toleration."[67] If death functions, as I argue, as a means of communion and incorporation, it is understandable that this religious figure, in his restricted conception of the church and the community, is supplanted by the twinned maternal deaths. One of these deaths belongs to Lady Arabella Johnson, whose celebrated arrival to the colonies quickly moves toward grief at her mortal withdrawal. Lady Arabella's rapid departure from life and the narrative may seem like a strange place to locate significant acts, but in the Lady's short appearance she manages to accomplish the fundamental task of dying. Immediately after her arrival, her health begins to fade and she languishes alongside the long-suffering Mrs. Conant. Mary's sentimental connection to the Lady and her physical proximity to her own mother ascribe to Lady Arabella a maternal role. She comes to share a single deathbed with the elder Mary, and so Arabella doubles the intimate experience of maternal loss. But Lady Arabella's death also influences a community greater than the immediate individual family unit. It is through Lady Arabella's death that the romance illustrates the conversion of sentimental attachment to the body into a similarly affective attachment to the land.

The new world seems to consume the Lady, and in her death she becomes part of the environment that seems so vampiric and threatening. But instead of lamenting her choice to follow her husband in his colonial venture, Lady Arabella dismisses the causal relationship between settlement and suffering. "The time of my departure hath come and what matters it whether it be in England or America?" she asks her husband when he voices regret at their relocation.[68] The question denies America's responsibility for the death of the loved object, displacing the idea of the dangerous environment that has already claimed so many lives. On her deathbed, her husband's complaint, "But for my selfish love, you might be living in ease and comfort," is answered with: "In the short space we have been allowed to sojourn together, I have enjoyed more than all my life beside."[69] The new world is in this way transformed into the site of desire as it represents the sacrifices made, the distances traveled in order to be with the one she loves, and Lady Arabella herself projects the landscape as the locus of love and its necessary self-abnegation. "I have come into the wilderness too," Lady Arabella tells Mary when faced with her first rough, meager meal, "but 'sweet is a dinner of herbs where love is.'"[70] Arabella declares the sacrifice of emigration and the foundation of a new community, here exemplified in the limits imposed on luxurious consumption, to be *in good taste.* The wilderness and her new life in it is "sweet." The family meal, the act of eating together, is thus a communal and communalizing act, one in which the participants consume shared objects and experience what Freud argues is the connection between the oral drive and identification. Here, narcissism is sublimated, allowing these individuals to gather in the bond of shared object choice. Sweet may be the meager meal where love is, but love is *there* because of the meal's ritual affirmation of that consuming drive.

While her "what matters it" statement serves to ameliorate her husband's relationship to America, its dismissal of location occults the cultural work that her death effects. Lady Arabella's death acts as a foundational, national narrative precisely because she dies in America. Despite the insistent Indigenous presence, made known through continual threats of violence, the land is described as vacant or tractless; through her interment, Lady Arabella comes to inhabit and domesticate it. The settlers continually invoke the image of the desert to describe their surroundings and, in a powerful statement of the "self-annihilating power of vacancy,"[71] the narrator's ancestral voice recalls the bewilderment at confronting the dark, expansive, and empty new world.[72] But as the novel moves forward, the land becomes increasingly habitable, marked by the population. The surviving settlers, happily greeting their newly arrived compatriots on the shore, are in stark contrast to the frightening void of the unmarked ocean and empty land initially met by the narrator; there, man "had rarely been upon these waves and the records of his boasted art were not found in these deserts." This unmarked space, his blank page, fills the witness with a sense of isolation and insignificance, causing him to shrink "from the contemplating of human nothingness."[73] It is not until death itself provides an inscribable surface that the settlers are able to locate and narrate their new community.

By inhabiting or becoming part of it, the Lady, as the object of desire for her husband, becomes the means for an intense, almost erotic attachment to the land itself. When he visited her grave he "laid down his head and wept. He arose, and for awhile rested his melancholy gaze on the bright sun and verdant earth"; afterward he prayed to God to forgive "this worship of an earthly idol."[74] In this ceremony Johnson mourns his wife by fetishizing her place of burial, displacing his desire, and its manifestation in worship, onto the land itself. His idol is not only his deceased partner, but also the earth in which she has been placed, asserting the space of the burial plot as a social one, not only of commemoration but also of communion. Mr. Johnson's fatal attachment allows him to continue the foundational work he started, not in Shawmut, but rather by locating himself permanently on his land at Tri-Mountain. "Bury me in the lot which I have laid out at Tri-Mountain," he says, "that at the great judgment-day I may rise among the heritage which I have feebly endeavored to build up."[75] Through this statement, Johnson manifests a distinctly historical consciousness, locating himself in a causal relationship with a future that he stands to inherit. The heritage is not familial (Johnson has no children in the novel) but rather communal; to that community location he gifts the constructive work of his life and similarly that of his death. Child attaches an extratextual note to this statement that shows the extent to which Mr. Johnson did indeed affect/effect the future community by his decision. "This request was complied with," the authorial voice notes, "and the first burying-place in Boston was laid out around his grave."[76] The act of burial consecrates a place, the "here" of community, by connecting that "here" to a body in the ground. The foundational moment for the city, the deaths taking place in 1629 and Boston's founding in 1630, is thus supported by the affective, structural work of death.

Like Cooper's *Pioneers,* one of the texts Child had imagined claiming readers as it moved across the land, her novel becomes a conquering discourse of its own. The interment of Arabella and her husband, like Natty's, *inhabits* the wilderness. In *The Pioneers,* Cooper's narrator puts forth that the groundbreaking work of the pioneer is "succeeded by the permanent improvements of the yeoman, who intends to leave his remains to moulder under the sod which he tills, or, perhaps, of the son, who, born in the land, piously wishes to linger around the grave of his father."[77] The work of death *grounds* the social establishment indicated by the "permanent improvements," marking first upon the ground and so locating a place onto which to project those pious wishes, a location around which to linger. *The Pioneers* further foreshadows Natty's foundational final act in *The Prairie* by replacing Natty's ruined home with a small cemetery. When Oliver and Elizabeth, the young couple united by Natty's efforts, visit the area, the Leatherstocking himself declares the graves to be "wholesome sights to young as well as old,"[78] indicating their reflective and educational purpose. These are sights/sites of devotion as well as incorporation; the gravestones are texts to consume both the living and the dead, bringing them together and tying the living to that sacred land. Just as Natty's monument on the prairie demonstrates to "traveler and the trader . . . a spot where a just white-man sleeps,"[79] Johnson's grave becomes a marker of white presence in the "desert" around which to establish the new outposts of "civilization." Death, as both of these foundational narratives show, is a sentimental marker on the land, one that strengthens and maintains settlements, providing an affective geography in which the community can locate itself.

The first of the twinned deaths at the heart of the novel, the death of Mary's mother, also effects this sentimental bonding but on a more intimate level. While Lady Arabella's death functions as an affective location for the community, Mrs. Conant's death works to consolidate its smaller constituent, the family, by giving the father and daughter a space onto which to inscribe the sentimental terms of conciliation. This consolidation is done in large part through Mr. Conant's sentimental education. While she was alive, Mary's mother functioned as a mediator between father and daughter; proclaiming love and loyalty to them both while neither seem capable of reconciling on their own. After the series of losses begin to affect Mary's mental stability, her father reflects on their distanced relationship: "He felt that he had, in reality, known very little of Mary, except through the medium of her mother."[80] The act of death and the sentimental injunctions of the deathbed provide new terms through which the father can relate to his daughter. His wife's death moves Conant, the cold, vitriolic Puritan, from his habitual harangue to the "language of tears."[81] At his dead wife's side, Conant abstains from filtering the experience through religious discourse and instead allows himself to cry. "He stood by the corpse of who for twenty years had lain in his bosom," the narrator says, "and he heeded not that the big, bright tears fell fast upon her bed."[82] This lachrymal release is repeated several times after the death scene and is posited against the emotional vacuum of the Puritan discourse. When Mary is assumed dead, Conant allows the release of "a few reluctant tears," letting them "lay undisturbed upon his furrowed cheek." This emotional act is quickly checked by the narrator, who asserts, "Perhaps had he known the near approach of his minister, they had never been shed."[83] Religion, or rather the public demonstration of religion, here acts as an impediment to sentiment, "the voice of nature" that Conant "stifled" in his public performance of grief where "[he] hid all his better feelings beneath the cold mask of austerity."[84] It is this cold mask that the religious leaders praise, the unemotional front lauded as an example of Christian grief. Skelton goes so far as to make this false Conant a model for the community. He says: "If every man bears his part of the public calamities as well as you have borne the death of your child, I have no doubt the Lord will smile upon our undertakings."[85] But this austerity is carefully constructed as unnatural, false, and the reader is privy to Conant's private emotional grief, his tearful "better feelings" in which he indulges away from the public eye. These tears represent a "softened state of feeling," and it is this sentimental awakening that allows him to recognize the limits of his dogmatic rhetoric and to question his intolerant positions taken in regard to Mary and Charles.[86]

This self-reflection is directly related to the spectacle of death; "There is nothing," the narrator asserts, "like the chamber of death to still the turbulence of passion, and overcome the loftiness of pride."[87] This is evident in Conant's reflections on Charles's assumed death when his conscience "inquired whether he had not in some measure mistaken obstinacy and pride for conscientious zeal; and in the humbleness of the moment, he acknowledged that christians were too apt to mistake the voice of selfishness for the voice of God."[88] This moderation of temperament is supported by the invocation of his wife's body: "His earliest enemies had been of the English church, and he had seen his wife drooping and dying amid the poverty which his religious opinions had brought upon her."[89] The specter of his wife thus continues to haunt Conant, he sees the text of his life written out on her body, and his sentimental invocation of her suffering form impedes his customary dogmatic expression.

The gap opened up in his previously rancorous discourse is not only the result of the suffering body but also of Mrs. Conant's powerful deathbed requests imparted to Conant (and Mary). "If Brown comes back," his wife tells him, "You must remember our own thwarted love, and deal kindly with Mary," to which her husband avers, "Verily, my dear wife, your dying request shall be obeyed."[90] His wife requests that he identify his position with that of his daughter, his wife translating the love affair into a repetition of their own. His concession to obedience speaks to the power cultivated by this dying figure as her behest forces Conant to "this softened state of feeling" with his daughter. He speaks to her with tears in his eyes and delights in his new conciliatory position,[91] in the prospect of sublimating the aggressive narcissism of his previous bigotry to his new identification with his daughter. When this concession to family is frustrated by the news of Charles's death he reflects: "Since the death of his wife, he had thought, with a good deal of concealed pleasure, how very graciously he would make a sacrifice to the peace of her only child; and now that there was no hope of making this atonement for his past harshness, he felt more disappointment than he would have been willing to acknowledge."[92] His actions toward Mary are filtered through his relationship with his wife ("the peace of her only child"; he is to deal with Mary in the terms of "our own thwarted love") and so require the affectionate, tender approach of the deathbed. The "concealed pleasure" and the consequently excessive and therefore unacknowledged disappointment, gesture toward the sentimental work of loosening the restrictive emotional bonds of Puritan society. These affective measures can maintain the family; it is the cruel disregard for sentimental attachment, the hardline, dogmatic stance that keeps its members from communion.

The dead mother's voice seems to gird this sentimental resistance to the divisive coldness of the Puritanical emotional divorce. After he attempts to destroy Mary's prayer book, Conant feels "the sting of self-reproach" because "the words of his dying wife seemed to resound in his ears, as she said, 'Be kind to Mary for my sake.'"[93] Mary had spoken the same dying request to her daughter as well: "*For my sake* . . . be dutiful to your good father as you have been to me."[94] The father and daughter thus become stand-ins for the mother herself, the sentimental power of her admonition is a logic of substitution under which the two are to treat each other as if they were her. If the Christian grief invoked by the Puritan elders indicates a complete separation from the dead, the continued presence of the dead body, the incorporation of her voice and presence into the bodies of the text, into the bodies of her husband and daughter, represents the possibility of a persisting responsibility to the dead, who, by being the shared love object between the two, impresses them into her service and thus creates a community out of that indebtedness. This protracted attachment introduces compassion into Conant's relationship with his daughter and it is this that allows him to change his posture toward her from one of censure to one of acceptance and reconciliation. "Come to my arms, my deare childe," he writes to her, and this "mixed feeling of compassion and affection" permits the consolidation of the family unit: patriarch, son-in-law, daughter, and grandchild, in the face of dogmatic and even racial difference.[95]

This softened, sentimental attitude represents a marked difference between Conant and the acrimonious schismatics, a difference that is both affected and produced by the presence of death. Previously, the contentious environment of the settlement was answered by three feminine reactions: Sally's unthinking gaiety and Mary's weariness both represent the failures of uncritical acceptance and foreclosed rejection in affecting change and conciliation in the social system. It is the third response, Mrs. Conant's revelatory yet sympathetic gaze, marked by the approach of death and "its calm, heavenly influence," that allows the subject communion through its sentimental posture. "She looked," the narrator says, "with compassion on the wild and ever-varying light of human doctrines."[96] The presence of death allows Mary to recognize and overcome the worldly, constructed boundaries that maintain schism, separation, in favor of a more humanist, inclusive sentimental gaze. It is this compassionate gaze, produced and reproduced by sentimental excitement, "the painful power of tragic representation," that allows the strident Conant to soften the tone of his rhetoric, to find release for his 'natural' sentiment, and through this, to affect the reconciliation that forms the basis of community. The sentimental construction therefore gestures toward a model of toleration; if the Conant-Brown family is the metonymic representation of the protonational community, then it is this affective ligature, not the cold Puritanical mask, that serves as the foundation from which Child, her narrator, his editor speak.

This shifting of the foundational narrative reenvisions the historical subject, remodeling the "heritage" left to the present community, changing emphasis from the harsh and intolerant Puritan community to the sentimental and inclusive family unit. This shift changes the relationship to the past for Child's audience, evincing what Bruce Mills refers to as the pervasive "disenchantment with Calvinism,"[97] that affected historical engagement with the Puritans for the Unitarian community of Boston. This change in the foundational narrative is therefore reflective of contemporary realities. "By the time Child's novel was published in 1824 . . .," Mills writes, "Calvinists suffered a second-class status and Unitarians controlled the institutions of power in Boston."[98] Mills sees this directly reflected in Mary's rejection of her community's affective neglect. He says, "[Mary] is unable to experience suitable companionship with her father and other villagers because they have attempted to govern her affections with harsh Calvinist doctrine."[99] "What drove Mary to despair," Mills says, "And in part compelled the Boston religious community to reform their faith was their heritage of a harsh and often unfeeling faith."[100] It is in this way that Child's book, according to Mills, "indicates that she understood prevailing Unitarian religious views. In significant ways, *Hobomok* writ large New England's, and especially Boston's, struggle to discard the remnants of an orthodox religious faith and thus resonates with the beliefs of those who directly inspired Child's work."[101]

But, as I have shown, Child's novel is not about negation or rupture, but rather recognition and reconciliation between the constituents of the white settlement. The novel does not "discard"; rather, it serves as an act of recovery. The narrator says: "In this enlightened and liberal age, it is perhaps too fashionable to look back upon those early sufferers in the cause of the Reformation, as a band of dark, discontented bigots. Without a doubt, there were many broad, deep shadows in their characters, but there was likewise bold and powerful light."[102] Instead of distancing the community from its "heritage," Child's novel recreates the foundational subject, shifting it from its previous location in the "stern and unsympathetic faith"[103] to the "bold and powerful light" of the inclusive, tolerant, and sentimental family bond. Unitarians wanting to throw off their Puritan past, wanting to reimagine the structures of their family, find, through their sentimental involvement with the text, their bond to this past renewed. This alteration creates a sense of continuity between the past of Puritan settlement and the present of Unitarian Boston; it strengthens the historical legitimacy of the Unitarians, who can then be seen as the rightful heirs of the "native"[104] community. Reading Child's historical romance requires one to reconsider, as Baym says, "national origins, characters, and values."[105] On the ground claimed by the maternal grave, Child's romance exalts the Puritan forefathers and fosters a sentimental paternity that denies the "barren" nature of Puritan history.[106]

This transfiguration, as both a transformation and a revelation, is produced by the historiographical posture taken up in the elaborately constructed narrative frame. A key figure in the nativist relocation is the unnamed narrator, the figure who initially takes up the project of writing history. He intends to place New England in the national narrative by recreating it in the historical romance, a form that, by its very popularity, threatens to "conquer" the American imagination, eliding the foundational importance of the Northeast. "Barren and uninteresting as New England history is, I feel there is enough connected with it, to rouse the dormant energies of my soul."[107] The project is thus formulated as one of recovery, predicated upon and reproducing a nativist sentimental location. The narrator has an intimate connection with the past through his ancestor, and by exhuming this body is able to claim (author)ity for the narrative and legitimacy for his national/nativist identification.

The narrator demonstrates this nativist exuberance in the opening paragraphs of the novel, in which he locates the reader by indicating his own ties to the land and community. He begins the narrative of the Conant family and Salem by stating: "I never view the thriving villages of New England, which speak so forcibly to the heart, of happiness and prosperity, without feeling a glow of national pride, as I say, 'this is my own, my native land.'"[108] The language of identification is coded by the language of ownership: "this is my own," he says, "my native land." The ownership claimed is not exclusive but rather communal, emphasized by the community-minded narrative but also performed in the confusion of voice in the frame. Who is the narrator? The frame sets him out to be an amateur writer who, with the help of an editor/friend, manages to publish the narrative of a long-lost ancestor. But the frame doubles up on itself, confuses the voices, the levels of mediation. One is never sure if the narrative voice of the story is this unidentified narrator, his ancestor, his editor, or the author herself. For instance, it is the editor who provides the historical pamphlets to his author/friend. Is it then the *editor's* ancestor, appropriated by the authorial voice, who speaks in the narrator's voice? Or did he serendipitously give the author back his own dead? Or perhaps the ancestor is a literary device of mediation in the novel that reflects that same device in the frame (the ancestor is, after all, not introduced in the preface but rather in the first chapter of the narrative). This multiplicity of voices multiplies claims to ownership, and the single ancestor becomes the communal ancestor: this spokesman for the past belongs to us all.

This *communal* ownership is important to the historiographical posture, as this posture is predicated on the power to take up the dead and write upon their bodies. In *Sensational Designs,* Jane Tompkins argues for the power of the dead in affecting the sentimental reform narrative, but the dead have no agency. In this way, I am claiming Tompkins's theory only to reassign the active subject. It is not the dead body that speaks, it is not the dead body that affects society, but rather those living bodies that would manipulate, torture, and exhume dead bodies for narrative purposes. These dead women do not write but are written upon and so function as the material medium through which the author asserts her author-ity over the text of history. In the writing of history, the selection of the object for analysis is self-referential; the historian, "haunted by presuppositions,"[109] "chooses 'subjects' conforming to its place of observation."[110] The body upon which one writes must therefore be recognizable, shared, in order to legitimate the historian's work.

The recognition of this body is double, an acknowledgment of the coherence of the historical representation, a recognizable figure of the past, that is also a figure of discourse through which the present can narrate. The present must believe that the dead can talk. "The dead," French historian Michel de Certeau says, "are the objective figure of an exchange among the living."[111] The dead allow the initial act of separation that permits one to speak, giving one a place onto which to impose this speech and, in such analytic discourse as history, the distance from the subject through which one is authorized to evaluate. Such speech remains "a discourse of the dead . . . a discourse in the third person,"[112] meaning that the mediation of the speechless body allows the historian to occult her narrative responsibility, the interested nature of her discourse. By speaking through or for the vacated body, the dead body, the "dead letter,"[113] the author elides her own construction of the narrative. In *Hobomok,* the long-dead ancestor apparently speaks, with only the substitution of modern speech; "I shall," the narrator tells the reader, "take the liberty of substituting my own expressions for his antiquated and almost unintelligible style."[114] But the confusing narrative interruptions, moving out of the chronological limitations of the ancestor, hint at the objectification of this body, its use as a space onto which the present writes, rather than one that speaks for itself. In making possible the writing of history and occulting its interested narrative, death valorizes the historical romance, making it the substantial "food for reflection," and not the "confection" of the overtly manipulated and manipulable novel.

The dead body thus creates a space onto which a foundational narrative can be written, one of validation for both the text as a cultural production and characters within the narrative itself. Death attaches the subject to the land, the community, and the narrative, allowing the sentimentality and nativist self-recognition through which nationality and nationalism is produced and reproduced. The sentimental ligature requires not simply the spectacle of death but more importantly the enduring memorial that both commemorates the loss and gives space to the community that gathers to mourn, affirming their community ties. This is significant because these sentimental foci conceal the marginalizing work that death also effects. The important cultural work of the two white women is in stark contrast to the death scenes narratively displaced from the texts. The most startling of these vanishing acts is that of Hobomok himself, who structures his departure from his family and the narrative as a death. "Hobomok will go far off among some of the red men in the west," he says. "They will dig him a grave. . . . I will be buried among strangers, and none shall black their faces for the unknown chief."[115] This removal-as-death effectively "disappears" the character, allowing him to leave no remains. The fetishistic object is therefore removed as well. The historical narrative excludes the Indian as a recognizable subject and the white community's own culpability for his disappearance. Hobomok *speaks his own death sentence,* and so he removes himself, the Native, as an obstacle for national consolidation. This unmournable death removes the problematic subject without leaving evidence of an un-narrated, silent space, an "open wound of secrecy."[116] Effacing the issue of racial toleration, the marginalized death of the Indian allows both the community within and the one without the novel to focus on the consolidation of a white, Christian, American subject.

AnOther Mother

Against this hearty reconciliation of the white, Christian American community lingers the specter of another mother, Hobomok's mother. This Native American mother has the potential to serve as a third mother figure for Mary, a potential substitution emphasized by the fact that Mary had served as a nurse not only for her own mother and Arabella but for this Native mother as well.

It is Hobomok's mother's ailing health and Mary's care for her that instigated the desire of the Indian chief for his future wife. "If something within taught him to copy . . . all the kind attention of the white man," the narrator says, explaining Hobomok's devotion to Mary, "'twas gratitude for the life of his mother which she had preserved."[117] It is this mother who celebrates the news of their marriage by dancing, singing, and caressing Mary with "frantic joy,"[118] it is this mother who nurses Mary in her deranged state,[119] and it is this mother who tends to Mary in her married life. "All the kind attentions which could suggest themselves to the mind of a savage," the narrator says, "were paid by *her Indian mother.*"[120] Having worked so diligently to demonstrate the conciliatory work of the maternal figure, the mother's role in the generation of community, the novel here seems to offer an alternative to the dominant structure, one birthed by the Other mother. But, in opposition to the generative acts of the two white mothers, this foundational potential is frustrated by the death of "the old squaw," a death that is disclosed but never narratively present. After the narrator's distant and brief description of Mary's life with Hobomok, spanning two years in two paragraphs and described as a period in which "nothing occurred of any importance to our story" save the brief note that Mary gave birth to a son,[121] she/he/I/We declare: "After this general view of things, we must now pass over to . . . 1633, and leave the interim to the reader's imagination."[122] It is within this span of silence, the narrator says later, that "the old squaw had lately died." Unlike her white counterparts, this mother gains nothing by death; this other mother shrinks into the shadows much like her son will do. These Native deaths thus demonstrate a melancholic disavowal that takes the form of the "never never," a refusal of acknowledgment described by Judith Butler in *The Psychic Life of Power.* This refusal denies both love *and* loss, saying, "I have never loved and therefore never lost the other." This silence forecloses the possibility of identification; the haunting Native American described by Renée Bergland might therefore be seen as a product of deep structure, an inability to grieve that girds the subject's fundamental social identification. This barred identification remains exiled through the ritual practices of mourning. Neither the characters nor the readers return "again and again to [the] defiled grave" of the Native.[123] Where is Hobomok or his mother buried after all? How can I return to *no* place? Rather, these readers return to the monuments dedicated to the white inhabitants of the land, the white deaths that endure as the "humic foundation" for contemporary communities.[124]

I would like to conclude by looking briefly at a similar interracial national romance that was produced and continues to be avidly consumed in a country whose definition of "national origins, characters, and values" depended and in some ways continues to depend heavily on the valorization of racial mixing.[125] José de Alencar was a Brazilian statesman who became one of the empire's most famous authors, producing romances, plays, and essays in a prolific twenty-year writing career. One of his most enduring works, *Iracema,* was published in 1865 and is the second of Alencar's Indianist trio that includes the works *O Guaraní* (1857) and *Ubirajara* (1874). These romances share a similar exaltation of the Indian and interracial relationships (save the last, which is set before contact), but they do not have interlocking plots or characters, like the Leatherstocking novels. Despite this, Alencar's Brazilian romances were considered remarkably similar to Cooper's works, some critics going so far as to charge the Brazilian with plagiarism.[126] But instead of Cooper's "dread of miscegenation," critics praise *Iracema* for its celebration of mestiçagem, particularly in comparison with this other prominent American author.[127] Critic Robert Stam writes, "Whereas U.S. tradition venerates the Euro American founding fathers, the Brazilian includes an indigenous mother. . . . Brazilian literature lauded cross-racial heterosexual romance . . . as the generative matrix of a mestiço nation."[128] I would like to reconsider *Iracema*'s "generative matrix" by looking at how death and mourning might function as a mode of redress for the categorical transgression of sexual miscegenation. Is the cross-racial romance actually lauded or generative in Alencar's work? What are the implications for a mestiço heritage if, in his most famous coupling, the foundational figure of this "indigenous mother" neither survives nor accomplishes the same kind of re*mark*able deaths as the white women in *Hobomok,* failing to give space through a Native *sema?* I argue that, like its North American counterparts, the Brazilian's "dream" of mestiçagem is overwritten by the work of death. The spectacle of "tragic representation" in this romance does work upon the mother, but not in the same influential manner as the white mothers in *Hobomok.* Here, the tragic representation of the Native mother's demise, Iracema's destruction and death, functions as a ritual of redressive machinery, a purging through consumption that participates in rather than overturns the "elimination logic" that Patrick Wolfe attaches to the project of settler colonialism.[129]

Alencar presents *Iracema,* as Child did for *Hobomok,* as his contribution to the search for a distinctly national literature, the desire, as Alencar describes it, for a "poesia inteiramente brasileira [an entirely Brazilian poetry]."[130] The national romance, Doris Sommer argues in *Foundational Fictions,* engages the reader in a sentimental entanglement of erotics and politics that functions as an allegory for national political organization. In the miscegenist romances under this banner, this sexual coupling could function as "a way of annihilating difference and constructing a deeply horizontal, fraternal dream of national identity."[131] But in this "dream" of flattening categorical hierarchies, new structures of distinction emerge. Structural anthropologist Claude Lévi-Strauss asserts that the use of such cultural mythology for cognitive resolution of contradictory or contestatory states "inevitably traps the human imagination in a web of dualisms." Wendy Doniger summarizes this argument by saying: "Each dualism (such as male/female) produces a tension that seems resolved by the use of a mediating term (such as *androgyny*), but then that new term turns out to be one-half of a new dualism such as androgyny/sexlessness *ad infinitum.*"[132] Mestiçagem, then, does not resolve or render horizontal the relationship but rather perpetuates the hierarchical strain of the binary; a focus on mestiçagem contains within it an oblique fixation on the idea of purity. This fixation can be seen in the intra- and extranarrative processes of redress. Those actions meant to resolve breach and crisis function as purification rituals, unsettling the resolution Alencar posits in the form of mestiçagem. Alencar's miscegenist romance maintains a fixation with purity much like Cooper's Leatherstocking, who insists over and over again that he is a "man without cross." As in Cooper's frontier novels, Alencar's narrative demonstrates instead a loyalty to and hardening of racial boundaries that is effected by the work of death in the novel. In *Iracema,* Alencar's mestiçagem is not the harmonious union of different groups but rather representative of what social anthropologist Victor Turner terms social drama, in which a disruption, or breach, occurs leading to a situation of crisis that must be redressed by some corrective measure. The apparent bridging offered by mestiçagem, the recuperation of marginal subjects in terms of race and gender through sexual reproduction, is undermined by the redressive machinery of death and desire through which Alencar effaces, evacuates, and makes impossible those subject positions.

In the prologue to *Iracema,* Alencar notes the origin of the novel to be the legends and traditions of his native region, Ceará, attempting in the narrative to reconcile history with fictional romance in order find a "native son" that is neither Indian nor European. "Subtitled a 'legend,'" Wasserman points out, "the book could also be called a myth of place, since it tells how certain topographical accidents received their names—what stories give them meaning."[133] I would argue that the mythical structure imbues not only the topographical aspects of the novel but also, according to Harrison's theory of *hic jacet,* the location of a legible human presence for the region. The work of mythology is "dialectic in its attempt to make cognitive sense out of the chaotic data provided by nature."[134] In the case of Alencar, the author must address the colonial encounter from a nationalist position that did not exist at the time. In so doing, he destabilizes or opens up the European/Indian or colonizer/colonized binary, attempting a cognitive resolution to a seemingly contradictory state: being Other but at home, being the invader and yet identifying with the invaded territory. He reconstructs the past to align with a contemporary imagined community in formation, explaining a Brazilian national sentiment that resides outside both terms of the colonial recognition (colonizer/colonized), an attempt that elides colonial violence in favor of a romantic vision of mestiçagem. Eduardo de Assis Duarte notes: "O embate entre nativos e colonizadores fica reduzido a pano de funda para o idílio amoroso establecido entre Martim . . . e a bela Iracema [the struggle between the natives and the colonizers is reduced to a background for the romantic idyll established between Martim . . . and the beautiful Iracema]."[135] It is upon this scene, that of European colonizers making contact with Indigenous people, those who will have been colonized, that Alencar attempts to locate a third term, resituating in history a contemporary conflict that impedes a social project, namely that of patriotic allegiance during the period of rising nationalism.[136] An elite citizen, writing from the urban center, Alencar must find a legitimate way in which to distance the white Brazilians such as himself from the other white, urban elite: the European, the Portuguese. But Alencar's third term, from which he can assert not only affiliation but also filiation, is not an independent term itself. The mestiço does not unite the binary white/Indian, colonizer/colonized, bridging the gap between the two identities. Instead, the term displaces the crisis into a new binary: mestiçagem/pureza, mixed blood and pure blood. Alencar's mestiço myth attempts resolution and succeeds only insofar as it represses the dualism on which the mediating term is predicated. This project of reconstruction, framed in the tone of a legend, "deixa ver a convivência do literário com o ideológico [allows one to see the coexistence of literature and ideology]."[137] As critic Djelal Kadir argues, the division between history and ideology is always an irreducible tautology when written upon the American landscape.[138] Kadir traces this back to the naming of America, or Amerige, as it was initially labeled on maps. This neologism, he argues, literally translates to "land of no-place" and so from its very beginnings the land is posited as a blank page, the material exposed to the inscription of the European imagination.[139] One could insist that this semantic discovery reflects the somatic construction of America as well, often represented as a woman (often naked, sometimes recumbent) in artistic depictions of conquest.[140] Following Kadir's discovery, it is possible to argue that this "no place" is in fact the Indigenous body, and more specifically the Indigenous female body that is conceived of as *only* a vacant surface, one that has no original wholeness for which to mourn. Alencar's machinery of redress pushes Iracema toward this identification with the land, not an inhabitation or marking by *sema* but rather a devouring, complete identification that annihilates the subject as she becomes one with it. She is always vacant, always waiting to be filled.

In *Iracema,* the area that most explicitly engages with the issue of purity is that of gender and the attendant issue of sexuality. In the author's own words, gender is central to Alencar's national project. In his "Carta ao Dr. Jaguaribe," Alencar describes the formation of his novel, noting that he had become engaged with the idea of creating a literary work inspired by the legends of his native region, as well as his recent historical and biographical work, when he made a trip to Ceará in 1848. He indicts the figure of the woman, though, as ultimately bringing the project to fruition. He says of existing history: "Faltava-lhe o perfume que derrama sobre as paixões do homem a beleza da mulher [it was missing the perfume that the beauty of women pours over the passions of man]."[141] The author notes that it is the corporeal figure of the woman, the physical affect, that catalyzes the expression of the work's project. The national project, creating an affective attachment to the land, is explicitly connected to desire for and desire cultivated by the female body. "O perfume" of the woman's beauty incites "as paixões" of mankind. To this end Iracema's body is written as connected to and expressive of the land that she inhabits, the "filha do sertão [daughter of the jungle]"[142] who erases the boundary between sexual and colonial desire. This appropriation of the female body by the author is the cultivation of imagined communities based on desire. Here, the libidinal connection to a shared object is explicit. But the family romance of the Brazilian national novel seems to take a strange turn as it appears to exalt the *maternal* figure, disregarding the father's role. But Alencar's narrative insists that the perfidious desire does indeed belong to the mother, reinventing the Native mother in the androgynous position of both exalted father and defiled mother. The narrative seems to offer her a subject position only to inscribe upon her the mark of abjection, to outlaw that very position as chaotic, confused, and, as the sign of abjection is a violent expulsion, connecting her to what is hailed in *Hobomok* as "revolting," or "very bad taste."

There are two women present in the novel who represent the object of desire for the colonizing male gaze but there is only one physical female body, that of the eponymous Iracema. The other woman, Martim's "virgem branca [white virgin]" or "virgem loura [blond virgin]," is continually invoked but never corporeally realized, a fact that does not diminish the importance of her imagined figure. Even though she is never physically present in the narrative, Martim's fixation on the white virgin provides a socionormative foil for Iracema, a comparison aggravated by the racially inflected aberrant sexuality of the Native woman.[143] This other woman, Martim's lost love object that he maintains as a site of desire, obscures the reader's sentimental attachment to Iracema herself, emphasizing her difference from a recognizable cultural heritage. When he is lying with Iracema in his arms, a sentimental moment in which the creole reader, aligned racially and linguistically with the Portuguese man, should herself feel love for and a connection with the Native woman, Martim distances the reader from Iracema by thinking of home. "Lá o espera a virgem loura dos castos afectos [There the blond virgin of chaste affection waited for him]," an image that he directly contrasts to Iracema, the "virgem morena dos ardentes amores [the brunette virgin of burning love]" with her "olhos negros [black eyes]" and "lascivo talhe [sensuous figure]."[144] Even though Iracema is continually referred to as the virgin of her tribe, the vestal keeper of the jurema, she is also explicitly sensual, most markedly in the contrast to the blond woman who represents Martim's social code of purity, virginity. Alencar presents the Indian woman's purity as aberrant from the European idea, estranged from and therefore dangerous to the white warrior's social structure. Iracema is pure, but she is also an object of sexual desire and a desiring subject herself ("ardentes amores"), a deviant subject in the terms of the "castos afectos" of the faraway blonde.

This aggressive sexuality, opposed to the white woman who passively waits, manifests itself explicitly in the initial sexual encounter between Martim and Iracema. While Martim desires Iracema, he does not act directly on it, asking instead for her to provide him with the sacred jurema, substituting one transgressive act of consumption for another. It is Iracema who goes to Martim while he sleeps, inverting the roles of male aggressor and female passive receptor. Iracema's aberrant concept of purity is also shown in her own self-misrepresentation after the sexual act. The narrator remarks that "Tupã já não tinha sua virgem [The Tupi now did not have their virgin],"[145] referring obliquely to the completed sex act. Iracema, though, continues to call herself chaste, a confusion of terms that indicates the disorder of the situation and Iracema's inability to understand the boundaries of purity and defilement. Martim, though, does understand, and recognizes in his decision to leave the Tupã that in their coupling they have clearly disrupted the social structure and that this disruption requires redress. Their act of contact and contamination results in a social crisis, the breach of their sexual contact forcing the two to remove themselves to the margins, the beach where they then set up their home.[146]

The aberrant sexual personae, Iracema the aggressive seducer and Martim the unconscious, passive object of seduction, also undergo a transformation following their transgression, what Duarte refers to as "o milagre do branqueamento de Iracema [the miracle of Iracema's whitening]."[147] When they arrive at their new home, Iracema is no longer the aggressive figure she was in her native environment. Instead, her agency becomes vacated; she becomes the passive object that approximates the figure of the white virgin: the quintessential agency-less subject, one who cannot act of her own accord because she exists only in the image, the desire of another. Duarte says of this process: "Transforma-se o amador na coisa amada, Iracema passa a ser movida pela paixão e pelo desejo de se transformar no objeto do desejo de Martim [Transforming herself from lover into a loved object, Iracema changes from being moved by passion and desire, transforming into the object of Martim's desire]."[148] This new Iracema he describes as "docemente rendido e conformado com a perda de sua identidade [sweetly surrendered and resigned to the loss of her identity]."[149] Iracema is both the author and material, the perpetrator and victim of seduction and, through its allegorical extension, of conquest as well. At the same time Martim gains in agency as he pushes away from Iracema, the body that represents the social crisis in which he finds himself. Instead he embraces socially normative masculine behaviors by fighting alongside Poti; abandoning Iracema at the cabin, he abjects domestic space and with it the Native female body.

What this transformation approximates is a purification ritual, one in which the aberration that threatens the established social order is expelled.

Julia Kristeva, expanding on Mary Douglas's work *Purity and Danger,* argues that the social aggregate is based on a logical order; that which is jettisoned from this "symbolic system" is that which escapes or threatens its rationality. The subject, in defense of such "dirt,"[150] becomes a "tireless builder,"[151] with a strict "adherence to Prohibition and Law."[152] Martim's rejection of Iracema thus indicts her as an object of this defilement, her agency and sensuality in contrast with his established social order represented by the blond virgin. Her "branqueamento" can therefore be read as an attempt to redress the crisis of contact between the European social order and the Indian other. It is also interesting to read the emphasis on Martim's purity in the light of the crisis of colonial contact. While Iracema is explicitly labeled as pure, Martim is so labeled implicitly and, more importantly, he maintains his purity through his innocence in the sexual contact. When Iracema tempts Martim (à la Eve, as Duarte reads it), the white soldier invokes God to expel the impure thoughts, as an injunction against acting in a transgressive manner: "O cristão repeliu do seio a virgem indiana.... Cerra os olhos para não ver; e enche sua alma com o nome e a veneração de seu Deus:-Cristo!... Cristo! [The Christian pushed the Indian virgin from his chest.... He closed his eyes so that he could not see; and his soul called out with the venerated name of his God:-Christ!... Christ!]."[153] The primer of his social structure, the "religião de sua mãe" [religion of his mother],[154] is the safeguard of the symbolic order that expels the threatened defilement. The name of God is the logos that orients his understanding of such binaries as purity and defilement. The Native is here designated as contaminative and irrational while Martim's own mother, recalled by his recourse to the "religião de sua mãe," becomes a sanitary refuge.

The verbal exorcism is accompanied by a creation of physical distance, "repeliu do seio a virgem indiana," showing that the crisis of the subject is one of contact; he will recreate this physical repulsion later when he "abandons" Iracema to fight with Poti and, when he does return home, his time spent away from the hut staring at the sea projecting both his national and sexual desire outward, to the Motherland. His consumption of the foreign body leads only to crisis in the social system. It is only in his soporific displacement that he can consume Iracema as he wishes. In his dreams "Podia amá-la, e sugar desse amor o mel e o perfume, sem deixar veneno no seio da virgem [he could love her and suckle from love the honey and perfume without leaving poison in the virgin's breast]."[155] What the jurema accomplishes is to rid Martim of consciousness, the injunction of social codes, that which places taboo between himself and the aberrant object.[156] The narrative, though, structures the transgressive sexual act in such a way to protect the white soldier's social codes of purity and defilement by displacing agency onto the Indian Other. The narrator describes Iracema's aberrant sexual agency as animal-like, comparing her to "a juruti, que divaga pela floresta, ouve o terno arrulho do companheiro [the *juruti* (bird) that wanders through the forest listening to the tender cooing of his partner]," [157] a comparison that places her outside not only the norm of gender roles, but also that of the human. In the act of transgression, Iracema acts and Martim is transformed into a victim: "Immersed in a fantasy state induced by the jurema, Martim can take pleasure from Iracema's body, without having to take responsibility."[158] As Duarte indicates, "a narrativa exalta a elevação moral de Martim e debita á [Iracema] a responsabilidade por aquela união proibida . . . à mulher e à sua magia telúrica todo o poder de sedução, fazendo do homem uma vítima [the narrative raises the moral elevation of Martim and makes Iracema responsible for that prohibited union . . . to the woman and her telluric magic all of the power of seduction, making the man into a victim]."[159]

It is therefore Iracema who bears responsibility for the couple's transgression, and it is she who must suffer and die because of it. Her death, labeled from the start of the novel as the ultimate mode of redress, is therefore the only resolution to the crisis that results from her actions. Iracema is conscious of her fate, telling Martim that in her death he will be free to pursue the white virgin. The foundational mother, the figure that critics use to set Alencar apart from Cooper, the celebration of heterogeneous society, is thus predicated upon her removal, an abjection of her racial and gendered otherness. Martim cannot be happy with her, in his state of transgression, and therefore even Iracema herself posits her own death, the death of the mother, as a liberating force. It is only through the birth of his son that Martim reattaches himself to the land; "o amor renascera com o júbilo paterno [love was reborn with the paternal glee]" (80),[160] and it is indicatively through the son that the threatening otherness, in the figure of Iracema, is vacated. Duarte remarks on the vampiric nature of the son, who feeds on his Amerindian mother, transforming the maternal care of nursing into an extraction of resources that strengthens the son even as it sucks the life from Iracema. But this vital sacrifice does not bind mother and child within a rhetoric of responsibility that typically attends such deaths. Instead, as she weakens, Iracema withdraws herself from the relation, handing her son over to Martim and calling him "yours," not "ours" or "my." The figure of the mother is in this way emptied of its claim as her physical body is emptied of its sustaining force.

The Amerindian mother is thus barred from her powerful relation to futurity as well, her important social role as the primary influence over the social and religious formation of the child.[161] Iracema's death, her vacated body, allows Martim to take his son back to his homeland, the educational role appropriated by the father, exorcising the potentially dangerous contamination of Indian influence. The religion of the Other mother is replaced by that of the father, or rather that father's mother, "a religião de sua mãe." This substitution shows how not only the transgressive gender but also racial otherness is excised in the final redress of Iracema's death and subsequent departure of Martim and Moaçir. The conspicuous racial absence, even that of the mestiço son who leaves with his father and does not return (to the narrative or Ceará), enacts a vacating of racial difference, an act of purification that rescues the racial binary from any blurring of its borders or from its seemingly carnivalesque inversion, restoring privilege and dominance to the white man as it marginalizes and effaces the Indian woman. Moaçir's departure from his Native parent coincides with that of little Hobomok in Child's novel. The Indian-ness of little Hobomok is progressively diminished as the boy loses his father, his name, and any connection to Native culture. This "whitening" plays a significant part in buttressing the sentimental attachment both between father/grandfather and child as well as Child's audience searching for a recognizable heritage.[162]

In this romance of erotic transgression and Native erasure, *Iracema* becomes a mode of redress for the crisis of colonial contact, the work a mediating term that approximates a liminoid cultural production.[163] The liminoid allows his urban readership an experience of society's margins, where the structure is questioned, crisis reenacted, and then resolved. Liminoid productions are not dangerous to the social structure, in that they are contained and framed as an imitation of reality. By presenting his audience with a sterilized recounting of the colonial encounter, occulting violence with romance and offering the "resolution" of a mestiçagem, the act of narration becomes an act of education. The audience, through its attachment to the Native characters in the liminoid production, nonthreatening because distant from the reader and, as I have shown, absent in the narrative, is given the gap necessary to cultivate desire. Instead of the anxiety of contact, the audience is given the erotics of exoticism, a discourse that allows one to approximate the Other but also to avoid the contamination of direct contact. This is because, as Wasserman states: "The exotic arises as a sign of interest on the part of the self in that which is not self. It is not, however, the complete other; it is the acceptable, complementary, renewing other. The exotic mediates between the defining self and a more radical otherness, which at the limit would fall outside the grammar of the defining discourse."[164] Alencar's exotic is predicated on empty bodies, transgressive forms vacated through acts of purification. Thus his very act of writing represents redressive machinery in its expulsion of the dangerous other. Mary Douglas states: "In perceiving we are building, taking some cues and rejecting others. The most acceptable cues are those which fit most easily into the pattern that is being built up. Ambiguous ones tend to be treated as if they harmonised with the rest of the pattern. Discordant ones tend to be rejected."[165] The act of inscription, "a convivência do literário com o ideológico," actively constructs a defense of the social system and, in Alencar, vacates the bodies of the racial and gendered others, perpetuating "the fiction of emptiness."[166] "A conciliação miscigenadora," says Duarte, "oculta a dominação e propicia o mito da democracia racial, ainda hoje vigente no Brasil [the miscegenist conciliation occults and perpetuates the myth of a racial democracy still popular today in Brazil]."[167] Alencar uses what he deems to be "uma raça extinta" [an extinct race],[168] appropriating what he sees as already dead, empty bodies to recreate a relationship that is only "generative" in terms of the dominant cultural power. The form of the narrative, its Indianist focus, occults its own insistence of difference, asserting its sovereign author-ity by bringing forth subjects that are then ritually vacated. Like Cooper's Indian John, Hobomok and Iracema speak their own death sentence, just as the dead body, and not the historian, seems to speak the past. The Indian is therefore removed as an obstacle for national consolidation, the history of Brazil and that of New England no more tainted with their resistant bodies than Cooper's frontier. These silent or unmourned deaths make the characters disappear; they leave no *remains.* In each romance, the author offers a reproductive cross-racial couple, pairs who produce a single child and so offer a historical narrative for the birth of an American subject. But each also engages in a strategic, sentimental deployment of dead bodies, and these romances that seem to produce love objects through birth refocus that libidinal energy through the spectacle of death. The Indian, and particularly the Indian mother, is a border experience, one that cannot be alleviated by the alternately loving and violent rejection of identification but can neither be sustained within the ordered world of the social. These mothers, the reader learns, exist in silence or vague whispers on the breeze.[169] Unlike the materialism of the white woman, these Native mothers lack the substantial means for foundation. The Other mother becomes, not the page upon which the fictional narrative of community is written but rather vacancy itself, the empty space the white mother will inhabit, the tractless land that her death will mark as the *place* of white settlement in the New World, the *sema,* the sign, of the nation to come.

4

Mother Tongues

Translating the Nation

Noo-chun kes-uk-qut-tiam-at-am unch koo-we-su-onk, kuk-ket-as-soo tam-oonk pey-au-moo-utch, keet-te-nan-tam-oo-onk ne nai; ne-ya-ne ke suk-qutkah oh-ke-it; aos-sa-ma-i-in-ne-an ko-ko-ke-stik o-da-e nut-as e-suk-ok-ke fu-tuk-qun-neg; kah ah-quo-an-tam-a-i-in-ne-an num match-e-se-ong-an on-ash, ne-match-ene-na-mun wonk neet-ah-quo antam-au-o-un-non-og nish-noh pasuk noo-na mortuk-quoh-who-nan, kah chaque sak-kom-pa-ginne-an en qutch-e-het-tu-ong-a-nit, qut poh-qud wuss-sin-ne-an watch match-i-tut.

—William Apess

I came west, in search of silence.

—Natty Bumppo

The Darkening Varnish

When Martim leaves the New World after Iracema's death, the Portuguese soldier takes two things in his "frágil barco [fragile boat]": his son and his faithful dog. The child is named as a new kind of Brazilian subject, "o primeiro cearense," he who, "ainda no berço, emigrava da terra da pátria [the first Cearense, still in the cradle, emigrated from the land of his homeland]."[1] The small boy disappears entirely from the narrative at this point, leaving both a text and a landscape marked so insistently with and as his mother's body, even as the author describes his homeland as his "pátria," his father's land. The child is taken east, not away from but toward the land of his father, his "pátria," toward the religion of his grandmother and perhaps even toward the blond virgin so frequently invoked against his mother's "selvagem" condition. It was this Other mother who named the child Moaçir, an appellation that Alencar explains in his notes to the text as "filho do sofrimento: de *moacy*—dor, e *ira*—desinência que significa saído de [son of suffering: from *moacy*—pain, and *ira*—designation that means deriving from]."[2] The native son, "o primeiro cearense," is in this way marked nominally as the mournful production of two races but also re-marked by a foundational displacement from the land of his painful birth, his doubled removal from his *país natal,* the scene of his creation, which has already become the "terra da pátria." Moaçir, the future of the Brazilian people, is thus exiled from the Tupi language and culture that he, by birth, should inherit, a historical loss that Brazilian nationalists like Alencar will reaffirm, a loss that will make space for the Brazilian nation to emerge. As I've traced throughout *Mourning the Nation to Come,* this nineteenth-century claim to an interrupted legacy allows the elite postcolonial population to distinguish their heritage from that of the European, producing the nation as simultaneously marked and made possible by a melancholic bond between an Indigenous past and its creole future. In this chapter, we turn to consider how romancers of the past retain this tension between loss and fulfillment through their engagements with Indigenous language. Just as Alencar intercedes in the text to translate Moaçir's name for the reader, tying the child to his mother's culture despite her passing, other nationalist writers frequently took on the mantle of translator in their texts. Serving as a mediatory figure who both makes Indigenous language available for consumption while at the same time overwriting Amerindian speakers, the figure of the translator functions as a boundary separating the present creole from the historical Amerindian by reproducing the experience of loss in (and as) language, even as his text appropriates its signifying power for a postcolonial readership.

By removing the Brazilian child, this new native subject is also excused from participating in the scene of conquest and conversion that follows his father's return to this land of "amarga saudade [bitter longing/nostalgia]."[3] Unlike his son, Martim reappears in Brazil, but instead of the small family consisting of man, son, and faithful hound that floated away from the Cearense coast, the soldier returns with "muitos guerreiros de sua raça [e] um sacerdote de sua religião [many warriors of his race [and] a priest of his religion]." Martim brings with him men who will establish Christian cities and "plantar a cruz na terra selvagem [plant a cross in the savage land]."[4] If Iracema's death functions as a purification ritual that cleanses the land of her mortal, maternal inscription, as I have argued in chapter 3, the final sanitizing act of bleaching or racial "branqueamento" in the novel is this coda to her death that contains Martim's return and the spectacle of Native conversion.

Poti, the faithful Pitiguara warrior, stands in Iracema's place after her death; like her, he waits for Martim to return to him; he pines for his "irmão branco." When his white brother does return, Poti resolves to eliminate all distance and difference between them by erasing his otherness in the ritual of religious conversion. The narrator remarks that "não sofria ele que nada mais o separasse de seu irmão branco [he would not suffer that anything more would separate him from his white brother]."[5] The Indian desires to become one with the European, but instead of demonstrating the consuming power of his own active identification, Poti concedes to cultural and linguistic consumption on the part of the European. The narrator describes the conversion as a ritual of re-naming, as "Poti" is rendered in this imported tongue, becoming a new subject by being subjected to the language of his brother: "Ele recebeu com o batismo o nome do santo, cujo era o dia; e o do rei, a quem ia a servir, e sobre os dois o seu, na língua dos novos irmãos [He received with the baptism the name of the saint whose day it was; and that of the king, whom he was going to serve, and added to those two his own, in the language of the new brothers]."[6] This communion with his brother is thus a linguistic erasure and reiteration; impressment into the service of religion and king is inscribed upon the Indian. While some critics have read this concluding event as an assertion of unity and the "possibility of combining radically different elements,"[7] insofar as Poti serves as a substitute for the dead Indigenous mother, this act of conversion represents not unity but capitulation, the violence of reconciliation made completely on the terms established by one part. In acceding to his new name, Poti endures the erasure required by communion with Martim. This cultural effacement, committed in the absence of Moaçir, the figure of the future, affirms the child's loss of Native culture by eroding its foundation in his homeland. The Brazilian can return to the land of his birth, but he cannot be restored to his maternal culture, which has been overwritten.

This chapter will look at how the historical romancers already presented in this study use their narratives as linguistic projects of New World nationalism, deploying the loss of Native language as a mode of asserting New World languages that distinguish their print communities from their European colonial counterparts. In "What Is a Nation," Renan denies the viability of a linguistic foundation for community, arguing that language is an insufficient cause for national consolidation. "There is something in man," he writes, "which is superior to language, namely, the will."[8] This explains, he argues, historical changes in the languages of communities as well as the disjuncture between philological divisions and political realities. But while Poti's conversion takes the form of a willed consent to community that Renan argues supplants linguistic ties, this consent is explicitly addressed as transformation in and by language. This nationalist discourse does not disregard language as a formative principle but rather affirms its communalizing power. Alencar's closing conversion demonstrates how, by translating the name, one becomes legible to and inscribed within in a new community, and so he emphasizes the linguistic claim of colonization upon the Brazilian land and people. In so doing, Alencar opens up the possibility of another linguistic conversion, one that might resurrect what was lost; if *Native* Brazil is unmade in and by language, then *native* Brazil could be deconstructed in a similar manner. Missing from this scene is the son who, while removed to Europe, participates in neither the Native's capitulation nor the linguistic violence of conquest. The child does retain the inscription of his mother in his name itself, remaining marked by the legacy of another language, of another land, and so the possibility of another community, albeit a community that has been silenced. The name Moaçir makes present a historicized social reality and so, even after Native Brazil's conversion, this surviving trace of *Moacy-ira*, a textual remainder, becomes an opening onto a state exterior and prior to the consuming forces of European conquest and conversion.[9]

This native subject, born in America and yet coming from Europe, exemplifies the position of the creole nationalist, and his linguistic isolation explains the contemporaneous fascination with Native languages shared among early nationalist literati. Whereas Indian grammars during the colonial period worked as tools for the same conversion and trade, studies of Indigenous languages, encouraged by early national organizations, belied the anxiety that sharing a linguistic heritage with the European colonizing forces would work against any assertion of cultural independence. This concern for linguistic independence produced the Spanish American *Gramática* and poetry of scholar and public servant Andrés Bello, who attempted to establish a unique and yet unified Spanish grammar that would form the basis of a national identification.[10] The same project was taken up in North America by Noah Webster, who declared that "a national language is a national tie."[11] His grammar, spelling books, and dictionary were all produced, as historian Jill Lepore summarizes, to address the issue that "inhabitants of the thirteen 'united' states were both too much like the English and not enough like one another."[12] While the altered standard orthography of American Spanish and American English offered by these projects met with limited success, the adoption of Indigenous terms into the national lexicon translated easily into contemporary literary projects and so this Native incorporation became an important part of the *print language* of the nation as it developed around these texts.

In his study of print and national culture in *Imagined Communities,* Benedict Anderson argues, following Renan, that language is an insufficient cause for national feeling, but against the French thinker in promoting the role of *print languages* in national formation. In doing so, Anderson separates out projects of linguistic nationalism, which he identifies as a European instrumentality, from the narratives of national culture produced by the increasingly professionalized discipline of History.[13] The proliferation of print culture, Anderson argues, not only made these emergent historical narratives widely available but also, in its objectification of living languages, consolidated and reified its linguistic construction. Because of technological limitations and the demands of its markets, print could not address every single vernacular in a given area. Anderson argues that print culture addressed this problem by consolidating these groups into communities of a dominant print language, thus producing monoglot reading publics.[14] He says that these mechanically reproduced languages, disseminated throughout the community, "unified fields of exchange and communication below Latin and above the spoken vernaculars," making those unable to communicate with their entire community "capable of comprehending one another via print and paper." In addition to this language-based imagined community, Anderson argues, "print-capitalism gave a new fixity to language, which in the long run helped to build that image of antiquity so central to the subjective idea of the nation."[15] That is, by stabilizing language itself, print lent language an archival function, making the history it produces universally accessible to its community of readers. "For three centuries now these stabilized print-languages have been gathering a darkening varnish," Anderson says. "The words of our seventeenth-century forebears are accessible to us in a way that to [the fifteenth-century reader] his twelfth-century ancestors were not."[16] But Anderson's separation of this scriptive economy from the work of its popular narratives, what this study has identified as its *scrypt*ive economy of loss and fulfillment in the national romance, keeps him from understanding its work of translation as itself a project of linguistic nationalism.

In the Americas, this "darkening varnish" was established not only by the standardization of American English, Spanish, and Portuguese through print but also "darkened" by this incorporation of Native signs into the national romance. In Cooper's important Leatherstocking novels, for instance, the reader not only consumes Native figures and white deaths but does so through a language unique to the land that those bodies inhabit. By using Indigenous terms, Cooper locates the reader in a history that, while written in an English that has its origins in Europe, remains tied to a distinctly American heritage. This "darkening" move can be seen in Cooper's 1850 addendum to his prefatory remarks for *Last of the Mohicans.* There, the author presents the American landscape as a territory marked by a linguistic struggle, one that he reveals in his confession regarding the name of the lake around which the action of the novel takes place. "There is one point," he says, "on which we would wish to say a word before closing this preface. Hawk-eye calls the *Lac du Saint Sacrement,* the 'Horican.' As we believe this to be an appropriation of the name that has its origin with ourselves, the time has arrived, perhaps, when the fact should be frankly admitted."[17] The author struggles with the existing names of the lake that, in its alternating European occupation, is burdened by either complicated French or monarchical English. It is in defending his territory from the latter that Cooper offers his innovative appellation:

> Looking over an ancient map, it was ascertained that a tribe of Indians, called "Les Horicans" by the French, existed in the neighborhood of this beautiful sheet of water. As every word uttered by Natty Bumppo was not to be received as rigid truth, we took the liberty of putting the "Horican" into his mouth, as the substitute for "Lake George." The name has appeared to find favor, and all things considered, it may possibly be quite as well to let it stand, instead of going back to the House of Hanover for the appellation of our finest sheet of water.[18]

Instead of asserting the foundational naming of colonial expansion, the name Cooper chooses reaches back, beyond the House of Hanover, to a prior occupation, by a people whose only trace is inscribed in a foreign language on an unspecified "ancient map." Cooper thus endows Bumppo, the frontiersman who strikes out for the wilderness in advance of civilization, with the Adamic power of naming. But he also locates that power historically: Natty does not name *ex nihilo* but rather retains in this new title the trace of lost worlds and lost words.

In this way, studies that focus on the emergence of print language in the Americas, particularly that language as it is deployed in the interest of community formation (as in Anderson's study), should be attentive not only to the "fatality" of languages read as the interplay of linguistic diversity and the creation of a monoglot mass reading public,[19] but also the "fatality" of language as it functions, in Robert Pogue Harrison's terms, to make present the work of death upon the living. In *Dominion of the Dead* Harrison declares that language itself, "the origin of our basic words," presses upon the subject his very historicity and indebtedness to the past, and so to the dead of which that past is comprised. Through language we inherit the meaning of words, established by their previous practitioners; our "basic words," he says, following Heidegger, "possess a plurality of meanings that derives from the plurality of prior worlds through which they have passed on their way down to us."[20] Language, in its barest sense, is our inheritance; the *lex* is our legacy that binds us to the past and, in its providential quality, to the unborn as well.[21] If we combine Anderson's theory of a capitalist print language and Harrison's philosophical consideration of the legacy, we see in Natty's philological wandering the struggle to lay claim to and thus institute a past, a legacy, for the nation whose beginnings he narrates.

But while Harrison argues for the thrownness of the subject as he confronts the historicity of the word, his being subject to the language that he articulates by recognizing himself as subject to the "authority of the past,"[22] Cooper's project usurps this position of authority through the figure of the translator. In taking up this figure, the national romance draws on what postcolonial critics have identified as the work of translation as a mode of power and colonial subjection. "In the colonial context," Tejaswini Niranjana writes, "a certain conceptual economy is created by the set of related questions that is the problematic of translation. . . . In forming a certain kind of subject, in presenting particular versions of the colonized, translation brings into being overarching concepts of reality and representation," concepts that simultaneously justify colonial incursion even as they occlude the violence of its work.[23] In *The Poetics of Imperialism,* Eric Cheyfitz describes this as the function of translation as foreign policy, its contribution to the work of colonial powers in managing sites of otherness by producing "figures of the other, not fact."[24] Drawing on the etymological history yoking translation with metaphor, Cheyfitz argues that translation functions as an extended form of figuration that is "grounded in the desire of what names itself *the domestic* to dominate what it simultaneously distinguishes as the *foreign*."[25] This translation thus works as an apparatus of order and control, dispossessing Indigenous figures of their language and any claim that language makes over the *proper,* the literal, the real.

While the resurgence of the translator in nativist narratives in the nineteenth century seems to invoke other ways of seeing and ordering the world, it withholds that authorizing potential by displacing Indigenous speakers. The confession that Cooper makes in his 1850 preface to *Last of the Mohicans* sheds light on this dispossession when read in conjunction with the author's footnotes to the narrative. In these paratextual remarks, the author makes his external authority known by providing the reader with historical, geographical, anthropological, and even etymological notes to supplement the work of his fiction. In the first of these notes, Cooper explains the name of this lake:

> As each nation of the Indians had either its language or its dialect, they usually gave different names to the same places, though nearly all of their appellations were descriptive of the object. Thus, a literal translation of the name of this beautiful sheet of water, used by the tribe that dwelt on its banks, would be "The tail of the Lake." Lake George, as it is vulgarly, and now indeed legally, called, forms a sort of tail to Lake Champlain, when viewed on the map. Hence the name.[26]

But while this detailed presentation attributes the descriptive name to one of a vague number of Indian languages or dialects, Cooper's preface exposes this explanation as a lie; it "has its origin," Cooper says, "with ourselves."[27] The name is his, its history invented. But what this footnote and even the confessional preface achieve is positioning the author as the reader's translator, the figure who mediates between this legacy of the past and the present upon which it bears. Cooper admits as much in the text itself when he says of Natty's speech, spoken to an Indian companion in a Native tongue, that he will give "free translation" of the words for the reader, retaining only the curiosities of speech that such language entails. Natty's translation is an incorporation into English of an imagined Native position and thus an affirmation of a dead Native language that has no dead at its core. The author claims the position of the translator, but in relation to a language that, while referencing the Native past, is created and contained within the narrative itself. He both translates and undermines that translation by revealing its invention and so ruptures words and legacy; Cooper "depopulates their underworlds, [disjoins] them from their antecedent speakers and thereby dispossessing the dead of their claims to language."[28]

Alencar, whose debt to Cooper is widely acknowledged by critics, even if denied by the author himself, establishes a similar position of author/translator in his Indianist romance, a position that both creates and guards a national print language. "A língua é a nacionalidade do pensamento," Alencar wrote, "como a patria é a nacionalidade do povo" [Language is the nationality of thought as the homeland is the nationality of the people].[29] In his project of establishing a national language capable of distinguishing a Brazilian way of thinking, Alencar also incorporates Native terms as a way of making an Indigenous language present. The language of *Iracema* seems to be overwhelmingly populated by the dead, as Alencar makes frequent use, not only of Indigenous terms, but also explanatory footnotes, prologues, and attached essays that draw attention to his role as the translator of these terms. Through these framing texts, Alencar "interfere antes, durante e depois do texto, participando exaustivamente na produção do sentido [interferes before, during and after the text, participating exhaustively in the production of meaning]."[30] But unlike Cooper's admission of creation *sui generis,* Alencar's footnotes are supported by extensive citation, including his recourse to the Tupi dictionary published by the poet Antônio Gonçalves Dias in 1858.

Unlike Bello, in his concern with Spanish, and Webster, with English, Gonçalves Dias foregoes remaking colonial language entirely and focuses instead on a single Indigenous language, Tupi. The dictionary, which the poet dedicates "Ao Instituto Histórico e Geographico Brazileiro,"[31] reflects the linguistic structure of national history as outlined in Karl von Martius's programmatic essay for the Instituto. In that essay, selected by the organization to set the agenda for historiography in Brazil, von Martius prescribed a thorough investigation of Indigenous languages to support a national history:

> Como documento mais geral e mais significativo [para uma história brasileira] deve ser considerada a *língua dos índios.* Pesquisas nesta atualmente tão pouco cultivada esfera não podem jamais ser suficientemente recomendadas, e tanto mais que as línguas americanas não cessam de acharse contìnuamente em uma certa *fusão,* de sorte que algumas delas em breve estarão inteiramente extintas . . . aproveito porém esta ocasião de exprimir o meu desejo que o Instituto Histórico Geográfico Brasileiro designasse alguns linguistas para

> a redação de dicionários e observações gramaticais sôbre estas línguas. . . . Neste respeito seria muito para desejar que se investigassem especialmente as *radicais* de língua Tupi e dos seus dialéticos, desde o Guarani. . . . Que para tal dicionário brasileiro servisse de modêlo o vocabulário que a Imperatriz Catarina mandou esboçar para las línguas Asiáticas, e que afinal e principalmente se coligissem em primeiro lugar todos os vocábulos que se referem a objetos naturais, determinações legais (de direito) ou vestígios de relações sociais.[32]
>
> [The language of the Indians should be considered as a more general and significant document [for a Brazilian history]. Research in this currently little-cultivated sphere cannot be recommended strongly enough, all the more because American languages have not stopped finding themselves constantly in a kind of *fusion,* so that some of them shortly will become completely extinct. . . . I take advantage of this occasion to express my desire that the Instituto Histórico Geográfico Brasileiro would designate some linguists for the purpose of writing dictionaries and grammatical observations on these languages. . . . In this respect I would very much wish that they would investigate particularly the roots of the Tupi language and its dialects, from Guarani. . . . The vocabulary that Empress Catherine ordered written for Asian languages could serve as a model for this Brazilian dictionary, and that mainly it would focus primarily on collecting words relating to natural objects, legal determinations (of law) or vestiges of social relations.]

Von Martius's recommendation is an imperial instead of a national model, framed by this final comparison to Empress Catherine that makes the study of language a tool in understanding and perhaps encouraging the consuming reach of Brazilian sovereignty. But while von Martius's impetus is to collect *living* languages before they die, before they "become completely extinct," Alencar's romance, written just twenty years later, adopts the mournful position that Tupi, along with its speakers, is already dead

In his essay "Carta ao Dr. Jaguaribe," explaining the origins of *Iracema* and his process of composition, a letter that is attached to the novel as a form of epilogue, Alencar declares that his text speaks in the language of "uma raça extinta [an extinct race]."[33] Nevertheless, these dead, "desentranhado" (disemboweled/withdrawn) from the earth in which they sleep, and their dead language are the "fonte que deve beber o poeta brasileiro [the fountain from which the Brazilian poet should drink]" in order to create a national literature.[34] "O conhecimento da língua indígena é o melhor critério para a nacionalidade da literatura [The knowledge of the Indigenous language is the strongest criterion for the nationality of literature]," Alencar writes,[35] and so he quaffs his thirst for "uma poesia inteiramente brasileira" with a language "haurida na língua dos selvagens [drawn from the language of the savages]."[36] In his novel, and in particular in his own intervention as the translator, the native son, the creole Brazilian, returns again to the scene of his creation and speaks in the tongue of his mother. His combination of dead Native language and living European tongue creates a uniquely Brazilian subject, and so his romance, as Phillip Rothwell notes, "may thus be read as the attempted consumption of the pre-Portuguese languages of what would become Brazil, in an effort to brazilianise Portuguese."[37]

Following the directive offered by von Martius, Alencar concentrates his use of Tupi on the naming of birds, plants, and tribal relations, the "objetos naturais" and "relações sociais" that von Martius indicates comprise the most important vocabulary to collect. There are 126 footnotes in Alencar's romance, ranging from etymological explanations of names of fruits (note 49) and trees (note 78) to the names and locations of rivers (note 86) and Indigenous sayings (note 47). But these paratextual notes do not seem to support a better understanding or knowledge of these exotic objects but rather serve as a means of merely collecting the words themselves. For example, in the text the narrator describes Iracema hiding something in her cotton *carioba* ("oculto sob a carioba de algodão entretecida de penas").[38] In Alencar's footnotes the author intercedes to translate this *carioba* as "camisa de algodão; de *cary*—branco, e *oba*—roupa. Tinha também a *araçóia,* de *arara* e *oba*—vestido de penas de arara [cotton shirt; from *cary*—white, and *oba* –clothes. She also has *araçóia,* from *arara* and *oba*—dress of macaw feathers]."[39] This explanatory footnote does very little to improve the reader's understanding of the object; it was, after all, already introduced as a covering made from cotton (algodão) and interwoven with feathers (entretecida de penas). But the footnote does call attention to the exotic word itself, even offering a supplement in *araçóia.* Alencar makes these notes over and over again: the object for which they fish in the river, *o piau,* is indeed a "peixe" or fish (note 121) and the nickname Iracema earns for being such a songbird, *jandaia,* is indeed a type of songbird (note 50). The selection and then translation of exotic terminology functions to estrange the Portuguese in which he writes and to tie that language to the unique features of the land itself.

Because this recovery excludes the Native speaker (who has either died, as Iracema, or lost his language, as with Poti), Alencar's use of Tupi is not a wholesale conversion to the language of "os selvagens," an unworking of the erasures of conquest. It is instead a mournful embrace of an originary loss that makes the contemporary postcolonial nativist position possible. This loss is marked by the figure of the translator, whose presence signifies the distance or gap that remains between the Brazilian reader and her Tupi heritage. This is not the resurrection of a "língua bárbara" but rather a memorializing of that language's disappearance within the dominant tongue, the "língua civilizada." By framing the original language as already dead, as previously exterminated, the author is able to access a lost language that holds no claim on the significance constructed from it in the present because, as the only means of accessing the dead, the translator retains sole authority in determining its meaning. Through his imposition of translation upon the native language, Alencar guards the reader from accessing those Native dead while constructing, through this amalgamated print language, a new linguistic archive, a location in which to assert *new* fatal figures, for the Brazilian reader to consume and become indebted to.

By choosing to focus his translation on Tupi, Alencar distances the reader even further from the threat of a Native heritage and thus responsibility to an Indigenous population. The language spoken by the Tupinambá, the language Alencar's translation pretends to access, was only one of approximately seven hundred Indigenous languages in Brazil at the time of conquest.[40] In order to facilitate religious missions and the advancement of white settlements in the interior of the colony, the Portuguese in Brazil appropriated Tupi, disseminating it among the other Amerindian tribes as the "Lingua Geral" (in the north "Lingua Geral Amazônica" and in the south "Lingua Geral Paulista"), a lingua franca imposed upon Indigenous communities and required in their interaction with the Portuguese state.[41] Through this imposition of "a unitary, all-encompassing discourse," a single legible figure substituted for diverse Indian bodies (and tongues),[42] Tupi had already been deployed as a hegemonic translation, one that dislocated Native bodies from their linguistic homes or dwellings. Tupi was itself a form of "glottophagic imperialism,"[43] a language that consumed and thus worked death upon other languages. Nonetheless Alencar chooses this language, fatal in its own right, as a way of changing the Portuguese in which he communicates, incorporating into it the mournful memorial of the "raça extinta." This Brazilianized Portuguese, he tells Dr. Jaguaribe in his letter, is the only foundation for a "literatura nacional."

The Question of What I Am Eating, a Cuisine of Contre-Tems

These nationalist literary projects, buffered by the position of the translator that is taken up by their authors, do not cease to be harried by sites of difference in language that the role of the translator simultaneously occults and reveals. In consuming Native language, the author/translator may intervene on his reader's behalf to guard her against dangerous exposure, but this liminal position also threatens to transform that barrier constructed by the translator into a conduit for the Other or other languages to wreak havoc upon the stability established by translation. While Alencar uses Native terms to establish his own position of authority, Phillip Rothwell points out that this incorporation actually *encourages* interrogation. "The languages on which the novelist dines," Rothwell writes, "leave him with a bad case of indigestion . . . they introduce a network of possible meanings beyond authorial control, despite Alencar's attempt to force the languages to submit to his own intentions."[44] In other words, through the translator's notes that discover meaning in exotic words, Alencar exposes the hermeneutical act of translation and thus the possibility of *other* interpretations and of Other interlocutors to whom the primary language is addressed. Rothwell traces the way Native language continues to haunt the text, despite Alencar's sanitizing footnotes, by revisiting the name "Poti," the warrior whose conversion marks the conclusion of the romance:

> Attention is drawn to the meaning of the Pitiguara's name, as Alencar seeks to foreclose it once and for all. The reader's suspicions should have been raised by Alencar's repetitive assertions throughout the novel with regard to the meaning of Poti. The Pitiguara are insultingly referred to as "potiguara, comedor de camarão [potiguara, eater of shrimp]." The author's notes once again seek to validate the etymological assertions of the body of the text: "*Potiguara—Comedor de camarão; de* poty *e* uara. *Nome que por desprezo davam os inimigos aos pitiguaras [Potiguara—Eater of shrimp; from* poty *and* uara. *Contemptuous name given to the Pitiguaras by their enemies].*" . . . One thing that is peculiar about Alencar's assertions is the thought that being

called a "shrimp-eater" is a term of abuse, particularly given the positive status bestowed shrimp. . . . The entries in the *Pequeno Vocabulário Tupi-Português* of Pe A. Lemos Barbosa are somewhat illuminating in this respect and speak for themselves:

poti—defecar; excremento [to defecate; excrement]
poti—camarão [shrimp][45]

Despite the assurances of the authoritative translation, Rothwell demonstrates here how the "network of possible meanings" defiles Alencar's authority by offering an*other* reading of the text. In consuming the language, the reader in turn becomes contaminated by the slippery text. Alencar uses translation as a mode of establishing a space for him to write; translation becomes a way to claim authority over languages that are both simultaneously familiar and foreign. But this authoritative space both relies on the translator's ability to interpret the word and, if it is to occlude the possibility of other authors, must at the same time deny that power, making the text seem immediate. Because of his insistent presence in the text, Alencar is unable to accomplish the latter and it is this failure that could, as Rothwell's example shows, make him sick.

If the interlinguistic struggle over meaning is giving Alencar digestive issues, it is *intra*linguistic communication that Cooper's mouthpiece Natty Bumppo finds hard to swallow. This is nowhere clearer than in Natty's final adventure on the prairie (before he is resurrected in the full bloom of youth in *The Pathfinder*). In *The Prairie* (1827), the Leatherstocking is an elderly trapper who has traveled to the vast "inland sea" in a final effort to outrun the settlements. While Natty had previously been attentive to language and his own skill in naming and translation, the prairie offers new challenges to the glossophilic frontiersman, making language itself an important scene for debate in the novel. French critic François Brunet argues, "Il y a, dans le cycle de Bas-de-cuir en général, dans *La Prairie* en particulier, une 'attitude de narration' particulière pour laquelle la réflexion sur les signes, et plus particulièrment sur le langage, est centrale, au point que, de la manière la plus visible, elle fasse ici et là l'objet de discours de la part de personnages et du narrateur [There is, within the Leatherstocking cycle in general, and especially in *The Prairie,* an attitude of the narrative, specifically through which reflection on signs, and even more so language itself, is central, to the point that, in the most visible manner, it appears everywhere (*ici et là*) as the object of discourse on the part of the characters and the narrator]."[46] The struggle over language has perhaps more to do with the introduction of new English language variants than the issue, present throughout the series, of translating between Indian languages and English. The American frontier in 1803 is a much more expansive space than the one Natty describes in 1757. Natty tells those in his company "America has grown . . . since the days of my youth, to be a country larger than I once had thought the world itself to be."[47] The Leatherstocking, then, must confront this emerging variety of American life and language in a manner quite different from his New York provincialism of *Last of the Mohicans* (1826) and *The Pioneers* (1823). On the vast prairie, Natty is joined, for example, by a bee-hunting Kentucky youngster, whose speech is formed around the jargon of his profession, and the squatter clan of Ishmael Bush, whose speech is short, bare, and undecorated. Between Paul Hover's references to queens and "lining" and Ishmael's repeated requests that Bumppo drop his wilderness metaphors and "speak plainly,"[48] Natty finds himself frustrated in his communications with fellow Americans throughout the novel. Even Cooper finds the idea of intralinguistic translation pressing. Keeping in mind audiences who don't speak American English, the author is careful to add (in 1832) a footnote to the narrator's description of "the brown and party coloured livery of the Fall," saying, "The Americans call the autumn the 'fall,' from the fall of the leaf."[49] The introduction of these new characters onto the scene, all of whom carry their own linguistic burden, makes of *The Prairie* "un analogue de la réalité linguistique et culturelle américaine, confuse et bigarrée [an analogy of the American linguistic and cultural reality, confused and motley (*bigarrée*)]."[50]

While critics have focused much of their attention on the issue of interlinguistic translation, as Natty very prominently functions as translator, negotiating relationships between Indian and white communities, this troublesome communication within the English-speaking community hints at a more subtle, but perhaps more threatening loss. While I have argued in chapter 3 that the communication of legacy and thus community is effected by the text of the memorial, the troubled intralinguistic communication in the novel hints at the possibility of misreading the text and thus the fragile position of the communities buffered by these print languages. In particular, Brunet singles out the signifying conflicts between the elderly trapper, our frontiersman Natty, and the naturalist Dr. Bat or, as he has named himself, Battius.[51]

When the reader first meets Dr. Battius, he is returning from an expedition of his own making, a search for something to name in the wilds of the frontier. But in the two days he has been missing from Ishmael and his family, in whose company he travels west, he has not seen "even a blade of grass that is not already enumerated and classed."[52] Obed Bat, who prefers his latinized "Battius," the classification he gave himself, wants to produce a "Historia Naturalis, Americana," a natural history of his native land that would rival Buffon and his imitators. But he struggles to find a blank page, an unnamed space in which to establish his authority; the dark unknown of the frontier has already been exposed and written upon by these European naturalists. Dr. Battius is a new character for the Leatherstocking novels, a figure, like Natty, who strikes out in advance of civilization. He and Natty are both "lovers of the same pursuits," men of the natural world, albeit distinct in that one imposes knowledge upon the wilderness while the other derives knowledge from it.[53] He seems, nonetheless, a patriot and devotee of the American landscape in a manner quite similar to Natty's, his rustic counterpart. He rails against the foreign scientist Buffon, who dismisses the potential of the American scene to produce greatness, and he actively celebrates the variety of animals (human and otherwise) that he encounters. But his greatest struggle, Cooper's novel seems to indicate, is that nobody understands him.

Battius is an American who seems to speak a foreign language. Cooper places this figure in conversation with characters who, though they share a common English, insist that they cannot understand the naturalist nor can they be understood *by* the naturalist. Describing the "monster" he encountered on the prairie, Battius tells Ellen Wade "there was a moment I acknowledge when the *fortiter in re* faltered before so terrible an enemy." The young country girl answers, "You speak a language so different than that we use in Tennessee . . . that I hardly know whether I understand your meaning. If I am right, you wish to say you were chicken-hearted." But while Ellen believes herself to be simplifying their discourse, exposing Battius's cowardice to the harsh light of plain English, her translation only further impedes their conversation as Battius now feels impelled to interrupt his narrative and explain that her statement is "an absurd simile, drawn from an ignorance of the formation of the biped. The heart of a chicken, bears a just proportion to its other organs, and the domestic fowl is, in a state of nature, a gallant bird."[54] The two, it seems, cannot agree on common terms and so their communication stalls. Battius thus acts as a site of difference within the English-speaking community and so an indication of the variety of positions within English that are mutually incomprehensible.

While Ellen understands enough of the Doctor's speech and intentions to share limited conversation with the naturalist, Natty is a different story. The scientist and the frontiersman cannot find a common tongue between them and nothing illustrates this failure better than their ongoing struggle over the most representative of prairie animals: the buffalo, also known to some as the bison, or the *bos ferus,* or the *bos sylvestris.* When the trapper and the naturalist first exchange words, it is because of this disputed animal. Natty, employing his usual natural tropes, compares the disappearance of the Sioux to that of "the herd of Buffaloe . . . chased by the Panther across this plain." Battius feels compelled to intervene when he hears Natty name the animal thus. "Buffaloe," Battius insists, is a "vulgar error," and he offers in its place two latin terms, finally concluding that "Bison is a better word."[55] But Natty refuses to concede to these scientific terms, arguing for the practical impracticality of naming ("Would the tail of a beaver make a worse dinner," he asks, "for calling it a mink?") in the face of Battius's insistence that all creatures should bear a title that immediately reveals its characteristics. I would argue that Natty's dismissal of naming and the importance of names is entirely disingenuous. Not only is Natty himself a "namer," as Cooper's preface to *Last of the Mohicans* reveals, but he is also an aficionado of the practice in general. In *Last of the Mohicans,* upon meeting David Gamut and judging him to have a strong name, Natty confesses to the singer that "I am an admirator of names."[56] This, along with his careful attention to the inscription of names and his privileging of descriptive Indian naming systems, to which I have drawn attention in chapter 3 of this study, all argue against this disregard he demonstrates in the face of competition. Naming is important to Natty; it is his legacy, the lingering trace through which, even after he has passed from the earth, he will continue to exercise influence over those to come. The language of the wilderness has, until this point in the series, been Natty's own, and if the dead continue to inhabit language, as Robert Pogue Harrison argues, this linguistic struggle at the end of his life threatens Natty's final resting place.

This crisis of inheritance is perhaps why Natty continues to struggle with the naturalist over the right to determine titles for the animals, people, and objects on the frontier. At their second meeting, the frontiersman tries again to gain the upper hand on "his rival," this time by challenging Battius to identify the game that he and Paul are eating.[57] The meat is none other than that of "a savoury bison's hump" that Natty had prepared according to its "particular merits," cooked on its own with none of the "foreign relish" to obscure the palate.[58] The buffalo hump is described by the narrator as "all the culinary glory of the Prairies," rendering it exemplary of the landscape, and perhaps even the work of expansion as a consuming of that space. In the pivotal year of 1803, these men sit down to dine on America, and perhaps, through this "consuming affection," incorporate this vastly expanded American frontier into their own sense of self. When Battius comes upon the scene, Natty challenges him to recognize this national feast, testing the scientist's knowledge of the land he is so driven to classify, to consume on his own terms. "Sit ye down," Natty says to the doctor, "and after eating of this morsel, tell me, if you can, the name of the creatur' that has bestowed upon you its flesh for a meal."[59] Dr. Battius accepts Natty's challenge, declaring faith in his classificatory powers, saying there are "many and infallible" signs by which he can determine the animal's identity:

> "You were saying, friend, that you have many ways of telling the creatur'?"—observed the attentive trapper.
>
> "Many; many and infallible. Now, the animals that are carnivorous are known by their incisores."
>
> "Their what!" demanded the trapper.
>
> "The teeth with which nature has furnished them for defence, and in order to tear their food. Again—"
>
> "Look you then for the teeth of this creatur'," interrupted the trapper, who was bent on convicting a man who had presumed to enter into competition with himself, in matters pertaining to the wilds, of gross ignorance; "turn the piece round and find your inside-overs."[60]

Battius's signs are unintelligible to the trapper and even a translation of the signifier "incisors" into "teeth" does not make the original term available to him. Natty can only understand the sound "incisores" as "inside-overs," and instead of pointing him in the direction of the mouth, Natty, following his own translation, tells the doctor to "turn the piece round." Natty understands neither the doctor's use of language nor the object the doctor seeks, and so it seems that the two cannot come to a common understanding.

A similar scene follows, in which Dr. Battius asks for the heart of the animal following Paul Hover's admission that Natty advised him to cut closer to the "heart" or center of the meat to get to the tenderest part, repeating the previous performance of slippage and misunderstanding. Finally, Natty declares Dr. Bat the loser and reveals that what they are eating is "as juicy a buffaloe-hump as a stomach need crave."[61] The doctor, though, is unable to concede defeat to the trapper. "Your system is erroneous," Battius says, "from the premises to the conclusion, and your classification so faulty, as utterly to confound the distinctions of science. The buffaloe is not gifted with a hump at all. Nor is his flesh savoury and wholesome, as I must acknowledge it would seem the subject before us may well be characterized."[62] As their earlier dispute has established, Dr. Battius does not know the animal Natty names "buffaloe" as such; the two, it seems, will never agree on what they are eating because they continue to function solely on their own terms. Each refuses to concede to the system of naming belonging to the other person and so they arrive at the irresolvable differend.[63] In the struggle to gain ground on their own terms, the signifying conflict leaves as its casualty a referent whose name always remains in dispute. Cooper attempts to intervene at this point and impose on the disputants his final judgment. In the accompanying footnote, the author offers a clarification for the reader: "It is scarcely necessary to tell the reader, that the animal so often alluded to in this book, and which is vulgarily called the buffaloe, is in truth the bison; hence so many contre tems between the man of the Prairies and the man of science."[64] Cooper here assumes the exterior voice of a common reason based on a common language; the clarification he offers "is scarcely necessary" and is located in an undisputed "truth." The scene, and Cooper's attempt to regulate it, belies the anxiety Brunet indicates around the desire for a single set of terms, a common language for the American people. "L'enjeu est en effet," Brunet says, "trouver entre tous les personnages un langage commun, fondé sur une autorité acceptable par tous [The issue is in effect to find between all the characters a common language, founded in an authority acceptable to all]."[65] Cooper, the outermost translator in the text, the last line of defense between the excess it contains and the reader it attempts to educate, offers here to serve as that determining authority, an authority that appeals to a "truth" that need hardly be spoken.

Translation Is a Form

While Cooper's own translation is a signifying violence against the sovereignty of the trapper, an elision of the Leatherstocking's power to "vulgarily" name the animals of his environment, the author's intervention does not overwrite the scene of dispute it attempts to address; it cannot remove from the frame of the story the idea of contesting interpretations. Like Alencar, he can't entirely cover up the possibility of difference, the possibility of seeing the scene otherwise. It was Cooper, after all, who endowed Natty with the power to name, and in Natty's resistance to the "sign" of truth, the reader has in her hands a character who asks her to read *other*wise.

In introducing his own translation of Charles Baudelaire's *Tableaux Parisiens,* Walter Benjamin essayed on this work of translation in "Die Aufgabe des Ubersetzers," which most English readers know as "The Task of the Translator." There, Benjamin described translation as "eine Form,"[66] an idea translated by Harry Zohn as a "mode,"[67] as a way of doing or experiencing something. But in the original the Form also resonates with the idea of a shape, form, or mold. To think of it only as a mode would be to lose the idea, at least in part, of its limiting force. As *eine Form,* translation both contains an original but also reshapes it according to the constraints it brings with it. These shaping forces are determined not only by the conscious directives of the translator but also by the "times in which they live, the literary traditions they try to reconcile, and the features of the languages they work with."[68] Connecting with what Harrison describes as the thrownness of the *lex,* these constraints are both produced and experienced by the translator. "The way in which I can try to mean," Paul de Man explains, "is dependent upon linguistic properties that are not only (not) made by me."[69]

The gap here between *mode* (Modus) and *form* (Form) signals what Paul de Man described, in summarizing Benjamin's work (including the translations of that work), as the fate (or fatality) of the translator: "the translator, per definition, fails."[70] This inherent failure is grounded in a primary lack of immediacy, the necessary distance between translation and original that marks the translation as secondary and so the translator as "lost from the very beginning."[71] De Man notes that we can read the *Aufgabe,* the *task* of the translator, differently. *Aufgabe* also means "one who has to give up. If you enter the Tour de France and you give up, that is the *Aufgabe*—'er hat aufgegeben,' he doesn't continue in the race anymore. It is in that sense also the defeat, the giving up, of the translator. The translator has to give up in relation to the task of refinding what was there in the original."[72] In her own consideration of Benjamin's essay, Carol Jacobs amplifies this slippage by drawing out this relation of *Aufgabe* to *aufgegeben.* It is not simply the act of giving up, Jacobs notes, but also the condition of being given up or abandoned. This reading moves beyond the figure of the translator entirely, who is not necessary for thinking through the idea of translatability itself, which is contained from the beginning in the original.[73] The failure de Man describes is located not only in the distance between translation and original but also in an essential instability that gives rise to the very idea of translatability. De Man grounds his essay on Benjamin on the seemingly remedial question "what does Benjamin say?" This question not only gestures toward the failures of Benjamin's translators but also the way that translation destabilizes the "original" as well, opening up sites of excess. "They disarticulate, they undo the original, they reveal that the original was always already disarticulated."[74] When Zohn translates *Form* as "mode," he is reshaping the original but also "giving up" on capturing what exceeds this new text. In asking us to attend to the work of translation, to the *Aufgabe* of translation, these romancers make manifest the figure, the form of the translator, and so make visible the often-invisible and always-troubled labor of moving between languages. By making present this figure, the text also gestures toward an *elsewhere,* to other texts and other speakers that cannot be contained within the shape, the mold, the form of this translation. The novels thus expose their readers to excesses of meaning. The author's position is revealed not as the author-ity but, like the prophecy that he inscribes into the text, as a mediatory position between the text and something greater, an *outre-mer,* a beyond in which lies the possibility of other meanings, other readings, other prophecies.

When Joseph Smith completed his translation of *The Book of Mormon,* he did so by placing a blanket between himself and his scribe. He never looked at the plates he dug up from the earth but rather through the urim and thummim, the tools through which the meaning of the text was revealed to him, a meaning that, once it was written down in English, disappeared forever from view. Fawn Brodie cites David Whitmer's testimony to this process:

> "Joseph Smith," he said, "would put the seer stone into a hat, and put his face in the hat, drawing it closely around his face to exclude the light; and in the darkness the spiritual light would shine. A piece of something resembling parchment would appear, and on that appeared the writing. One character at a time would appear, and under it was the interpretation in English. Brother Joseph would read off the English to Oliver Cowdery who was his principal scribe, and when it was written down and repeated to Brother Joseph to see if it was correct, then it would disappear, and another character with the interpretation would appear."[75]

Smith's process emphasizes the barrier necessary for translation to take place, the gap in meaning that becomes the burden, the task of the translator to guard against by making barriers out of words, mounds or fortifications of the *lex,* the dead as Harrison argues. But what these barriers bring with them is the awareness of an *autre,* an outside that the reader of translation is forbidden, that the reader of translation could not understand. Smith's process of receiving and translating revelation is thus itself revealing: in order to comprehend what is being said, we need the veil. But while the veil may serve to obscure the sublime from sight, the trope necessarily includes a *beyond* the veil, the possibility of rending the partition that stands between man and the abyssal non-sense of the past or the divine.

Natty, as both translator of texts and a text to be translated, contributes to the national structure of print community, as I have outlined throughout this study, a figure in whose historical situation and death the reader can recognize legacy of a familiar community-to-come. But Natty also reveals the *unworking* at the heart of that mournful experience. If Bumppo's troubled communication with his fellow (white) man implies the struggle of language to occult the division and difference in which it operates, Natty's death scene has something else to say about the mortal experience, the experience that will be taken up by the survivors, translated and memorialized as the mournful consumption of community. The everyday miscommunications and proliferation of language systems, even within English itself, can only hint at the experience of overwhelming excess that Natty experiences, not dying or dead, but meeting death itself at the instant of his passing.

After he has rejected Pawnee burial rites, after he has made arrangements with Captain Middleton to be passed on to the future through his memorial marker, Natty has to die. He lies still and quiet for over an hour after this deathbed activity when suddenly, supported by his grieving friends, Natty rises to his feet: "For a moment, he looked about him, as if to invite all in presence to listen, (the lingering remnant of human frailty) and then, with a fine military elevation of the head and with a voice that might be heard in every part of that numerous assembly he pronounce the word –'Here!'"[76] In the instant of his death, Natty hears a call coming from elsewhere. Natty answers to a missing call or interrogation, a "where?" or "when?" in an inquiry of presence to which he responds, locating himself in respect to a beyond, *au-delà*. But this is not the *hic jacet,* the spatializing and temporalizing "here lies" of the living mourning the dead. It is rather a "here stands" of the encounter with death itself. Despite the appearance of an invitation to listen in, the living do not hear the voice to which the trapper responds. Natty's experience of death is incommunicable, beyond words and therefore beyond the reiteration of testimony. The final event remains one that, despite its deployment in the national narratives described in this study, is ultimately untranslatable.

Coda

What Remains

> As Pummíssin. | He is not yet departed.
>
> —From "Of Death and Buriall, &c.," in Roger Williams, *A Key into the Language of America*

> Today, at the hour of our awakening, we must be our own historians.
>
> —Justino Quispe Balboa (Aymarà), quoted in Michel de Certeau's *Heterologies*

William Apess Is Afraid to Die

On January 8, 1836, an impossible speaker took the stage at the Odeon Theater in Boston. William Apess, Pequot by birth, Mashpee by adoption, Methodist minister by occupation, had come to speak about the Indian dead and the American people. Apess had gained some notice in recent years, particularly for his advocacy for the Mashpee community during their dispute with the Massachusetts government.[1] His most recent book, a narrative of the Mashpee Revolt as well as other supportive documents titled *Indian Nullification,* had received more public attention than any of his previous writings.[2] But that night at the Odeon, Apess seemed to focus less on the lived experience of Indian communities in the present than on the figures of the past.

William Apess had come to speak about American history. Following from "the first inquiry," the question "Who is PHILIP?," Apess retraced an extensive history of Native-European contact for his audience, recounting tales of accommodation on the part of the Indian and violent conflict on the part of colonists. But this was not a simple retelling of the past. Apess used this revised history as an opening onto present action, a gesture not only toward the unstable foundations upon which national culture had been built but also to the lived experience of memory in the present time, one that insisted upon subjects that the nationalist narrative had disavowed. In Apess's speech, Philip is made present as the shadow of other storytellers; he "yet lives" in the hearts of those "remaining few" who would proudly declare (as Apess does) that "the blood of a denominated savage runs in his veins."[3] William Apess had come to tell a different story about the past, one that *will have made* space for the figure speaking at the Odeon. William Apess had come to mourn.

Apess stood before the gathered crowd and presented what he later published as his *Eulogy on King Philip* (1836), an encomium of the seventeenth-century Wampanoag chief whose resistance to colonialization had made him an important subject for creole nativist historiography. Philip was depicted in the scryptural economy of national discourse as a tragic figure who had fallen over and over again on the stages and pages of the early republic, giving white audiences and readers a space to mourn and a body upon which to inscribe an affective inheritance.[4] These early national consumers of the text distinguished themselves from their European heritage by valuing what the British had destroyed, by mourning what they had condemned. But on that winter night at the Odeon, Philip's body was not offered in the interest of making possible the sovereign tears of the creole nationalist but rather in calling attention to the Indian himself as mourning subject. Apess accomplishes this shift by making explicit the necropolitical terms of New World nativism. "There is a deep rooted popular opinion in the hearts of many, that Indians were made, &c. on purpose for destruction," Apess told his audience, "to be driven out by white Christians, and they to take their places; and that God had decreed it from all eternity."[5] Apess makes clear that this sacred history, one that forecloses Indian survivance,[6] betrays a lack of faith in God's providence; such claims misunderstand "that the favor of the Almighty was good and holy, and all his nobler works were made to adorn his image, by being his grateful servants, and admiring each other as angels; and not as they say, to drive and devour each other."[7] Unworking the trope of disappearance, Apess restores the translation of dispossession as divine inheritance to its original terms: "those who are in possession of [Philip's] soil" are there "only by the right of conquest." Apess uses the affective work of lamentation to highlight rather than obscure the violent displacement of colonization.[8] The figures who make this re-vision of national history possible are "those few remaining descendants who now remain as the monument of cruelty of those who came to improve our race and correct our errors." "Let every man of color wrap himself in mourning," Apess writes. "Let the children of the pilgrims blush, while the son of the forest drops a tear, and groans over the fate of his murdered and departed fathers."[9]

In presenting Native American historiography, in making spectacular the figure of Native American mourning, Apess's *Eulogy on King Philip* unworks the scryptive economy of New World nationalism by engaging with rather than resisting its central figurations, by opening the narrative up to the possibilities of revision, insisting upon its violent appropriations by making present the irony of erasure, of cloaking the giving of death in a narrative of affection. But Apess's earlier writings also show how this broader project of retelling the history of the nation was connected to the more intimate work of autobiography, of telling the history of the self. In 1829, years before he stood before a Boston audience to tell the history of the nation, William Apess published the story of his life, a book he titled *A Son of the Forest.*[10] In that text, the history of William Apess's life begins in 1676, in recalling a treacherous dispossession that he would return to over and over again in his writings. Tracing what historians have named a specious connection between his Pequot heritage and King Philip,[11] Apess begins his autobiography by reminding his reader of the betrayal that ended Philip's war against the colonists, an act of treachery that allowed "the whites to possess themselves of the goodly heritage occupied by this once peaceable and happy tribe."[12] This foundational displacement, Apess goes on to say, was doubled by a "more intense and heart corroding affliction—that of having their daughters claimed by the conquerors." The loss of territory, culture, continuity is in this way written upon the defiled bodies of tribeswomen who, once appropriated by "the conquerors," mark a loss that cannot be recuperated. "However much subsequent efforts were made to soothe their sorrows in this particular," Apess writes, "they considered the glory of their nation as departed."[13] Following directly upon this assertion of irremediable loss, Apess describes his more immediate lineage as a reflection of this earlier history. His grandfather, he says, "was a white, and married a female attached to the royal family,"[14] and he further repeats this yoking of dispossession and sexual violence as he describes the abuse he suffered at the hands of his maternal grandparents. Apess attributes the cruelty "in part to the whites, because they introduced among my countrymen ardent spirits." He adds:

> [Whites] seduced them into a love for it, and when under its baleful influence, *wronged them out of their lawful possessions—that land where reposed the ashes of their sires—and not only so, but they committed violence of the most revolting and basest kind upon the persons of the female portion of the tribe,*

> who until the arts, and vices, and debauchery of the whites were introduced among them, were as happy, and peaceable, and cheerful, as they roamed over their goodly possessions, as any people on whom the sun of heaven hath ever shone.[15]

To tell the story of his life, Apess places himself within a history of annihilation, a long story of Indian removal that marks Pequot land, culture, and person as already departed. But, as testified to by the story that follows, William Apess remains.

Apess's connection to death functions as a strong narrative thread in the story of his life. In the spiritual autobiography that takes up most of Apess's narrative, he grounds both his relationship to God and his Native heritage in a deep and resilient fear of death. After abuse at home led to his being bonded out to the local Furman family at four years old, Apess recalls one of his earliest and strongest memories as the pious Mrs. Furman's reminder that he too might die. Against his protest that only the elderly die, Mrs. Furman points young Apess to the cemetery "where many younger and smaller persons than myself were laid to moulder in the earth." Though he could not fully understand what she meant at the time, Apess notes that this instruction weighed heavily on him throughout his childhood. "I trembled and was sore afraid," he writes of himself at six, "and for sometime endeavored to hide myself from the destroying monster, but I could find no place of refuge."[16] When he begins his more formal religious education at church meetings, this fear continues to afflict him. He describes himself as "overcome by the fear of death," translating what he describes as his depressive state produced by religious meetings and the "mental agony" of being forbidden them as an abiding mortal dread, his own vulnerability to this "destroying monster" from which he cannot hide. Apess's terror only increases when he experiences mourning for the first time. "About that time," he writes, "death entered the family of Mr. Furman and removed his mother-in-law." Apess feels this loss acutely. "The old lady," he tells the reader, "had allowed me to call her mother" and he mourns her alongside and in equal measure to her children. It is the death of this "mother" that objectifies the abstract concept of death for the young Apess. "I was much affected," he says, "as the old lady was the first corpse I had ever seen."[17] In presenting him with the material fact of death, Apess's "mother" seems to function as the figuration necessary for understanding what had previously remained elusive about the looming and yet inarticulate idea of his own mortality. "Shortly after this occurrence," Apess writes, he falls sick himself and becomes convinced of his own impending death. Recalling a persistent feeling of suffocation, he writes, "I believed that I was going to die."[18]

Apess describes his existential dread as abnormal for children his age (all the events described above happened between six and eight years of age), exhibiting signs of piety and religious leanings despite the community's belief that he was "too young to be impressed with a sense of divine things."[19] But put in conversation with his opening meditation on dispossession and destruction, there is more here in Apess's fear than can be ascribed to established forms of spiritual testimony. Intervening in the narrative between his initial education in death at six and his own miraculous recovery from its precipice at eight, Apess identifies another source of dread in "the great fear I entertained of my brethren."[20] Just as the reminder of death serves to recall him to right action in the household, so too does "a mere threat of being sent away among the indians into the dreary woods."[21] If Apess imagines himself pursued by a "destroying monster," then, this figure is made manifest in his flight from the dark-complected women he encounters in the woods who inspire in him "a tale of blood" and drive him to abandon his party and flee to the Furman house. This fear, Apess writes, "was occasioned by the many stories I had heard of [Indian] cruelty toward the whites—how they were in the habit of killing and scalping men, women and children."[22] Apess traces out this fear of death via a history that envisions Indigenous bodies as an apparatus for destruction even as it marks him in advance by dispossession and disappearance.

It is from this doubly disavowed place that Apess writes the story of his life into a national print culture that would otherwise exclude him. In telling of "the great fear I entertained of my brethren," Apess remarks on what remains untold in those stories that frightened him. "The whites did not tell me," he writes, "that they were in a great majority of instances the aggressors—that they had imbrued their hands in the life blood of my brethren." This untold story identifies the conditional terms of seeing Indigenous people—and white Americans—otherwise.[23] "*If* the whites had told me how cruel they had been to the 'poor indian,'" Apess notes, "I *should have* apprehended as much harm from them."[24] This re-visionary approach, the conditional shifting of the past that *would have* produced a different future, opens up that historiography of the nation that otherwise forecloses the possibility of Apess's own scriptive perdurance. Referring more broadly to his work, Lisa Brooks argues that Apess's "praxis-based framework" asks us to "restore Native networks, texts, and histories to American literature, to look with new eyes at a story we think we already understand."[25] Following Brooks's reading of his method, we might argue that Apess's autobiography not only testifies to the presence and present of Native life, offering a "here" and "now" that counters the popular discourse of Indian extinction, but also serves as an erratum that chronicles what has been left out in considerations of the past.

In crafting his life into a text, Apess was participating in what Phillip Round describes as proprietary authorship, "a special social category of writing in which the creator has secured copyright, becoming 'visible' in the public sphere as a political entity given legal rights by statute law."[26] Round argues that the distinct legal rights accorded to copyrighted authors allowed Native Americans to instantiate a sense of personhood that was in other ways socially and legally denied them.[27] It is for this reason, Round says, that we should attend to the ways that American Indian writers negotiated the "formal gestures" that comprise proprietary authorship, including "legal and material efforts put forward by the authors in the marketplace, as well as rhetorical and physical properties of the books themselves."[28] In addition to the copyright notice and title page of *A Son of the Forest,* Round pays particular attention to the portrait of Apess added to the front matter in the second edition of his autobiography. In that frontispiece, Apess is depicted wearing "a coat and cravat, and his hair is cut short and styled like most Euro-Americans of the emerging middle class." Beneath the portrait he is identified as "Mr. William Apes, a Native Missionary of the Pequot Tribe of Indians." "It would appear," Round notes, "that Apess's frontispiece portrait served to ground his authorial identity firmly in middle-class respectability, concrete labor, and the physical properties of textual production."[29] Together with the copyright and title pages, these affirmations of identity and the attachment of that identity to the text comprise the authorial gestures that prefigure Apess as a subject even as they affirm the legal recognition attendant with the rights of ownership. These images of the author (in portrait and copyright notice), preceding as they do the narrative of the author's life, ground the story in an assertion of the self that stands in for being even as it instantiates legal personhood.

Apess's inclusion of the portrait in the revised edition of his autobiography also presents an important counterpoint to the appropriative collecting of Indian lives in contemporaneous print culture. Not only were Native Americans rendered signs without referents through the vanishing discourses of the national romance, as I've traced throughout this study, but this work carried over to projects in the visual arts and the more "substantial" work of history and biography.[30] Round compares the frontispiece to those included in two other Indian autobiographies, George Copway's *Life, History, and Travels* (1847) and Black Hawk's dictated *Life of Black Hawk* (1833).[31] The former captures an anonymous, romantic Indian standing on a distant hill and staring off to one side, an idealized figure resonant with the national imaginary, while the latter reflected a body of work that aimed to collect "real" Indian lives. The frontispiece is based on a painting by Charles Bird King, one of a set of almost 150 paintings completed as part of a government effort to document Indian lives before they became extinct. The bureaucrat responsible for the commission, Thomas McKenney, had already established a collection of artifacts for his "Archives of the American Indian"; placed alongside the artifacts, the King portraits rendered explicit contemporary representation as a form of capturing and preserving not just individuals but an abstracted idea of the subject.[32] The McKenney collection and its federal funding encouraged other artists like George Catlin to travel west and capture Indian life in painting. Catlin's "Indian Gallery," a traveling show featuring salon paintings of Indigenous life, became yet another way for audiences to consume Native American figures as already-historical artifacts. The project to document Indian life in history and biography had similar archival goals, seeking to preserve lives that were considered fading if not already lost. One of these, Samuel Gardner Drake's *Indian Biography* (1832), even attempted to capture Apess in its own version of the "Indian Gallery." Nestled in Drake's extensive consideration of Philip is a brief sketch of Apess himself:

> If Indian tradition do not err, some of the blood of the immortal *Philip* now circulates in this city. The Rev. *Wm. Apes,* of the Independent Methodist order, a Pequot, is preaching occasionally among us. He has seen a chequered and various life, as appears by a book which he has published, entitled, "A Son of the Forest." He contemplates giving the traditionary, as well as the real history and antiquities, of the Pequots; which must be a work desired by every one. Mr. *Apes* is thirty-four years of age, very active and intelligent. He makes a wide mistake in his life, by calling *Philip* king of the Pequots; for *Philip* was not born when the tribe was destroyed. And there is no tradition that the Wampanoag chiefs ever claimed dominion over the Pequots, but on the contrary the latter were "a terror to all their neighbors."[33]

Drake's sketch of Apess is notably marked by a suspicion of Apess's own self-presentation. His conditional affirmation of Apess's claims about his life ("*If* Indian tradition do not err . . .") and his critique of Apess's historiography ("he makes a wide mistake in his life") demonstrate how the voice of "real history," as Drake names it, can both contain and revise a subject on its own terms. In light of Drake's portrait and in conversation with the archiving of images, we can understand how the political work of proprietary authorship can function as a counternarrative to these appropriative projects, insisting on a subjectivity in excess of the subjects captured in these images and narratives.

We can broaden our considerations of Apess's resistant authorial gestures to include his later decision to publish the *Eulogy* with a single illustration. While galleries, museums, and libraries filled up with Native figures, Apess offered his own image of Philip, not as the proud yet fallen leader (as Round describes the portrait of Black Hawk), but as an uncanny sentimental object, one that echoed the scryptive work of creole nativism even as it unworked its assumption of Indian extinction. Jill Lepore, who places Apess's dramatic history in the *Eulogy* alongside Edwin Forrest's phenomenally popular play *Metamora,* says that "like *Metamora,* Apess' address, his *eulogy,* also fetishized Philip's dire end; the frontispiece engraving of the pamphlet version of his speech depicted Philip's death scene."[34] In making the comparison to Forrest's work, Lepore asks us to think of the etching as a translation of the pathetic scene, to see in its arrangement a theatrical staging, bodies facing out to the audience for consumption of the tragedy. I would like to draw out another connection to a powerful figuration of Native presence and speculate on Apess's etching as a significant "authorial gesture," one that not only signals his cultivation of textual production (and thus legal personhood as author) but also revises the work of others. By including the engraving of Philip, Apess offers his own translation of nativist figuration, drawing attention to the ways in which the troping of the nation is subject to revision and so "contesting settler epistemological privilege."[35]

The arrangement, characters, and action featured in Apess's frontispiece would have seemed familiar to his readers. In 1807, Joel Barlow published his epic poem *The Columbiad,* complete with eleven engravings by Robert Smirke, illustrations of particular scenes from the text. One of these scenes could be found in book 6 of that work, where the reader encounters the pathetic death of one Lucinda at the hands of two Mohawk men. Lucinda was Barlow's "romantic sounding pseudonym" for the historical Jane McCrea, who was murdered and scalped during the Revolutionary War.[36] That Apess was familiar with Barlow's epic poem is likely. If he had not read or heard the work directly, his central resource for his revised history, Samuel Gardner Drake's *Indian*

Biography, cited Barlow's descriptions in support of its narrative portraits, and the image Smirke produced was copied and circulated broadly on its own. Art historian Samuel Edgerton notes that while other narrative and visual interpretations of the event existed, "Smirke's sentimental treatment apparently appealed to American taste for it became the single most important representation in forming a popular image of the murder of Jane McCrea during the nineteenth century."[37]

William Truettner notes that this image of McCrea's death was itself old-fashioned, an "uncomfortable departure" from the sentimental figure of the vanishing American.[38] Instead, the illustration offered an older image of Indian violence and white victimhood even as its narrative gestured toward the moral failures of the British in funding violence against white colonists. In the illustration (fig. 2), Lucinda appears in the lower right, restrained by two Indians. She throws her arms up, head back and chest bared to the viewer as the men, behind and beside her, raise knife and tomahawk, the mechanisms of her imminent death. In the background, opposite these three figures, the viewer sees her fiancé, Heartly, in the distance, running to save Lucinda. His distance affirms that he will arrive too late, but his presence also assures us that her death will be witnessed. It is Heartly who makes possible the later testimony to this moment and thus makes possible our own consumption of her death. Placing Apess's frontispiece to the *Eulogy* (fig. 3) next to Smirke's illustration of Lucinda's death, the influence of the McCrea visualization is clear. Philip, like Lucinda, appears in the lower right, head back and chest exposed while restrained by two figures, this time two English colonists. Like the Lucinda illustration, the two men stand over and behind the central figure, although in Apess's image the men are dressed anachronistically, in breeches and bicorne hat more appropriate to the latter part of the eighteenth century than to the seventeenth. As in the Smirke image, the men menace the victim with the tools of death; the man to the side holds a sword instead of a tomahawk while the crouching man behind him still holds a knife that hovers above Philip's head now instead of Lucinda's.[39]

The power of Apess's authorial gesture is not simply in the inversion of subjects that makes the Native American the locus of sympathy instead of abjection. There is also a significant shift in translating the McCrea image to fit Apess's project. Instead of a single figure coming upon the scene (always too late), there are two. Together the Native and white men depicted in the upper left bear witness to the event, already defined by the title attached to the image as "King Philip Dying for His Country." This foundational sacrifice is, in this re-visionary image, structured as a debt belonging not just to the creole subject, the horrified Heartlys who come onto the scene too late to save the victim from extinction but just in time to commemorate, to mourn the loss. Instead, this event is also witnessed by a still-living Native American, and

Fig. 2. Robert Smirke, "The Murder of Lucinda," from Joel Barlow's *Columbiad* (1807)

Fig. 3. "King Philip Dying for His Country," from William Apess's *Eulogy on King Philip* (1836)

so Apess makes space for those whom the other collections of Native figures exclude. Apess insists on Other witnesses who will have Other stories to tell.

One event that seemed beyond narration, evading objectification and consumption via the print narratives of nation and subject, is that of Apess's own death. At first, it seemed to contemporary historians that William Apess had disappeared. When Barry O'Connell offered a biographical introduction to his unprecedented collection of writings by Apess in 1992, he lamented that "known records locate him only until 1838." After that date, O'Connell notes, "no trace has yet been found of his movements, of his life, or of his death."[40] Scholars often repeated this lament, even after archival discoveries led O'Connell to revise his history in 1997 to include evidence from an inquest into Apess's death.[41] In "Once More Let Us Consider," O'Connell concludes his revision of Apess's history by noting that scholars "must be not only provisional about what we think we know but fully alive to the mystery of others' lives, the fullness of which will always elude us."[42] In 2004, Robert Warrior published a brief article that used the obituaries and inquest recently "emerged in archival research" in order to reconsider Apess's death as well. In that piece, Warrior offers to "speculate" on Apess's death, opening up what had become a foreclosed place in the archive that is too frequently marked by a historical insistence on "Native invisibility."[43] Warrior's framing of his work as "speculation" allows him to craft a narrative that includes within it the possibility of its undoing. His article is marked by what is not shown, what cannot be known, the justifiable conjecture, and the unresolved dispute.[44] Just as Apess's work seems to resist simultaneously the work of exclusion from and containment within national narratives and the institution of national memory, so modern scholars are invited to turn from the invocation of settled truth or totalizing knowledge of the subject in favor of being alive to mystery and the work of speculation.

The twentieth-century restoration of Apess's death touches on what remains excluded from the institution (and institutions) of national history, the gaps and silences that surround figures rendered extinct or impossible by the dominant narratives of early national life. In O'Connell's biography of Apess, we see these gaps in the series of questions that make up the two paragraphs following Apess's sudden disappearance, although Apess's singularity rather than his vanishing frames these queries. "Are there records and events," O'Connell asks, "inside histories of native communities in these years, continuities in oral traditions that historians have failed to uncover?" Were Native Americans practicing a strategic withdrawal in order to "keep intact whatever could be hidden of their own existence and culture? Were they there and lost because, for the most part, historians did not bother to look?"[45] O'Connell offers these questions as provocations for further research, gesturing toward the common acceptance of the "vanishing" thesis traced earlier in this study ("the common assumption that most Indians had disappeared from southern New England by the nineteenth century") that grounds the scryptive national memory. "Native Americans," O'Connell writes, "have been kept, and remain largely outside the written histories of the United States."[46] "Indians cannot be accommodated in the available ideological frameworks. . . . Neither the indigenous histories and concerns of native peoples nor the complex relations between them and the Euro-Americans can be comprehended by the providential history that has generally passed for the actual history of the United States."[47] What *Mourning the Nation to Come* has attempted to outline in the previous chapters is how this providential history gained ground in the early republic, highlighting the way that creole patriots transformed colonial subjects into postcolonial citizens by translating historical Indigenous claims to land in North and South America into a proleptic narrative that included Euramericans. But the discursive structure of this affective interpellation cannot be reduced to a purely symbolic exchange. As a productive apparatus for the nation, the book itself, the massively reproducible printed artifact, functioned as a crucial mechanism not only in proliferating these new histories but also as an imaginary limit identifying what can and should be preserved in institutions of cultural memory. The scryptural economy of print nationalism, in its figurations of loss as much as its own conception of the monumental work of writing, creates an exteriority that its institutions of memory seem to foreclose.

A full accounting of Native American history would require looking askance at the archive, as O'Connell's questions indicate and his *reconsideration* and Warrior's *speculation* perform. In reflecting on her own reconsideration of King Philip's War, Lisa Brooks offers the image of the "looking glass," a term borrowed from Apess's 1833 essay "An Indian's Looking-Glass for the White Man," as a way of conceiving of a scholarly method that "should not lead us to a definitive new interpretation, but rather should provide a lens to multiple interpretive possibilities." Brooks writes:

> A clear portrait of the American literary and historical landscape, I suggest, can only be achieved by joining the two sides of the looking glass that are in relational opposition: the striving for "clear sight," and the recognition that, even as we strive with integrity for radiant lucidity, the text or landscape that we read, the scenarios that we reconstruct, can never represent a singular historical reality. Instead, we can aim to discern that world, as if through a prism, acknowledging and embracing the many images that are refracted through the multifaceted "looking glass."[48]

This prismatic approach requires us to look elsewhere for traces of what has been excluded or rendered impossible not just by national histories written since the nineteenth century but also by its privileged form, the book as the arresting tomb, the memorial of national life upon which both the narrative and its affective obligation are inscribed. It is the centering of archives around these monumental inscriptions that leads Rodrigo Lazo to acknowledge that "historical memory in the Americas is always fragmentary,"[49] a recognition not only of the limited framework of the archive (the problem of space in an insistently materialist project), but also of the partial, fragmentary quality of that which survives in such spaces. "What remains," Lazo notes, "is not complete."[50] It is only through the acceptance of this "fragmented and incomplete materiality," Lazo writes elsewhere of his own research, that he has been able to "read in a way that looked for what was possible in those fragments."[51] These fragments are what Lazo names as "textual remains," traces that can lead us to unfamiliar places, exposing the potential for "disjunction and contradiction" already present in the archive.[52]

We can see this tracing of remains as well as its attendant epistemological shift with respect to the discourse of national memory in recent work by Robert Dale Parker on the poetry of Jane Johnston Schoolcraft. Narrating his archival searches for the Ojibwe poet (a narration required, he notes, by a general astonishment that her work could be found at all), Parker teases out Schoolcraft's manuscripts by untangling the notes of previous scholars, sifting through the "stew of randomness and confusion" that characterized her husband's papers for signs of her work, and making the serendipitous discovery of a new catalog of "a bunch of old stuff that had been sitting in boxes" by librarians on the verge of moving their collection.[53] The agon of Parker's search is matched by the vicissitudes of the sources he discovers, marked as they are with inaccuracies as well as "mysteries and uncertainties" that preclude him from telling a story of Schoolcraft's work or life that can be characterized as totalizing or authoritative.[54] Instead, the story he tells of his work is marked by hedging statements like "so far as we know at present," which we might read as an ethical opening up within literary history. When Parker goes through a more formal list of Schoolcraft's titles, a location of her significance familiar to readers of literary history, one notices this opening up in the repetition of a particular phrase: Schoolcraft, Parker writes, was "among the first American Indian writers. She was also the *first known* American Indian literary writer, the *first known* Indian woman writer, by some measures the *first known* Indian poet, the *first known* poet to write poems in a Native American language, and the *first known* American Indian to write out traditional Indian stories."[55] The qualification of "known" marks his assertions within a structure hospitable to new developments, new discoveries, and new (or renewed) figures who might displace Schoolcraft's primacy in these vaunted categories. The archive that Parker describes and to which he contributes is in this way characterized by a radical openness, one that retains the possibility of revision, an inscription that is marked by a pending return. If the archive functions as an institution akin to the national monuments and cenotaphs that arrest Anderson and his reader in the opening of his study, then Parker presents us with a tomb whose stone has been noticeably rolled away, not in the promise of an apocalyptic totality, but rather in recognition of the dead who do not (yet) remain.[56]

Words Are (Not) Things

In the first of his collected lectures on American literature, published in the same year as Apess's autobiography, Samuel Knapp opens with a brief epigraph: "Words are Things," a phrase he attributes simply to "Mirabeau."[57] Knapp, a lawyer, military leader, sometimes legislator, and member of the American Antiquarian Society goes on to explore the importance of language, and in particular *print* language, to the development of a national literature, locating the importance of the *thingness* of words in the durability of inscription necessary for keeping "language alive in its purity."[58] "The language that is addressed to the ear alone is soon changed or lost," he writes, "but that which is addressed to the eye as well as the ear, is long preserved by a twofold impression upon the mind. The sight is more faithful than the ear, and preserves her knowledge longer."[59] Knapp, like many of the authors in this study, imagines the work of the press as infusing language with a sense of endurance, of futurity, and so marries his work of tracing out literary history for a present reader to an idea of monumental inscription, the durability of a scriptural economy. He ends his lecture with a brief meditation on the collecting of Native American languages and the advancing material economy of letters among Indigenous communities represented by the creation of the Cherokee syllabary.[60] He sketches a history of Sequoyah and his invention, claiming to have received this history "from the lips of the inventor himself," although later admitting to two other sets of lips, those of the interpreters who mediated between himself and "the American Cadmus."[61] He concludes that Sequoyah understood and "felt the advantages the white man had long enjoyed, of having the accumulations of every branch of knowledge, from generation to generation, by means of a written language, while the red man could only commit his thoughts to uncertain tradition."[62] Print had rendered personal and cultural history more stable, more faithful, and so by entering print culture Sequoyah had secured for the Cherokee a form of enduring legibility that seemed to guarantee an acknowledgment of the Native American as *perduring* subject.

All of this follows, both in format and function from Mirabeau's pithy equation. The French aristocrat and revolutionary had stood at the opening of the first French National Assembly and had dared to declare the *thingness* of words, allowing Knapp to argue forty years later about the power of language as a physical phenomenon, opening and closing a consideration of American language and literature with declarations of fidelity. The sight is more faithful than the ear, Knapp avers; print has rendered history more certain. The trouble with locating this power in Mirabeau's evocative speech, though, is that the French statesman never said that words are things. He said that words *aren't* things. Early transcriptions of Mirabeau's speeches record him advising against "la facilité de l'esprit humain, à prendre des mots pour des choses,"[63] and the English translations appearing at the same time retain this collapsing of distinction as a source of critique.[64] By 1800 the distinction between words and things seems to be under pressure. In a letter to William Godwin, Samuel Taylor Coleridge wrote that he "would endeavor to destroy the old antithesis of *Words & Things*," a Romantic desire to acknowledge the sensual life of language separate from its referential labor, a desire that posits itself against an established acceptance of their division. By 1814, another Romantic poet, Lord Byron, seems to have rewritten the history of this distinction altogether. In a letter to Samuel Rogers, Byron refers to "[Sheridan] saying of Mirabeau that '*words* are *things*,'"[65] an idea that shows up in Canto 3 of Byron's *Don Juan* (1821), in which the poet meditates on the *thingness* of words, not as Coleridge or Wordsworth would have it in the boundless creative potential of the mind, but rather as the material afterlife of print itself. "But Words are things," the poet writes. "'Tis strange, the shortest letter which Man uses/ instead of speech, may form a lasting link/ of Ages." Somewhere along the way, in the circulation of transcription and translation, Mirabeau's words had shifted. In their shift, they testified to the *unfaithful* records of print.

The ironic shift indicated here, in pronouncing one's faith in print's memory and stability through a misremembered transcription of an oratorical event (what is in its nature singular, unrepeatable), exposes a gap in the record, a gap produced by the record, through which the "fullness" O'Connell describes escapes us. Locke names the conflation of words and things as an "abuse of language" precisely because of this gap, one he insists upon. "Words in their primary or immediate Signification," Locke writes, "stand for nothing but the Ideas in the Mind of him that uses them, how imperfectly soever those Ideas are collected from the Things, which they are supposed to represent."[66] If words are then incapable of coinciding seamlessly with their referents, mediating but not connecting precisely the distinct realms of idea and object, then we could extend this to a distinction between figure and figuration, the subject and the idea of the subject. When Round offers us the political work of proprietary authorship, he is engaging with a Byronic commodification that gathers from the material environment of print culture a sense of thingness without insisting on the transcendent immediacy of language. Apess's statements of copyright, his frontispieces, his title pages all work with his narratives to proclaim the figuration of the text, creating with it a powerful argument about rights by making visible claims to ownership over the property created by printed words. But if we stop there we also accede to an idea of the primacy and stability of print's memorial function that maintains its violence of encapsulation. Pictures of William Apess are not William Apess. The words William Apess are not William Apess. And so in tracing a *being before the law,* an idea of the subject produced through legal categories of copyright and proprietary authorship, we should also be listening for a *Being* before the law, one that antecedes or exceeds figuration, the shadows of survivance that gesture toward a fullness that the text cannot contain.[67]

In *Manifest Manners,* Gerald Vizenor offers "shadows of survivance" as a way to think through that which resists representation or simulation in colonial forms. From what he invokes over and over as the "ruins of representation," we are invited to "[uncover] traces of tribal survivance, trickster hermeneutics, and the remanence of intransitive shadows," a residual effect (or affect) from a withdrawn catalyst.[68] "Shadows tease and loosen the bonds of representation in stories," Vizenor explains; they are "the sense of presence in the name and the trace to other stories."[69] Using this framework, we can understand not only how print produces its own shadows but also the ways it is shadowed in turn by an excess, a trace, a remnant of what it cannot contain. These are its failures, the ruins of representation from which we hear the invitation to unsee, to think otherwise.[70]

This can be particularly effective for tracing the (non)presence of orality in printed texts. "The wild unities of heard stories, and the pleasures of performance," Vizenor writes, "are unbodied in translations . . . are transformed in publications that are *seen* as cultural representations."[71] This unbodied transformation of the event of orality remains a significant space for thinking through the instantiating gestures through which Apess's subjectivity emerges on the page. Philip Gura names Apess's performances of the *Eulogy* "one of the most powerful and radical public pronouncements in a golden age of American oratory."[72] Jill Lepore remarks that the significance of Apess's work resides in its powerful work of *speaking* the past.[73] As Tim Cassedy has recently shown, this attention to medium cannot be dismissed as merely a presentist theory of communication. As print became more widely available in the eighteenth and nineteenth centuries, readers became more sensitive to distinctions in affect, status, and trustworthiness between this mechanized communication and those more intimately associated with the body, from handwritten manuscripts to "orally transmitted texts." "Convinced that even though voices, manuscripts, and print can all transmit verbal texts," Cassedy writes, "those texts that had been transmitted mainly by voice were of a different order of meaning because of their different medium of transmission."[74] Following Round's attention to the apparatus of print, if Apess can be said to be making "authorial gestures" in the production of his corpus, gestures that make present his claims to legal personhood, then in the textual remains of his performance at the Odeon, what arrives to us as *Eulogy on King Philip, as pronounced at the Odeon, in Federal Street, Boston, by the Rev. William Apes, an Indian,* we can follow meaningful *oratorical* gestures, shadows or traces of presence that retain markings of the event in all its singularity and irreproducibility.[75]

Returning to the *Eulogy,* we can shift our attention from Apess's revisionary history to the oratorical gestures through which the text retains traces or shadows of the event. The most prominent marker is the way Apess presents his history as a visual display, drawing attention to the speaker on the stage and what he *shows* even as he tells his story. Identifying his primary exigence, what brings him to the stage, Apess says he is there "to bring before you beings," and the bodies he invokes weep and blush, cry out and shed tears in the somatic tableau of his speech. "Let us look a little further," he says of his accumulating evidence, "we will present before you the words," "we will lay before you" the pathetic scene.[76] When he tells the story of the brokenhearted Indian father who, feeling abandoned by his white neighbors, dug up the bones of his child and left his home, Apess tells his audience "Hear his own words," and then speaks the man's lament.[77] In these moments, the printed text gestures to the sensual witnessing of the event, the appeals to sight and sound offered by and through Apess's body at the Odeon. The transformation of the performance into a print artifact does not exclude the trace of those voices, the speaker on the stage (and the voices he presents) nor his audience, who is doubled as "the reader or hearer," who is referred to the records, who is invoked in the "now" of "even now in this audience," and whose response is required, although withheld from the text ("what say you, judges").[78] Despite the transformation into print, Apess maintains the shadow of his own figure, that which presides over the text. In doing so, Apess demonstrates a keen sense for the spectacle of his own body, which bridges the "let us see" of the *Eulogy* to the famous passage from his autobiography in which he described crowds flocking to his service, "some to *hear* the truth, and others to *see* the 'Indian.'"[79] These oratorical gestures point us toward a spectacle that cannot be contained in the text or consumed by the reader but rather remains attached to other places and times, to the unrepeatable event that itself is mediated by *ideas* ("Indian") that are not *things.*

This shadow, the presence of nonpresence, is nowhere better understood in the text than in the very opening of Apess's *Eulogy,* the invocation of an apophatic presence: "I do not arise," Apess tells his audience, "to spread before you the fame of a noted warrior, whose natural abilities shone like those of the great and mighty PHILLIP of Greece, or of ALEXANDER the Great, or like those of WASHINGTON,—whose virtues and patriotism are engraven on the hearts of my audience."[80] Even as he invokes but never names Philip, in a comparison he won't (but does) make, Apess recalls (by denying) his own presence. Apess, standing, insists he does not arise; Apess, standing, asks his audience (still without naming his subject) "who shall stand?" Instead of the place-making work of the *hic jacet,* the "here lies" of the epitaph that gives the reader a time and space in which to dwell, Apess's apophatic presence undoes the incorporations of identification even as it gives him a *negative* space from which to create his own text. From a ruin of representation, both Philip's and his own, Apess builds monuments of mourning, not as stable signifiers emanating from the past but in the present and presence of *those who remain.* Apess invites us to hear, to see, to feel, to speak, to recall the excesses of the text, to re-mark that "what has been published and seen is not what is heard or remembered."[81]

Noo-chun kes-uk-qut-tiam-at-am unch koo-we-su-onk

In *Writing Indian Nations,* Maureen Konkle recounts the disappointment of young Bostonians at *seeing* Elias Boudinot speak. Boudinot was in Boston to raise support for Cherokee resistance, but when he took the stage some in the crowd were shocked by his speech and dress. Louisa Park describes the reactions of her companions as "great astonishment and disappointment" touched as well by resentment. "Little Charlotte Coolidge seemed to think she had been imposed upon," Park reports, "and declared she 'would not have stirred a step if she had known'; mighty was her wrath at not beholding a 'real wild Indian with his hair streaming down his back, a tomahawk in his hand, and a wampum belt, making a speech to us in Cherokee.'"[82] Ideas, the women were finding out, are not things, a disjuncture between figure and figuration that led some in the early Republic to disqualify as "Indian" those who failed to realize an exotic fantasy about subjects from other places and other times. Philip Deloria describes the dismissal of Indian subjectivity in favor of Indian figuration as a desire for "Indianness, not Indians." "The only culture allowed to define real Indian people was a traditional culture that came from the past rather than the present."[83] Mark Rifkin describes this "supposed anteriority of Native lifeworlds" a "model of perverse fixity." "From this perspective," he writes, "Indigenous duration can only be the carrying forward of what properly should be past, an inversion of 'real' time or 'natural' time which implicitly is that of Euramerican historicism."[84] Such ideas of an always-historicized authenticity seemed a ready dismissal for contemporary Indian voices and present experience in favor of a white authoritative (and authorizing) vision. Samuel Gardner Drake's correction of Apess's autobiography in his biographical note seemed symptomatic of a community in which white Indian "authorities" judged Native Americans against impossible standards. Apess's possible collaborator and associate in Boston, Joseph Snelling, for example, proclaimed that Apess could not be considered an authentic Indian voice because "he had so assimilated to white culture."[85] In comparing Apess's work to the recently published *Life of Black Hawk,* Snelling noted that the Pequot minister lacked the "wild, unadulterated savage, gall yet fermenting in his veins." Apess, Snelling declared, wrote only "in the character of a white man."[86]

By tracing the ways in which Apess's corpus resists even as it contributes to a national print culture, what I hope to have shown are the myriad ways in which William Apess, in marking out a space of disqualification, in casting the shadow of (non)presence from the ruins of representation, makes possible an opening onto what Derrida called *impossible mourning,* a means of commemorating loss that resists the incorporative violence of identification. As opposed to possible mourning, that "which would interiorize within us the image, idol, or ideal of the other who is dead and lives on in us," Derrida describes impossible mourning as "leaving the other his alterity, respecting thus his infinite remove, either refuses to take or is incapable of taking the other within oneself, as in the tomb or the vault of some narcissism."[87] In the "looking glass" of Apess's *Eulogy,* the reader is confronted by an unsettling and inherently unsettled narrative of national history, one that undermines authoritative visions of the past while also pointing to other places, other times, and other voices that cannot be contained within the memorials of print culture.

To consider this work, I want to return to the Odeon, to an evocative moment later captured in print but also advertised in advance as a highlight of the night's performance. According to an advertisement in the *Boston Daily Evening Transcript,* "At the close [Apess] will give a specimen of Philip's language."[88] This "specimen" appears on stage as the Lord's Prayer in Massachusett, an untranslated translation that testifies both to the colonial appropriations described in the *Eulogy* and an estrangement that unworks any attempt at identification. In her comparison between Apess's performance and Edwin Forrest's *Metamora,* Jill Lepore cites this oration as an "attempt to 'out-Indian him,'" that in order to do this Apess "fell back on the most authentic Indian speech recoverable to him in 1836."[89] But what I want to trouble here is what Lepore names as both "authentic" and "recoverable." When Apess takes the stage to deliver his *Eulogy,* the history he describes, his embodied position as speaker, the passage he quotes, and the audience who listens to him speak all complicate this moment in a kind of prismatic refraction or infinite regress from meaning in which we neither "*hear* the truth" nor "*see* the Indian."

There is a vein of scholarship that sees Apess's recitation in the *Eulogy* as evidence of his own language retention from childhood, that sees in this moment a coalescing of two facets of Apess's identity, that of minister and Indian.[90] In this reading, an idea of authentic expression attaches to his prayer, seen as a moment of "true" expression that restores him to a culture from he has been removed. But in making this assumption we ignore the expressive potential of simulation evident in the connections Apess maintains between his recitation and other writings, other figures, as well as a distinction he himself draws between himself and Philip that allows the fallen chief to speak. While Massachusett and Pequot belong to the same language family (Algonquian), and so share phonemes, words, and phrases in common, they cannot be collapsed into a single language. In his *Eulogy*, Apess in fact distinguishes between his words and Philip's language.[91] When Apess ends his history, he announces, "We will now give you his language in the Lord's Prayer,"[92] offering but making no claim on the language that follows; it is "his" language that "we" will give. It is not (only) Apess, but (also) Philip who speaks.

Even as Apess offers Philip's language, the message he speaks alienates us from the subject it purports to reveal. The Lord's Prayer he offers has its origin not in Philip but in his contemporary, John Eliot, and Eliot's translation of the Bible, a tool designed to make possible the conversion of Native peoples to Christianity. Apess had already documented Philip's resistance to Christianity in the history that preceded the specimen, as well as the corrupted work of missionaries among the Indians, so the text is strained by its attachment simultaneously to Philip and Eliot. And even as we trace the work to Eliot we come upon another figure, that of John Sassamon, a figure Apess condemns in his *Eulogy* as a "traitor," a man who was known by his people to be "false," although the nature of his betrayal remains unclear in Apess's text.[93] Sassamon, a translator mediating between the Wampanoag and English, had converted to Christianity at an early age and contributed to Eliot's translation of the Bible. In the conflict of 1671, what Jill Lepore describes as a "dress rehearsal for the events of 1675," Sassamon had been key in winning Philip's concessions to the British, playing both "messenger and missionary" for the colonial forces.[94] He was also likely murdered by Philip's men, an action Apess both attributes to his hero ("doubtless by the order of Philip") and concedes as a just killing.[95] Tracing the prayer to Sassamon, the language becomes a treacherous speech, not simply for his unfaithfulness in relation to Philip, but also perhaps for another role Sassamon played that Apess felt more acutely. In 1637, Sassamon interpreted for and fought alongside the British colonists in the Pequot War,[96] the war that would only conclude with a treaty outlawing the very existence of the tribe Apess claimed as his own. It is not (just) Sassamon we hear. It is (also) Apess.

The recitation moves from Apess to Philip to Eliot to Sassamon in a receding genealogy of figures who each contribute in their own way to distinct readings of the text. But even to pause at Eliot's Bible, to "unmask" the translation and return again to its origin in the Geneva Bible, we find a mire instead of meaning. The Lord's Prayer is an instruction ("Lord, teach us to pray," Luke 11:1), an exemplum of proper prayer offered in the interest of clarity and efficacy. In "The Day Breaking" (1647), John Eliot identified the uncertainty surrounding language and prayer as an impediment to Indian conversion. Eliot cited discouraged Indians who believed "Jesus Christ understood not what Indians speake in prayer" because God was only acquainted with the English tongue.[97] But in Apess's *Eulogy,* he cites an impediment to prayer among the English rather than the Indians. There, Apess refers to Increase Mather's "piety" in noting that the pilgrims prayed faithfully for Indian deaths and damnations, seeking divine license for their destructive acts or naming them in retrospect as the work of God. Deploying the ironic mode he uses throughout his speech, Apess proclaims, "It is also wonderful how they prayed, that they should pray the bullet through the Indian's heart and their souls down into hell. If I had any faith in such prayers, I should begin to think that soon we should all be gone."[98] Apess goes on to remind his audience of a few verses that would have served Mather and the others better in understanding prayer, scripture that would "utterly condemn them." The return to instruction in prayer thus becomes a reminder of this earlier moment of the text, a recursive moment in which the audience is reminded once again of Indian piety in contrast to European corruption.

Finally, the text Apess cites may indicate an additional level of mediation, one that diverges from the historical genealogy and reflects more precisely the contemporary work of historiography and the collecting of Indian lives. Just as the advertisement proffered a "specimen" of Philip's language in Apess's performance, so did Samuel Drake's *Indian Biography,* now revised and reissued as *The Book of Indians of North America* (1835). The year before Apess presented his prayer in Philip's tongue, Drake added a concluding section to his own "Life of King Philip" that contained a similar offering. "In bringing our account of this truly great man towards a close," Drake wrote, "we must not forget to present the reader with a specimen of the language in which he spoke. The following is the Lord's prayer in Wampanoag: . . ."[99] By comparing the Eliot translation with Drake's later "specimen" of language (table 1), it is clear that Apess's recitation bears a closer relation to the latter. While there are slight differences in spelling or hyphenation, the overall orthography and structure maintain a closer bond with Drake's text than with the Eliot original, which would have been difficult for Apess (but not necessarily Drake) to access. The "we" in "we will now give you" could in this way reference Drake himself, whose writing Apess had drawn on throughout the *Eulogy* and whose supposed mastery of Philip's life Drake had demonstrated through his prolific publications on the topic. But in his performance Apess had managed something that Drake's writings could not. He had spoken the words before they had been printed, marking them indelibly by a voice that appears, even as a lack, in the printed text that memorialized the event.

In this web of citation and mire of meaning, Apess gives his listener and then reader a kind of successful failure of mourning, an experience of alterity that, spoken through Apess, the medium of other worlds and other words, makes present the *disfigurations* of the past that resist incorporation. Apess presents the prayer as a "specimen," as an exemplum that should serve as a model, a representative passage from which the reader can infer the character of the person or the structure of its language. But there is too much left unsaid in the "looking glass" of citation; what should be familiar (the Lord's Prayer) remains helplessly enigmatic in its signification, pointing in a number of sometimes contradictory directions without offering an authoritative voice that makes it ultimately "recoverable." Instead, Apess's prayer presents the audience and the later reader with an *unreadable* event that seems to say (and yet nowhere confirms) more than what it says, "the trace of speech," as Derrida describes it, "that comes from the other":[100]

"Noo-chun kes-uk-qut-tiam-at-am unch koo-we-su-onk, kuk-ket-as-soo-tam-oonk pey-au-moo-utch, keet-te-nan-tam-oo-onk ne nai ; ne-ya-ne ke-suk-qutkah oh-ke-it ; aos-sa-ma-i-in-ne-an ko-ko-ke-suk-o-da-e nut-as-e-suk-ok-ke fu-tuk-qun-neg ; kah ah-quo-an-tam-a-i-in-ne-an num-match-e-se-ong-an-on-ash, ne-match-ene-na-mun wonk neet-ah-quo-antam-au-o-un-non-oh nish-noh pasuk noo-na-mortuk-quoh-who-nan, kah chaque sag-kom-pa-ginne-an en qutch-e-het-tu-ong-a-nit, qut poh-qud-wus-sin-ne-an watch match-i-tut."

Table 1: Specimens of the Lord's Prayer

John Eliot	Matthew 6 9. Noo-shun kesukqut, quttianatamunach koowesu-onk. 10. Peyàumooutch kukketassootamóonk, kuttenantamónk ne n nach ohkeit neane kesukqut. 11. Nummeetsuongash asekesukokish as-samaiinean yeuyeu kesukod. 12. Kah asquontamaiinnean nummatchese-ongash, neane matchenehukqueagig nutah-quontamounnonog. 13. Ahque sagkompagunaiinnean en qutch-huaonganit, webe pohuuohwussinnean wutch matchitut	Luke 11 2. Noo-shun kesukqut, quttiánata nunach koowesu-onk, a kukketassootamóonk peyaumooutch, kutcenantamooonk ne naj neyane kesukqut kah ohkeit. 3. Assamáiinnean kesukodae nutasekesuk-okke petukqununk. 4. Kah ahquoantamaiinnean nummatchese-onganonash, newutche nenawun wonk nut-ahquoantamauóunnonog nishnoh pasuk noo-namontukquohwhonan, kah ahque sagkom-paginnean en qutchehettuonganit, qut poh-quawussinnean wutch matchitut.

Table 1 (*continued*)

Samuel Drake	Noo-shun kes-uk-qut, qut-tian-at-am-unch koo-we-su-onk, kuk-ket-as-soo-tam-oonk pey-au-moo-utch, kut-te-ndn-tam-oo-onk ne nai, ne-ya-ne ke-suk-qut kah oh-ke-it. As-sa-ma-i-in-ne-an ko-ko-ke-suk-o-da-e nut-as-e-suk-ok-ke pe-tuk-qun-neg. Kah ah-quo-an-tam-a-i-in-ne-an num-match-e-se-ong-an-on-ash, ne-wutch-e ne-na-wun wonk nut-ah-quo-an-tam-au-o-un-non-og nish-noh pasuk noo-na-mon-tuk-quoh-who-nan, kah ahque sag-kom-pa-gin-ne-an en qutch-e-hhet-tu-ong-a nit, qut poh-qua-wus-sin-ne-an wutch match-i-tut
William Apess	Noo-chun kes-uk-qut-tiam-at-am unch koo-we-su-onk, kuk-ket-as-soo-tam-oonk pey-au-moo-utch, keet-te-nan-tam-oo-onk ne nai ; ne-ya-ne ke-suk-qutkah oh-ke-it ; aos-sa-ma-i-in-ne-an ko-ko-ke-suk-o-da-e nut-as-e-suk-ok-ke fu-tuk-qun-neg ; kah ah-quo-an-tam-a-i-in-ne-an num-match-e-se-ong-an-on-ash, ne-match-ene-na-mun wonk neet-ah-quo-antam-au-o-un-non-oh nish-noh pasuk noo-na-mortuk-quoh-who-nan, kah chaque sag-kom-pa-ginne-an en qutch-e-het-tu-ong-a-nit, qut poh-qud-wus-sin-ne-an watch match-i-tut
Pequot	Co shunōngone āhe suck cuck ābot. Na naw ūi e coom shaw ims nūskspe coūe so wūnk. Kuck sudamong peamook. Ecook Aiootoomomon ukkee tawti ee ōok ungow. A geescuck meē se nam eyew kee suck askesuck mysput eo honegan. A quon to mi nun namat to ōmp pa wōn ganuksh nō. Awe ah goon to mi nad macha. Chook quoe e guck, ah greead macon jussūon mattum paw oon ganuck pukkqueaw hus nawn woochet. Match-etook kee kucks sudamong, cumme ekē go wonk, ah kōont seek coomsakō oh woonk. Mackēeme, mackēme Eeats.

Sources: Eliot, *The New Testament of Our Lord and Saviour Jesus Christ* (Cambridge, MA: Samuel Green & Marmaduke Johnson, 1661); Drake, *The Book of Indians of North America* (Boston: Josiah Drake, 1835); Apess, *Eulogy on King Philip* (Boston, 1836). The specimen of Pequot comes from John W. De Forest's *History of the Indians of Connecticut* (Hartford: Wm. Jas. Hammersley, 1851). De Forest's history notes that this specimen was "obtained by Governor Saltonstall, of Connecticut, in the year 1721." The following translation is offered: "Father ours above in Heaven. Admired in highest manner be thy name. Like done thy will on earth as like in Heaven. Let us be forgiven evil doings of ours, as we would forgive wrong doers to us. Not guide us into snares but help us to escape from evil. Thine thy powerful kingdom, thine the strength, thine the greatest glory. Always, always me wish so" (39).

Notes

Introduction

1. Anderson, *Imagined Communities,* 9.

2. Ibid., emphasis added.

3. Ibid., 10.

4. "This is why," Anderson notes parenthetically, "so many different nations have such tombs without feeling any need to specify the nationality of their absent occupants. What else could they be *but* Germans, Americans, Argentinians . . . ?" (ibid., 9–10, emphasis in original).

5. Ibid., 11.

6. "To feel the force of this modernity," Anderson writes, "one has only to imagine the general reaction to the busy-body who 'discovered' the Unknown Soldier's name or insisted on filling the cenotaph with some real bones" (ibid., 9). In the United States, there was in fact a famous "discovery" or naming of an unknown soldier made possible by DNA testing. The soldier was returned to his family and reburied in his hometown without a patriotic rebellion or a destruction of the monument. "The outrage Anderson predicted," historian Michael J. Allen summarized, "failed to materialize" ("Sacrilege of a Strange, Contemporary Kind," 92). In tracing the history of this event, Allen notes that the identification and reburial of Michael Joseph Blassie's body did not undermine the affective project of the unmarked body as one "all could claim" (99). "Few seemed to have their sense of national identity shaken," Allen notes. "To the contrary, those asked to comment on the identification usually responded in ways that reaffirmed their sense of national belonging." The discovery confirmed for mourners the material grounding for the cenotaph, affirming its reality as a resting place for the dead and so the site of an obligation or response that is owed to the dead; the identification was seen as "something we needed to do as a nation" (118). It is notable of course, that while Anderson remarks upon the power of the tomb, on the burial of those within, he simultaneously identifies the tomb as a simulation, lacking "real bones."

7. Anderson, *Imagined Communities,* 22.

8. Ibid., 22–26.

9. In making this association, I do not mean to flatten out a deeper intellectual history. In his survey of the field of hemispheric studies, Ralph Bauer traces its origin in more distant work, including Herbert Eugene Bolton's 1932 presidential address to the American Historical Society and Lewis Hanke's *Do the Americas Have a Common History?* (1964). But Bauer also marks the "decisive development in hemispheric studies" as "the 'discovery' of the hemisphere by American studies in the wake of that discipline's turn from a United States-centered

multiculturalism and toward a trans- and postnationalist approach during the 1990s" ("Hemispheric Studies," 235). The "landmark works" that he cites from this period—Amy Kaplan and Donald Pease's collection *Cultures of United States Imperialism* (1993), Donald Pease's *National Identities and Post-Americanist Narratives* (1994), Joseph Roach's *Cities of the Dead* (1996), Walter Mignolo's *Local Histories/Global Designs* (2000), John Carlos Rowe's *Post-nationalist American Studies* (2000), and Shelly Streeby's *American Sensations* (2002)—all use Anderson's "imagined communities" as a way to frame portions or even the entirety of their work. By making the nation itself an object of study, then, Anderson seemed to facilitate a skepticism about national disciplinary boundaries.

10. Chatterjee, "Anderson's Utopia," 131. Homi Bhabha also addresses this heterogeneous temporality as the ambivalent enunciations of "minority discourses that speak betwixt and between times and places" ("DissemiNation," 309). For more on the temporal heterogeneity within the context of the United States, see Allen, *A Republic in Time.* In *Beyond Settler Time,* Mark Rifkin shifts this discussion of temporal heterogeneity in a significant way, insisting instead on a consideration of temporal *plurality* that does not take for granted the givenness of US territoriality that he associates with the settler time of "modernity" (vii–xii).

11. Loughran, *The Republic in Print,* 438.

12. Holland, *Raising the Dead,* 22; Roach, *Cities of the Dead,* 17, 105.

13. Wald, *Constituting Americans,* 2.

14. Rifkin, *Beyond Settler Time,* 42.

15. Luciano, *Arranging Grief,* 35–36.

16. Ibid., 29. Luciano goes on to describe the way that the mourning manuals and other writings that comprise this consolation literature worked to contain the unproductive diversion of time by moving the sufferer toward a restorative future. In this study, I do not focus on the shattering experience of personal loss that Luciano addresses as grief, but rather on the communalizing work of what she describes as "monumental time." See "The Living and the Dead" in this Introduction and chapter 3 of this study for more on the monumentalism of national mourning.

17. In his *Narrative Discourse,* Gérard Genette insists on separating out a sterilized idea of analepsis from what he describes as the "psychological connotations" of terms like retrospection that, according to Genette, "automatically evoke subjective phenomena." I collapse these here intentionally because, as I will argue throughout, the experience of time itself is helplessly entangled with subjective phenomena, and indeed intersubjective phenomena. See Genette, *Narrative Discourse,* 39–40.

18. Anderson, *Imagined Communities,* 24, 9. In raising the idea of response I draw heavily on Derrida's attention to responsivity, an idea that not only structures an ethical posture but also a precondition for the emergence of the subject. While the idea is discussed in a number of his works, including *The Animal That Therefore I Am* and *Specters of Marx,* an important inspiration for the current study is his idea of responsibility outlined in his meditation on memory following the death of Paul de Man ("Mnemosyne").

19. Anderson, *Imagined Communities,* xiv.

20. Ibid., 197, emphasis in original.

21. The phrase "gardien des tombeaux" comes directly before the long citation of Michelet

that Anderson includes in his work. He traces this citation through Hayden White's *Metahistory,* although he uses the original French because he finds the translation in White's text wanting. White takes this section from Roland Barthes's book on Michelet, whose translator Richard Howard uses the phrase "guardian of the graves" (instead of the equally available "guardian of the tombs"). See White, *Metahistory,* 158–60; Barthes, *Michelet,* 101–2. The passage of Michelet cited by Anderson and White comes from the prefatory essay to the second volume of his *Histoire du Dix-Neuvième Siècle,* titled "Des justices de l'histoire." For the complete essay see Michelet, *Œuvres Complètes,* XXI (1872–74), 267–78. In the essay, Michelet imagines the historian in the role of magistrate or administrator of the property of the dead ("J'ai parlé ailleurs de l'office qu'occupa Camoëns sur le rivage meurtrier de l'Inde: *Administrateur du bien des décédés.* . . . Cette magistrature, c'est l'Histoire").

22. Michelet, *Œuvres Complètes,* XXI (1872–74), 268.

23. Pratt, *Archives of American Time,* 111–12.

24. Ibid., 113.

25. Ibid., 115. In his critique of Pratt's work, Mark Rifkin summarizes this assumption of modernity as a form of "chrononormativity": "Pratt insists on the 'hybrid' character of the experience of time in the United States, but what engenders relation among these experiences is their mutual participation in 'the heterochronic time of modernity,' with whatever modernity might designate providing a regularity and orientation amid these other differences" (*Beyond Settler Time,* 205, n.147).

26. Gellner, *Nations and Nationalism,* 55.

27. Anderson grounds his theory of print capitalism's centrality to nationalism in an extended reading of the rise of nationalism in North and South America ("Creole Pioneers"), because he insists that they cannot be sufficiently explained alongside the later European models. His extended study of the region comes back as a turning point in his subsequent discussion of language ("Old Languages, New Models") and in the aforementioned appended chapter "Memory and Forgetting." In placing Anderson's "imaginary" within the realm of affect, I draw on the significant body of criticism focused on sentiment and sentimentality, particularly in American literature. Lauren Berlant described this project as shifting attention away from the deliberative and toward the body, and in particular its capacity for suffering. Sentimental works, "the world of feeling politics," draw alliances through "the capacity for suffering and trauma at the citizen's core" ("Poor Eliza," 636). While Berlant focuses on the flourishing of sentimental works after 1850, more recent work such as Peter Coviello's consideration of intimacy and Chris Castiglia's study of interiority and a "federalizing affect" have shown this to be an effective framework for understanding earlier texts as well (Coviello, *Intimacy in America;* Castiglia, *Interior States*).

28. Certeau, *Practice of Everyday Life,* 131–53. In calling this apparatus an economy, I follow Certeau's use of the term not simply as a financial organization of production and exchange but rather as the organization of a complex unity. See Ahearne, *Michel de Certeau,* 52–59.

29. Genette touches on this perdurance—the existence through time—of the written text in his consideration of the time of reading, although he is less concerned with print as the apparatus that not only makes this fracturing of time possible but requires it (33–35).

30. Certeau, *Practice of Everyday Life,* 144–47.

31. There has been ample critique of Anderson's argument regarding the efficacy of regional newspapers in terms of curating national identity, for example Guerra, "Forms of Communication, Political Spaces, and Cultural Identities"; White, "Early American Nations as Imagined Communities"; Loughran, *The Republic in Print.* Here I preserve his original focus in order to demonstrate the challenge in understanding print culture, even in this calendrical form, as residing completely within the "meanwhile" of homogenous empty time.

32. To follow Anderson's theory of colonial and early national print communities, we are required, as Trish Loughran has recently shown, to ignore the historical realities of their production and circulation, which was significantly more factional than unifying, characterized by "haphazard and uneven" circulation in the years leading up to and directly following the American Revolution (*The Republic in Print,* xix).

33. Benjamin, *Arcades Project,* N3, 1, and N2a, 3.

34. For more on this cultural work of preservation including early national reprints, see DiCuirci, *Colonial Revivals.*

35. Michelet, *Œuvres Complètes,* XXI (1872–1874):268; n.4.

36. All translations in *Mourning the Nation to Come* are my own unless otherwise noted. I chose to take on this work, even when popular translations are available, in order to limit the number of interlocutors in the text. For more on the work of translation and the figure of the translator as an interlocutor, see chapter 4 of this study.

37. In positing this experience of loss as the condition of possibility for the social I am distinguishing the particular project of *Mourning the Nation to Come* from those studies that focus on the shattering experience of personal grief (an alienation from the social that Dana Luciano draws out in her *Arranging Grief*), as well as from those studies of national culture that have focused on its mortifying effects, like Russ Castronovo's *Necro Citizenship.* While Castronovo sees the death as a means of structuring political life, he emphasizes its isolation as well as a deadened state, a passivity and lack of feeling that runs counter to the pathetic engagement I will trace in the national narratives.

38. Harrison, *The Dominion of the Dead.*

39. Rifkin, *Beyond Settler Time,* 1.

40. Pérez Vejo, "La construcción de las naciones como problema historiográfico," 290; Chasteen, "Introduction," xiv–xv; Guerra, "Forms of Communication, Political Spaces, and Cultural Identities."

41. Guerra, "Identidad y Soberanía," 231.

42. Chasteen, "Introduction," xv.

43. Wald, *Constituting Americans,* 121.

44. Sommer, *Foundational Fictions.*

45. Coviello, *Intimacy in America,* 167. Coviello's study is primarily concerned with the ways in which race becomes a site of affiliation in antebellum America. He notes that the Native American is aligned with or defined as the nation itself, which excludes Native peoples from the kind of racialization he describes. *Mourning the Nation to Come* explores this alignment and erasure of Native American with native (creole) American.

46. Wolfe, "Settler Colonialism and the Elimination of the Native," 388.

47. Mbembe, "Necropolitics."

48. Redfield, "Imagi-Nation," 69.

49. Ibid., 71.

50. Anderson, *Imagined Communities,* 196–97.

51. Cheyfitz, *The Poetics of Imperialism.*

52. Round, *Removable Type.*

53. Derrida, "Mnemosyne."

54. I attempt to follow Mark Rifkin's critique of the linear periodization that imagines "certain national events, like the Civil War, as moments of transition in which the country breaks away from a degraded past (slavery in the case of the Civil War), as opposed to tracing the regularities of settler violence in which the past appears less as a space of alterity than in a relation of continuity with the present" (*Beyond Settler Time,* 39).

55. Byrd, *The Transit of Empire,* xix.

Prolegomenon

1. *The Battle-Pieces of Herman Melville,* 202.

2. In his introduction to Melville's *Battle-Pieces,* Hennig Cohen notes:

> The figurative use of battle-pieces as a literary term is now more common than its use to indicate a genre of painting, but when Melville took it as the title for his collection of war poems, he did so with an awareness of its primary meaning. . . . Its visual connotation was important to him, and to make certain that his readers were apprised that he was presenting a series of pictures, he added the subtitle "Aspects of the War," ibid., 15.

3. Ibid., 202.

4. The object Melville offers for this exchange is not simply the individual sketches of the War, but a shared loss in the form of the past itself, the historic nature of the tragedy ("the terrible historic tragedy") that removes the community from trauma, transforming the morass of the recent past into history or History.

5. *The Battle-Pieces of Herman Melville,* 35.

6. Kent Ljungquist also notes that the poem does not appear in the table of contents in the first edition of Battle-Pieces ("'Meteor of War,'" 674).

7. Certeau, *The Writing of History,* xxv–xxvi.

8. Ibid., 2.

9. Harrison, *The Dominion of the Dead,* x.

10. Robert Penn Warren made this notable connection between Melville's Brown and the "weird," prophetic sisters of Shakespeare's tragedy (*Selected Poems of Herman Melville,* 351).

11. Certeau, *The Writing of History,* 46, emphasis in original.

12. Preston, "Letter."

13. Jackson, "Letter to Mary Anna Jackson."

14. In *Demeure,* Derrida argues the following about testimony:

> The technical reproducibility is excluded from testimony, which always calls for the presence of the live voice in the first person. But from the moment that a testimony must be able to be repeated, *technē* is admitted; it is introduced where it is excluded. For this, one need not wait for cameras, videos, typewriters, and computers. As soon as the sentence is repeatable, that is, from its origin, the instant it is pronounced and becomes intelligible, thus idealizable, it is already instrumentalizable and affected by technology. And virtuality. It is thus the very instance of the instant that seems to become exemplary: exemplary in the very place where it seems unique and irreplaceable, under the seal of unicity. And it is perhaps here, with the technological both as ideality and prosthetic iterability, that the possibility of fiction *and* lie, simulacrum *and* literature, that of the right to literature insinuates itself, at the very origin of truthful testimony, autobiography in good faith, sincere confession, as their essential compossibility. (*The Instant of My Death/Demeure,* 42.)

Here the very textuality is itself the technology of circulation and reproducibility. Its virtuality is a function of the mediation of the object (letter) as Mary Anna is made present to the instant through the consumption of the text.

15. Brown, "An Idea of Things in Kansas (1857)," 61.

16. Howe, *Reminiscences,* 254.

17. Quoted in Reynolds, "Cultural Biography," 87.

18. Emerson, "Speech by Ralph Waldo Emerson," 120. Recent revivals of the John Brown corpus have also focused on John Brown, Puritan. Criticism surrounding Russell Banks's Cloudsplitter (2006) focused on Brown as the figure who marshals the "transition from Puritan to Yankee" (Hutchison, "Representative Man," 68). Even David Reynolds's recent biography sees Brown's Calvinism as a notable factor in his development and reception, with an entire section of the biography devoted to developing a theory of the Puritan abolitionist called, in his alliterative structure, "The Puritan" (*John Brown: Abolitionist*). But while Reynolds insists that Brown's strict Calvinism functioned to divide or isolate him from his community, statements such as that made by Child and others show that Brown's physical (Howe) and spiritual (Emerson) connections formed the basis of a shared history and thus a locus of identification with Brown (and through Brown to an American History itself). Reynolds, though, marks a clear distinction between "life facts" and a "literary personae," arguing that the work of the Historian is to "[separate] person from literary personae," the latter he declares to be "the lie of literary voice" ("Cultural Biography," 85, 84). I would forward that Reynolds distrusts the "literary personae" too much, particularly in the case of a man such as John Brown, whose "reflection" of and "impact" on his era, as well as his "transcendence" of that social scene (Reynolds's three key concepts of cultural biography), depend greatly on who he was as a textual figure. Reynolds's desire for (and belief in his privileged access to) presence, though, is indicative of the Historian's narrative in general, as Michel de Certeau argues in *The Writing of History.*

19. Brown, "Prison Letters," Nov. 19.

20. Howe, *Reminiscences,* 254.

21. Quoted in Cabot, *A Memoir of Ralph Waldo Emerson,* 597. This was a spoken comment not included in the published version of "Courage" delivered on November 7, 1859. A controversy circulated based largely on the confusion of articles (between "the" cross and "a" cross). The *New York Daily Tribune* reported on the speech and this statement the following day, writing that Emerson said that Brown "will make the gallows as glorious as the cross" while most biographers, including Cabot, insist that Brown said "like a cross" (McDonald, "Emerson and John Brown," 386, emphasis added). Hawthorne famously "shamed" Emerson for his statement in an article in the *Atlantic Monthly,* saying, "I shall not pretend to be an admirer of old John Brown . . . nor did I expect ever to shrink so unutterably from any apophthegm of a sage . . . that the death of this blood-stained fanatic has 'made the Gallows as venerable as the Cross!'" ("Chiefly About War Matters"). When Emerson reviewed the reported words, he only said "That's about what I said" (quoted in McDonald 387). McDonald notes that despite the statement being expunged from the written record of his speeches, Emerson's gallows statement "did not die an easy death—it was printed in Redpath's biography of Brown (1860) and in at least one of Emerson's obituaries" (388). The survival of the statement (beyond its own death in print and the death of its author) speaks to both the salience of the sacrificial economy to which it attests as well as the diminishment of an exterior referent in favor of the text or narrative. It does not matter exactly what was said—even Emerson denies resolution in his statement—but rather what is circulated and consumed.

22. Thoreau, "A Plea for Captain John Brown," 121.

23. Ibid. Thoreau first delivered the speech in October and the printed version had the following head note: "read to the citizens of Concord, Mass., Sunday evening, October 30, 1859; also as a fifth lecture of the Fraternity Course, in Boston, November 1, 1859" (38). It is notable that Thoreau addresses his plea to a citizenry, a plea that emphasizes the moral character of a social body, one that feels together. He uses Brown to develop an idea of national character, a return to native subjects that "the poet will sing . . . the historian record," subjects that "will be the ornament of some future national gallery." "We shall then," Thoreau argues, "be at liberty to weep for Captain Brown" (121). Brown's death is posited here as a future heritage, the imminence of a national body produced by a mourning to come.

24. Ibid., 117, emphasis added.

25. Ibid., 118.

26. Ibid., 120.

27. Ibid., 121, emphasis in original.

28. Scheidenhelm, *The Response to John Brown,* 91.

29. Brown, "Prison Letters," 90, 95, 97. John Rogers was the first Protestant martyr under Mary I of England. He was burned at the stake on February 4, 1555, and is remembered for the brave, even joyful manner in which he met his death (Daniell, "John Rogers").

30. Brown, "Prison Letters," 97.

31. Whittier, "Brown of Ossawatomie" l.11, l. 16.

32. Hawthorne, "Chiefly About War Matters."

33. Jackson, "Letter to Mary Anna Jackson."

34. Lacoue-Labarthe and Nancy, "The Unconscious Is Destructed Like an Affect," 198.

35. Howe, *Reminiscences,* 256, emphasis added.

36. Thoreau, "A Plea for Captain John Brown," 115.

37. Ibid.

38. Ibid., 111, emphasis added.

39. Certeau, *The Writing of History,* 3.

40. In *The Gift of Death*, Derrida draws upon the economy of sacrifice in order to understand how the individual is made responsible (or response-able), made "to respond to the other and answer for oneself before the other" (3). The gift of death, he argues, "puts me into relation with the transcendence of the other," exposed to the gaze of God (6) which calls internally rather than externally. In the following study, I will draw out these ideas of history as a "call to explain oneself" (3) and the particular mode of this response-ability provided by the historical romance. By studying this genre, we are able to witness or testify to the ways in which these texts create community out of death, drawing on the Body that "links historicity to responsibility" (4).

41. Harrison, *The Dominion of the Dead,* ix.

42. Lacoue-Labarthe and Nancy, "The Unconscious Is Destructed Like an Affect," 199.

43. Thoreau, "A Plea for Captain John Brown," 114, emphasis added.

44. Freud, *Reflections on War and Death,* 41.

45. Nudelman, "'The Blood of Millions,'" 28.

46. Browne, *The Story of Our National Ballads,* 142.

47. Borch-Jacobsen, *The Emotional Tie,* 30.

48. Celebrant here is meant to evoke celebration as ritual, specifically as the word references the person who officiates the Eucharist ("Celebrant"). Christians who partake in this rite consume the body and blood of Christ which functions to simultaneously commemorate a past event (the Last Supper) while consolidating and testifying to a community (of the body with the Lord, of the body with/of the Church). In my argument, the cathected dead body (Brown in this case) becomes a similar site of consumption, one that incorporates the consumer into a larger body or community.

49. Brown, "Prison Letters," 93.This "sword" has a more literal interpretation as well. One of Brown's prisoners at Harpers Ferry was Colonel Lewis Washington, George Washington's great grand-nephew, who owned the sword presented to Washington by Frederick the Great. Many of the accounts of the raid have Brown carrying this relic, connecting him again to the national heritage.

50. Robert Scholnick notes that there were only thirteen reviews of the work and only 486 of the 1,260 printed copies had been sold by February 1868. It was at that time that Harper's wrote to Melville that, having guaranteed the publication expenses, he owed them $338.93 ("Politics and Poetics," 422).

51. William Dean Howells, "Reviews and Literary Notices," 252.

52. Ibid., 253.

53. Ibid., 252.

54. Quoted in Scholnick, "Politics and Poetics," 425.

55. Maurice Lee argues that Melville's *Battle-Pieces* "subversively quarrels with presumptuous notions of American destiny," that Melville's view of the recent past is more troubled than those pieces (he cites "Battle Hymn of the Republic" specifically) that display a dogmatic

confidence in the Union's divine/divinely guided victory ("Writing through the War," 1125). Lee argues that Melville is more uncertain about the War (its causes and effects) and the contemporaneous criticism of his poems indicates the adherence of the general public to "the self-fulfilling logic of American providence" described by Sacvan Bercovitch in *Rites of Assent* (ibid., 1126). My argument is not that Melville supports this providential attitude, but rather that critics like Howells fail to acknowledge the intermediary work of the historian or author at work in all texts, a "providential attitude" that inheres to the work of history itself. It is my argument that Howells's complaint is that Melville speaks instead of being spoken through, as a true prophet. While several critical reviews focus on Melville's political views, for instance the *Independent*'s review on January 10, 1867, that condemned Melville's prose "Supplement" and the poet himself as "mischievous" (quoted in Scholnick, 430), Howells's column focuses instead on the error in affect. Melville's failure is one of historiographical posture (whether intentional, as a disturbing or subversive "distancing," or, as Howells seems to imply, an unintentional consequence of Melville's style), his inability to remove his own voice, to speak "in the third person" as Certeau describes it, and so give us the body or bodies (within the text and of the text itself) in which to invest the libidinal energy of mourning. Because of this, Melville's role in the translation (and transmission) of prophecy is evident to critical readers, thus mediating and therefore dampening the testimony of the dead.

56. Whitman, "Leaves of Grass (1867)."

Chapter 1

1. In her *Victorian Astronomy* Agnes Clerke estimated that at least 240,000 meteors fell during the nine-hour shower (*A Popular History of Astronomy during the Nineteenth Century,* 376). In a recent article on "religious sky reading," Zach Marshall describes the 1833 Leonid meteor storm as a display in which "viewers from across the United States . . . saw anywhere from 50,000 to 150,000 meteors per hour or fourteen to forty-one meteors per second," with descriptions of the stars "falling like snow" ("Signs in the Heavens and the Distress of Nations," 289). In his testimony of the event, Elder Samuel Rogers recalls someone looking out the window and declaring it "almost broad daylight. 'That can not be,' another answered, 'For it is scarcely three o'clock.' 'I can't help what the clock says,' replied the first speaker, 'my eyes can not deceive me; it is almost broad daylight." This story captures not only the confusion of the moment but also the conflict between the overlying narrative of time (the clock that marches forward at a uniform pace and marks an objective time) and the experience of or testimony to time (the lived experience and the authority of the witness). This event is particularly interesting in light of the theory that this chapter will lay out because of its assertion of an affective narrative of time over a scientific or objective/dehumanized standard of time.

2. Rogers, *Autobiography of Elder Samuel Rogers,* 134.

3. Ibid., 133–35.

4. Certeau, *Writing,* xxvii.

5. Spicer, *Our Day in the Light of Prophecy,* 92.

6. *Doctrine and Covenants,* 154 [D&C 57]. The Elders of the Church published the first edition of *Doctrine and Covenants* in 1835 as a way to share the revelations of Joseph Smith

with the community, as well as brief lectures on faith. The original text is divided by section but not arranged chronologically (the revelation cited, for example, was given in Zion itself in 1831 and presented in section 27, while the revelation revealing the location of Zion, given after a conference in Kirtland, Ohio, earlier that year, is presented later in the text in section 66). In preserving and transcribing the text, the Church Historian's Press notes the modern enumeration of the revelations, which are given parenthetically in the citation.

7. Bruce Van Orden, an Associate Professor of Church History at Brigham Young University, points out that the Church lacks primary evidence for this assertion, i.e. the "holographic writing" of Smith himself in his journal. (The term "holographic writing" is used by Jessee to describe Smith's journal entries written in his own hand and unmediated by posthumous editors.) But Van Orden argues that this location of Eden is correct, citing the language in Revelation 57 in the *Doctrine and Covenants* as well as statements by contemporaneous Church elders Brigham Young and Heber Kimball. Young testified in 1857 that "Joseph the Prophet told me that the garden of Eden was in Jackson [County] Missouri" (quoted in Van Orden, "I Have a Question," 54).

8. Bushman, "Mormon Persecutions," 14, 18–20.

9. "Gentile" is the Mormon term for the white Christian population, the population from which they emerged and yet from which their religion made them distinct. The use of the term "Gentile" to describe the non-Mormon population emphasizes the filial transformation that accompanied conversion, the conversion into an older, native community that will be discussed in this chapter.

10. Smith, *Documentary History of the Church,* 437.

11. Noah Webster's *American Dictionary of the English Language* (rev.1848) defines "wigwam" as "an Indian cabin or hut, so called in *America*" (*An American Dictionary of the English Language,* 1137, emphasis in original).

12. *The Autobiography of Parley Parker Pratt,* 110.

13. Shipps, *Mormonism,* 33, 36–39; Underwood, "Early Mormon Millenarianism," 217.

14. Lewis, *The American Adam; Innocence, Tragedy, and Tradition in the Nineteenth Century,* 14.

15. Ibid., 13.

16. Shimeall, *Age of the World,* xviii, emphasis in original.

17. McCormick, "Notes on a Comparative American Literary History," 171, emphasis added.

18. Ibid.

19. There is, in Anderson's argument, the attendant implication that the New World itself, in its new economic structures and documentary mania, was experienced as the *newness* of Europe itself, freed from older structures of authority, even before the new national structures were fully developed. See White, "Early American Nations as Imagined Communities," 2004, 52. New World nationalism, then, arises without the burden of competing historical structures. Instead it is the expression of an ever-present modernity that contributes to the famous continental theorist's claim that America has no history (Baudrillard, *America,* 7).

20. Quoted in Lewis, *The American Adam,* 159.

21. Appleby, *Inheriting the Revolution,* 3.

22. Smith and Jessee, *The Personal Writings of Joseph Smith,* 11 (sic).
23. Van Orden, "I Have a Question."
24. Benjamin, *Illuminations,* 83–84.
25. Ricœur, *Memory, History, Forgetting,* 2004, 137–40.
26. Brennan, "The National Longing for Form," 52; Anderson, *Imagined Communities,* 35.
27. Renan, "What Is a Nation?" 19.
28. "Conference Minutes."
29. "7 April, 1844 (2) (Sunday Afternoon)," n.1. "Traditionally considered the Prophet's greatest sermon, the King Follett discourse was delivered at a time when both anti-Mormon and apostate sentiment was intensifying. "Accusations were repeatedly being made," notes B. H. Roberts, "that President Smith was a fallen prophet. On this occasion he coolly claimed that this single discourse would vindicate his prophetic calling. Although the sermon contains no new doctrine, never before had Joseph Smith so thoroughly, eloquently, and with such power presented what by now had become the very life-blood of Mormon theology."
30. Smith, *Documentary History of the Church,* 6:312.
31. Brown, *In Heaven as It Is on Earth;* Davies, *The Mormon Culture of Salvation.* Brown does an excellent job in considering Smith's interest in "grave artifacts," those relics connected to the "problem of death," but his focus remains the theological rejection of or escape from death. I think that the fetishism of the artifact (which requires death) evident in Brown's study might be better understood by looking at the ways that our relationships to the dead are not solely defined by *lack* and *rupture,* but rather intimacy and continuity.
32. Smith, *Documentary History of the Church,* 6:313.
33. Ibid., 6:310.
34. Ibid., 6:313.
35. Ibid., 6:314.
36. Ibid., 6:319.
37. Ibid., 6:303.
38. Ibid., 6:310.
39. *Doctrine and Covenants,* 193 [D&C 52].
40. Smith, *Documentary History of the Church,* 6:318.
41. Ibid., 6:319.
42. Ibid., emphasis in original.
43. "Accounts of the 'King Follett Sermon.'"
44. Brodie, *No Man Knows My History,* vii.
45. Certeau, *Practice of Everyday Life,* 137.
46. Anderson, *Imagined Communities,* 6.
47. The Books of Remembrance contain personal histories submitted and kept by the church (Bitton, "Guide to Mormon Diaries and Autobiographies," 2). According to the Book of Moses (an inspired gospel separate from *The Book of Mormon* and dictated by Joseph Smith in 1830), Adam kept a book that documented his descendants and included a genealogy. Such books were kept by the faithful throughout time (*The Book of Mormon* can be read as such a book, as I will show in this chapter) for the purposes of final judgment of the dead (*Doctrine and Covenants,* 128:7). *Doctrine and Covenants* 85:9 reads, "And all they who are not found

written in the book of remembrance shall find none inheritance in that day, but they shall be cut asunder, and their portion shall be appointed them among unbelievers, where are wailing and gnashing of teeth." Salvation itself is thus a *textual* production, one that is itself to be consumed by future readers. Twelfth President of the Church Spencer Kimball wrote to the faithful: "Please follow the counsel you have been given in the past and maintain your personal journals. Those who keep a book of remembrance are more likely to keep the Lord in remembrance in their daily lives. Journals are a way of counting our blessings and of *leaving an inventory of these blessings for our posterity*" (Kimball, "Listen to the Prophets," emphasis added).

48. Bitton, "Guide to Mormon Diaries and Autobiographies," 1. The report then goes on to document *only* those known, published materials in public collections, *excluding* personal histories submitted to and kept by the church; it is over a thousand pages long.

49. Ibid., 5.

50. Ibid., 6.

51. Certeau, *Practice of Everyday Life,* 134.

52. Pratt, "The Latter-Day Saints Millennial Star." Following the title page description of its contents, Pratt also included a passage from the book of Daniel to emphasize the apocalyptic framework of the community and its writings ("How great are his signs, and how mighty are his wonders!").

53. White, "Early American Nations as Imagined Communities," 2004, 53.

54. Anderson, *Imagined Communities,* 35.

55. Ibid., 7.

56. Ibid., 24. Anderson cites Benjamin as his source for the terms "homogeneous empty time" and "messianic time." Benjamin uses both terms to juxtapose the work of history (former) and the possible work of historical materialism (latter) as a revolutionary irruption that breaks the steady progress of historical time.

57. Ibid., 24–25.

58. *Doctrine and Covenants,* 154–155 [D&C 57].

59. Anderson, *Imagined Communities,* 11. In "DissemiNation" Homi Bhabha develops a critique of this historical progressivism around Anderson's insistence that the ability to imagine the nation through print is opened up by the destabilization of the sign due to the erosion of religious faith in sacred languages ("DissemiNation," 291–322).

60. Anderson, *Imagined Communities,* 24.

61. Benjamin, *Illuminations,* 254–55.

62. Harrison, *The Dominion of the Dead,* ix.

63. Ibid., 90.

64. Ibid., ix.

65. Ibid., 94.

66. Renan, "What Is a Nation?" 19.

67. Smith, *Documentary History of the Church,* 11.

68. Smith, *Teachings of the Presidents of the Church: Joseph Smith,* 58.

69. Smith's First Vision is recorded as an event, three years previous, in which he sought

council from God regarding which sect of Christianity to join and was answered by a vision of heaven and a command from God not to join any of them. See Bushman, *Joseph Smith,* 56–59.

70. Anderson, *Imagined Communities,* 24.

71. Jefferson, *Notes on the State of Virginia,* 104–7.

72. Bryant, "Thanatopsis," l. 50.

73. Sayre, "The Mound Builders and the Imagination of American Antiquity," 244.

74. Dahl, "Mound-Builders, Mormons, and William Cullen Bryant," 178.

75. Sayre, "The Mound Builders and the Imagination of American Antiquity," 226. As I show in chapter 2 of this study, this attachment to an Indigenous prehistory includes Mexico and South America, not only as a patriotic historical narrative for Spanish American nationalism but also as part of the broad claims to an ancient Indigenous culture from within the United States. For example, Eric Wertheimer has shown how this fetishized idea of ancient America played an important role for the way early national writers like Joel Barlow and Philip Freneau imagined the Inca and Aztec as distinguishing an American classical history, sometimes seen as anticipatory of later Euramerican republicanism (Wertheimer, *Imagined Empires).* For more on this in the context of Spanish American nationalism, see Castro-Klarén, "The Nation in Ruins."

76. Quoted in Dahl, "Mound-Builders, Mormons, and William Cullen Bryant," 181.

77. Dahl notes that the archaeological interest in the land was very much driven by the desire to answer not only cultural objections to the "barbaric" American landscape but also scientific ones by Buffon et al. Some of the more "informal" excavations were of course done for the purpose of material gain. The number and availability of the mounds made grave digging and treasure hunting a popular frontier activity. For more, see Southerton, *Losing a Lost Tribe,* 23–26; Silverberg, *Mound Builders of Ancient America.* Before finding and translating *The Book of Mormon,* Smith himself participated as a "seer" for such frontier excavations. For more on Smith's participation in these activities, see Quinn, *Early Mormonism and the Magic World View.* Fawn Brodie also discusses this era of Smith's life (*No Man Knows My History,* 16–37).

78. Dahl, "Mound-Builders, Mormons, and William Cullen Bryant," 181. While there is not an extensive history of mound excavations among LDS communities, there is a record of just such a discovery as Dahl describes in the excavation of the remains of the white Lamanite Zelph in an Illinois mound (*History of the Church* [vol. 2], 79). For more on the Zelph account, see Brown, *In Heaven as It Is on Earth,* 88–90.

79. Dahl, "Mound-Builders, Mormons, and William Cullen Bryant," 180–81.

80. Ibid., 181–82.

81. Ibid., 179.

82. In this way, the mound builder theories are deeply entangled with what critics have named the "Vanishing American" thesis of the frontier and historical romance, which is discussed at length in chapter 2 of this study.

83. Sayre, "The Mound Builders and the Imagination of American Antiquity," 229.

84. Smith, *Documentary History of the Church,* 11.

85. Smith, *The Book of Mormon.* This copy of the first edition preserves the use of capitalization for "Record," a distinction that is not preserved in the text edited by Royal Skousen (New Haven and London: Yale University Press, 2009).

86. A sample of this criticism includes: Bloom, *The American Religion;* Forsberg, "In Search of the Historical Nephi"; Hansen, *Mormonism and the American Experience;* Noll, *America's God.* Jan Shipps shifts this criticism by reading Mormonism as a *new* religion on par with Christianity and Islam, rather than a sect of the former, in *Mormonism : The Story of a New Religious Tradition.*

87. Gutjahr, "The Golden Bible in the Bible's Golden Age," 276.

88. George Dekker's *American Historical Romance* is a thorough study of Sir Walter Scott's influence in North America in which he traces the development of a Scott model for national fiction in the United States. For more information about the rise and popularity of the historical romance in the Americas, as well as its contribution to national culture, see: Balderston, *The Historical Novel in Latin America;* Bell, *Hawthorne and the Historical Romance;* Echevarría, *Historia y ficción en la narrativa hispanoamericana;* Gould, *Covenant and Republic;* Sommer, *Foundational Fictions;* as well as chapter 3 of the present study.

89. Hart, *The Popular Book,* 73.

90. Quoted in ibid., 74.

91. Quoted in ibid., 73.

92. In substituting the historical romance for the regional newspaper in Anderson's idea of imagined communities, I follow scholars such as Fernando Unzueta who have argued that the novel provides more fecund evidence for broad imaginings than Anderson's favored artifact of print ("Scenes of Reading").

93. Hart, *The Popular Book,* 80.

94. Bloom, *The American Religion,* 101, emphasis in original.

95. Skousen, *The Book of Mormon: The Earliest Text,* 1 Nephi 1:9–15. Further citations of *The Book of Mormon* come from this edition and will be referenced parenthetically in the text by book, chapter, and verse.

96. Kipp, "Introduction," vii. Maffly Kipp does not italicize the title in her introduction.

97. Shipps, *Mormonism : The Story of a New Religious Tradition,* 26.

98. Brodie, *No Man Knows My History,* 63. My own scan of the html text of *The Book of Mormon* returns 1,092 results for the exact phrase, climbing to 1,322 for "it came to pass."

99. Smith's text echoes and expands upon the historicist opening of the Bible itself by relying on this structuring of time. In the book of Genesis (KJV) the phrase "and it came to pass" is repeated sixty-two times, often as a way of structuring narrative progression, as in Jacob's journey to "the land of his people" and his marriage to Leah and Rachel (29:1–25).

100. Flanders, "To Transform History," 110.

101. There is a third group, the people of Zarahemla (called the Mulekites), who come to America around the same time as the Lehites and are absorbed into that group.

102. The promise implied here is not only the land held in covenant with the Lord, a land promised to a people, but a land *of* promise, one that will bear fruit. In an early revelation, Smith recorded God's word to his followers as "I hold forth and deign to give unto you greater riches, even a land of promise, a land flowing with milk and honey, upon which there shall

be no curse when the Lord cometh" (*Doctrine and Covenants,* 119 [D&C 38]). Elsewhere in *Doctrine and Covenants* Missouri is listed as the place of promise and fulfillment, as in D&C 62: "Behold I the Lord have brought you together that the promise might be fulfilled, that the faithful among you should be preserved and rejoice together in the land of Missouri. I the Lord promised the faithful and cannot lie."

103. Nyman, *I, Nephi Wrote This Record,* 1.

104. Ibid., 637. For more on this revelation, see *Doctrine and Covenants* 86 and 109.

Chapter 2

1. The edition notice in the text published by the Recovering the U.S. Hispanic Literary Heritage Project (1995) lists the exiled Cuban priest Félix Varela as the author of the romance in the cataloging information, but there remains significant skepticism about this attribution. In *Transamerican Literary Relations* (2004), for example, Anna Brickhouse connects the text instead to José María Heredia, suggesting the Cuban poet collaborated with Vicente Rocafuerte to produce the text (*Transamerican Literary Relations,* 49–57). In his forthcoming book, Rodrigo Lazo also casts doubt on the Varela attribution, noting that Varela himself denied that he had published anything anonymously (*Letters from Filadelfia*).

2. Baquero Arribas, "La conquista de América en la novela histórica del romanticismo español," 128.

3. Lindstrom, *Early Spanish American Narrative,* 2.

4. The review is not attributed to Bryant, but Gilbert Muller has noted that Bryant was producing most of the content for the struggling literary magazine at the time. His translation and publication of José Maria Heredia's poem "Niagara" in the previous issue indicates Bryant's awareness of and access to Spanish-language publications from the same area (and possibly the same author) as *Jicoténcal* (*William Cullen Bryant,* 65).

5. In *Ambassadors of Culture,* Kirsten Silva Gruesz describes Bryant's own creative work as flourishing during a period of "neighborliness in the New World," which was being formalized as a political relation through the Monroe Doctrine (*Ambassadors of Culture,* 54). Eric Wertheimer has also chronicled this interest of US Americans in pre-Columbian Central and South America in his *Imagined Empires,* tracing it through earlier texts by Freneau and Barlow as well as later writers like Melville (*Imagined Empires*). Gretchen Murphy extends this by tracing an interest in a hemispheric "family" through the end of the nineteenth century in her study *Hemispheric Imaginings.*

6. Bryant, review of *Jicotencal,* 336–37.

7. Ibid., 337.

8. Ibid., 339.

9. Mbembe, "Power of the Archive," 23.

10. Ibid., 24.

11. Ibid., 21.

12. Ibid., 24.

13. Ibid., 22.

14. Mbembe, "Necropolitics."

15. Bryant, review of *Jicotencal,*" 339.

16. *Jicoténcal,* 131.

17. Ibid., 132. The gag creates a spectacle of his suffering in front of Cortés's Indigenous allies, and after a Texcocan faints at seeing blood instead of words leave the general's mouth, it is removed and the hero drugged (131).

18. Ibid., 144.

19. Mbembe, "Necropolitics," 37.

20. Said, *Reflections on Exile,* 173.

21. Byrd, *The Transit of Empire,* xxi, xvii.

22. Sedgwick, *Hope Leslie,* 1:1.

23. Eliza Lee Follen née Cabot (1787–1860) was a close friend and correspondent of Sedgwick's, as well as a fellow abolitionist. Sedgwick described her in an 1825 letter as "a superior spirit, the reality of what I long and sometimes resolve to be" (Sedgwick and Dewey, *Life and Letters,* 174).

24. Follen, *Poems,* 15.

25. This equating of Indigenous figure with landscape functions both as a way to naturalize Indigenous disappearance (as a geological or geographical shift) and in presenting the Indian and Indigenous history as passive landscapes against which the drama of creole nationalism can be projected. In her study of this rhetorical move in Ecuadorian national imaginings, Christa Olson describes this *criollo* rhetoric as "[blending] indigeneity into the land, claiming its romance without granting indigenous people separate agency. To the extent that indigenous people appeared as integral to the landscape yet passively pastoral, both Indians and territory became available for national purposes" (*Constitutive Visions,* 62).

26. Sedgwick's selection is slightly different from the complete version in Follen's *Collected Poems* (1839). In this later collection, the poet writes "Here stood the *aged* chieftan" instead of "Indian chieftan." The former perhaps naturalizes a removal (translated as death, as I will argue) while the latter privileges difference from the temporally and racially displaced other (against ageing as a shared fate). But while the former indicates a shared mortality, it is only through the displacement onto the Indian that this mortality can itself be grasped. The Native American therefore functions as a legible sign of death, an inscribable figure that stands between the subject and the aporia of her own death, as with John Brown in the Prolegomenon to this work.

27. Follen, *Poems,* 11. 21–24.

28. Ibid., 1. 27.

29. Ibid., 1.40.

30. Baym, "Putting Women in Their Place," 33.

31. Sedgwick, *Hope Leslie,* vol. 2. As the novel progresses, Hope is increasingly referred to as "our heroine," a title she merits only eight times in the first volume of the work (197, 198, 201, 203, 223, 255, 270, 271) but thirty-four times in the second volume (7, 17, 23, 41, 56, 57, 66, 68, 80, 84 (twice), 88, 89, 103, 108, 114, 116, 120, 122, 151, 166, 168, 177, 217, 220, 234, 235, 269, 274, 282, 284, 290, 291 (twice), 292). The only mention of "heroine" that is not attached to Hope Leslie is the single instance in which Magawisca is referred to as "the heroine of Everell's imagination" (2:24). The distinction between the two is drawn even sharper in this

displacement from the reader, who is strongly marked in Hope's title (the "our" of "our heroine") but withheld from Magawisca, who is the heroine of an idea or memory ("Everell's imagination") and not an identifiable or sympathetic character.

32. Ibid., 266. Because it is her own father's violent act in which she intervenes, Magawisca's sacrifice also works to affirm instead of deny Indian violence, her disfigurement an enduring reminder of the Native American threat at the borders of the colony.

33. Ibid. 274.

34. Said, *Reflections on Exile,* 176.

35. In *Paper Machine* Derrida connects the limits of the narratable subject to the material platform that is both expressive and affirmative, drawing together the contemporary panic surrounding the "sans-papier" or undocumented person and a larger theory of the subject under the state (*Paper Machine,* 2).

36. Sedgwick, *Hope Leslie,* 2:289.

37. Said, *Reflections on Exile,* 173.

38. Sedgwick, *Hope Leslie,* 1:vi.

39. Ibid.

40. In one of the earliest and most influential methodological outlines of historiography, French positivists Langlois and Seignobos insisted on the absolute centrality of the written record to our knowledge of the past. "l'histoire se fait avec des documents . . . pas de documents, pas d'histoire [History is made with documents . . . no documents, no history]," they wrote in their *Introduction aux études historiques* (1898), 1–2. This codification of documentary evidence and the state archive as the limits of historical knowledge overlooks the work of the archive in sustaining colonial and imperial occupations (Stoler, *Along the Archival Grain;* Mbembe, "Power of the Archive"), and is frequently cited as the counterpoint to poststructuralist historiography that reimagined the "trace" beyond the document, as gesturing to a lived experience that eludes reification in the archive (Certeau, *The Writing of History;* Ricœur, *Memory, History, Forgetting,* 2004; Glissant, *Caribbean Discourse).*

41. Sedgwick, *Hope Leslie,* 1:vii.

42. Wolfe, "Settler Colonialism and the Elimination of the Native," 393.

43. Orians, *The Cult of the Vanishing American.* Orians is frequently cited as the origin of the "Vanishing American" term (see, for example, Romero, "Vanishing Americans" and Dippie, *The Vanishing American*). An investigation of the same trope in sociology seems to have developed independently. Renato Rosaldo calls this latter development "the doctrine of salvage ethnography—record the precious culture before it disappears forever" (*Culture and Truth,* 81).

44. Orians, *The Cult of the Vanishing American,* 5.

45. Irving, *The Sketch Book of Geoffrey Crayon, Gent.,* 2:235.

46. Ibid., 2:216–17.

47. Bellin, "Apostle of Removal," 11.

48. Quoted in ibid.

49. Ibid., 13.

50. Dippie, *The Vanishing American,* 13.

51. Ibid., 12.

52. Fiedler, *Love and Death in the American Novel,* 179.

53. O'Brien, *Firsting and Lasting.* This genre of writing can be traced through frontier romances to romantic poetry to historical treatises, but the structure of this language also permeated everyday life; Thoreau, in his journal, recorded his visit to Martha Simons as a "lasting" fantasy, remarking on her exceptional status as "the only pure-blooded Indian left about New Bedford" (*The Writings of Henry David Thoreau,* 6:247).

54. Cooper, *Last of the Mohicans,* 6-7. The paragraph is from the introduction to the 1831 edition, a revision of his original preface, in which the author writes "[The Mohicans'] claim to be the 'eldest son' of their 'grandfather' was freely allowed. Of course, this portion of the original proprietors of the soil was the first dispossessed by the whites. The few of them that now remain, are chiefly scattered among other tribes, and retain no other memorials of their power and greatness, than their melancholy recollections" (2). Written after the death of his hero Natty Bumppo in *The Prairie* (1827), the later introduction revises this (diminished) recognition of survival/scattering and instead insists not only on the naturalized vanishing (as verdure before the frost) but also on the complete disappearance of a subject. The shift is significant here: the mourning "scattered" remnant becomes the melancholic chronicler who records "historical truth."

55. Ibid., 33.

56. Longfellow, *The Song of Hiawatha,* 293.

57. Ibid., 281.

58. Romero, "Vanishing Americans," 392.

59. Longfellow, *The Song of Hiawatha,* 145.

60. Ibid., 146.

61. Debray, "Marxism and the National Question," 26.

62. Bergland, *The National Uncanny,* 3.

63. Rosaldo, *Culture and Truth,* 70.

64. "Jackson 1830 Annual Message to Congress," x.

65. Follen, *Poems,* 1. 19.

66. It is not surprising, then, that Jackson makes use of this trope after articulating a year earlier that the issue at the heart of the Cherokee/Georgia conflict is in fact state and national sovereignty: "A portion, however, of the Southern tribes, having mingled much with the whites and made some progress in the arts of civilized life, have lately attempted to erect an independent government within the limits of Georgia and Alabama. These States, *claiming to be the only sovereigns within their territories,* extended their laws over the Indians, which induced the latter to call upon the United States for protection" (Jackson, "First Annual Message, December 8, 1829," emphasis added).

67. Mbembe, "Necropolitics," 36.

68. Bancroft's *History,* published between 1834 and 1874, says of the Vanishing Indian: "The weak demand sympathy. If a melancholy interest attaches to the fall of a hero, who is overpowered by superior force, shall we not drop a tear at the fate of nations, whose defeat foreboded the exile, if it did not indeed shadow forth the decline and ultimate extinction of a race?" (*History of the United States,* 3:236).

69. Jackson continues to imagine "philanthropy's" response, saying that this noble

sentiment would not wish for a restoration. He says: "What good man would prefer a country covered with forests, and ranged by a few thousand savages, to our extensive republic, studded with cities, towns, and prosperous farms; embellished with all the improvements which art can devise, or industry can execute; occupied by more than twelve millions of happy people" ("Jackson 1830 Annual Message to Congress," x). Jackson's response to lack, to foreground the population boom and therefore overwhelming presence of the white American community, emphasizes again the survivor logic at work in this rhetoric. Here, Jackson directly opposes both numbers as well as their qualifiers. Jackson counts the Indigenous population as "a few," while the "happy people" that replaced them are estimated at "more than," thus lending to the numbers themselves a feeling of depletion followed by a swelling or excess.

70. Benítez-Rojo, "The Nineteenth-Century Spanish American Novel," 423.

71. Brading, *Origins of Mexican Nationalism,* 39. Ralph Bauer traces this back to protests over the New Laws of the 1540s ("The 'Rebellious Muse,'" 448–49).

72. Benítez-Rojo, "The Nineteenth-Century Spanish American Novel," 423. Benítez-Rojo has argued that this fixation with origins, "the tendency of nationalist practices to connect an event in the present with a rationally unconnected past" (420), produces an irreducible tension that he calls "Nationness/Modernness," a simultaneous, paradoxical assertion of an antique heritage on the one hand and complaint against antimodern (monarchical) political and social forms on the other (422–24). By focusing on the doubled work of mourning, as both an affectionate claim but also an assertion of difference/distance through the body of the survivor, we can see how historical romances used the death of the other as a way to negotiate an emergent future within this seemingly paradoxical structure, a national subject who *will have been,* who is initiated by this original loss.

73. Brading, *Origins of Mexican Nationalism,* 3.

74. Earle, "Creole Patriotism and the Myth of the 'Loyal Indian,'" 127. See also López García, "Visiones de la conquista en el teatro del exilio." Tomás Pérez Vejo describes this movement as creating an ethnocultural group of belonging: "Se territorializó la historia de manera que todo lo ocurrido en el territorio delimitado por las fronteras de los nuevos estados se convirtió en el pasado de la nación misma, en una genealogía definida no por la sangre, sino por la tierra [It territorialized history in such a way that everything that occurred within the territory delimited by the borders of the new state was turned into the past of the nation itself, in a genealogy defined not by blood but rather by the earth]" ("La construcción de las naciones como problema historiográfico," 291). Ralph Bauer sees the creole epic, and Olmedo's *La Victoria de Junín* in particular, as effecting this "territorialized history" through an "environmental argument" that embraced theories of environmental determinism but reversed its terms. In these works, "the natural environment of the New World makes its creatures, cultures, and political institutions, not weaker and degenerate—but more vigorous and virtuous" ("The 'Rebellious Muse,'" 456–57).

75. Bustamante, *Cuadro histórico de la revolución mejicana,* II:341–42.

76. The *mitote* is defined by the Real Academia Española dictionary as an Indigenous dance/celebration, from Nahuatl *mitoti,* meaning dancer "Mitote." A contemporary dictionary of "nahuatlismos" gives the original Nahuatl as *mitotli,* citing Clavijero (Montemayor et al., *Diccionario del náhuatl en el español de México,* 89). Bustamante is referring specifically

to the celebration of Toxcatl in Tenochtitlan on May 20, 1520 (JD) during which Alvarado slaughtered the celebrants gathered for the religious festival.

77. In *American Pentimento,* Patricia Seed describes this distinction as grounded in a distinction between English- and Spanish-speaking colonial projects: "The English had conquered property," she writes, while Spaniards "had conquered people" (*American Pentimento,* 2). This, Seed argues, carries over into the way that Indigenous peoples were treated during the independence period, consigning Native Americans to the past in North America while Spanish American independence carried Indigenous people into the future with them, evincing a "new attitude toward native people" in rejecting Iberian colonial policies such as tribute. But as Charles Walker notes, "For the indigenous population, continuity more than change marked the Andean republics' rupture with Spain. Well into the republican era, 'Indians' continued to pay tribute, euphemistically renamed the Contribution, and thus continued to constitute a unique fiscal and political category" ("The Patriotic Society," 275). In offering this comparison between the vanishing discourse and creole patriotism, I hope to show how neither recuperates Indigenous peoples from colonial violence, despite such seemingly inclusive proclamations as San Martín's, but rather produces an interior-exteriority, a nonrecuperative liminality that makes possible the national subject by connecting it to the land (as a terrestrial archive of foundational loss).

78. See, for example, König, "El indigenismo criollo"; Earle, "Creole Patriotism and the Myth of the 'Loyal Indian.'"

79. López y Planes held the office as "caretaker" after the beleaguered Unitarian Bernardino Rivadavia, the first president of Argentina under a tenuous Unitarian-authored constitution, resigned (Shumway, *The Invention of Argentina,* 107).

80. "Marcha patriótica,"11. 37–39.

81. Ibid., 11. 13–14.

82. Ibid., 11. 17–20.

83. Literally unable to be written. In the preface to his *Historia Antigua de México* (1780), Francisco Javier Clavijero (S.J.) argues that, because of the loss of historical artifacts, writing the history of Mexico was a task he deemed "difícil, si no de imposible ejecución" (*Historia antigua de México,* 1:v). Clavijero's history was influential to the creole patriot movement and was an early example of the elevation of pre-Columbian Indigenous societies as complex, advanced civilizations.

84. Shumway, *The Invention of Argentina,* 3.

85. Earle, "Creole Patriotism and the Myth of the 'Loyal Indian,'" 129.

86. The literary movement described as *indianismo,* the nineteenth-century romantic interest in the figure of the Indian, is distinct from the modern *indigenismo.* José Carlos Mariátegui described the latter as a concern for contemporary Indigenous communities demonstrated in its "attempts to vindicate the Indian socially" (Gold, "'Indianismo' and 'Indigenismo,'" 462).

87. The area that comprised the Viceroyalty of Peru was a stronghold for royalists and remained under Spanish control during the Peninsular War (Lynch, *The Spanish American Revolutions;* Fisher, *Bourbon Peru, 1750–1824;* Cotler, *Clases, estado y nación en el Perú*).

88. *Obras poéticas de d. José Joaquín Olmedo,* 20. All citations refer to page number rather

than line of verse. Quotations retain all spellings and diacritics of the original, presented by the publisher as the "Única colección completa, revista y correjida por el autor."

89. Ibid., 33.

90. Ibid., 34.

91. Ibid., 24, 30.

92. Ibid., 33.

93. Ibid., n.14, 186.

94. Ibid., 35.

95. Ibid.

96. Ibid., 37.

97. Ibid., 36.

98. Ibid., 36–37.

99. Ibid., 38.

100. Ibid., 34.

101. Ibid., 38.

102. Ibid., n.20, 188.

103. Ianes, *De Cortés a la huérfana enclaustrada,* 91.

104. *Obras poéticas de d. José Joaquín Olmedo,* 193.

105. Ibid., 193–94.

106. Quoted in Smith, "The Sacred-Historical Role of the Inca in Olmedo's 'Canto a Bolívar,'" 212.

107. König, "El indigenismo criollo," 748.

108. Quoted in Smith, "The Sacred-Historical Role of the Inca in Olmedo's 'Canto a Bolívar,'" 212.

109. Quoted in Bernal Medina, "Analisis comparativo de las críticas de Bolívar y de Bello," 120.

110. Freud, "Mourning and Melancholia," 249.

111. Quoted in Minguet, "El concepto de nación, pueblo, estado y pátria," 64.

112. *Obras poéticas de d. José Joaquín Olmedo,* 35–36.

113. Ibid., 35.

114. Ibid., n.14, 186.

115. A level of distinction implied here, one which space disallows a thorough investigation, is the class-based identification implied by the lost savage trope. Several critics have noted that recuperated Native figures are most frequently kings, sachems, and other characters of a recognizably aristocratic social standing. This would serve as an obvious distinction for nineteenth-century creoles, as contemporary Indigenous populations were then (as they continue to be in many ways to this day) severely limited in their financial resources, or their ability to function in colonial and post-colonial economic markets. The recuperative function of the noble savage, it seems, was his very nobility.

116. Earle, "Creole Patriotism and the Myth of the 'Loyal Indian,'" 133.

117. Quoted in ibid.

118. Méndez, "Incas Sí, Indios No," 12.

119. Ianes, *De Cortés a la huérfana enclaustrada,* 95.

120. Minguet, "El concepto de nación, pueblo, estado y pátria," 64.
121. *Obras poéticas de d. José Joaquín Olmedo,* 45.
122. Ibid., 40.
123. Ibid., 47.
124. Ibid., 49.
125. *Jicoténcal,* 14.
126. Ibid., 15.
127. It is interesting to note, in addition to the chronological violation of *la americana* that reveals the voice of the narrator and his own historical context, the moment of contact is not attenuated by linguistic divisions. There is no translation necessary; communication between the parties is direct and immediately understood. Language, then, is not asserted as a definitional characteristic. See chapter 4 in this study for a discussion of the role language and translation play in the New World historical romance.
128. *Jicoténcal,* 15.
129. Ibid., 16.
130. Ibid., 21.
131. Ibid., 83.
132. Ibid., 109.
133. Ibid., 4.
134. Ibid., 5.
135. Ibid., 8.
136. Ibid., 23.
137. McPheeters, "Xicoténcal, símbolo republicano y romántico," 404.
138. *Jicoténcal,* 27.
139. Ibid., 17.
140. Ibid., 109.
141. Ibid., 28.
142. Ibid., 6.
143. Ibid., 109–10.
144. McPheeters, "Xicoténcal, símbolo republicano y romántico," 407.
145. *Jicoténcal,* 111–12.
146. Here we see how the definition of sovereignty offered by Mbembe (following Foucault) that "to exercise sovereignty is to exercise control over mortality" (11) is not limited to the exercise of the fact of life or death but the condition under which this is experienced. The revulsion cultivated by Magiscatzin's deathbed speaks to the sovereign's power over horror, the spectacle of suffering not merely the reminder of the power over life but also the terror of a state of exception in which torture takes place, an abandoned state that exceeds the binary of life and death, a "creaturely" state. Tracing the focus on creaturely life in within a German-Jewish tradition, Eric Santner describes this as a "peculiar proximity of the human to the animal" rendered by man's subjection to a "traumatic dimension of political power and social bonds," itself a distinctly biopolitical circumscription "where life becomes a matter of politics and politics comes to inform the very matter and materiality of life" (*On Creaturely Life,* 12). See also Agamben, *State of Exception.*
147. *Jicoténcal,* 10.

148. Ibid., 120.

149. Ibid., 76.

150. Ibid., 126.

151. Ianes, *De Cortés a la huérfana enclaustrada,* 95.

152. *Jicoténcal,* 131.

153. McPheeters, "Xicoténcal, símbolo republicano y romántico," n.5, 405.

154. *Jicoténcal,* 117.

155. If one assumes the Varela attribution is correct (chapter 2, n. 1), this reading allows us a new critical view of the novel in the context of Varela's native Cuba. By seeing creole patriotism as aligned with the "elimination logic" of the Vanishing American, we can see how his geographical and chronological displacement of the Indigenous community (they are Mexican and they are historical figures only) could contribute to the continuance, up until the middle of the twentieth century, of the belief that the Indigenous population of the island was already extinct, or that their complete extinction was a historical fact. Such assertions continue even today despite ethnographical surveys that offer sufficient proof to the contrary. See Yaremko, "'Obvious Indian': Missionaries, Anthropologists, and the 'Wild Indians' of Cuba. Representations of the Amerindian Presence in Cuba," especially 449–50. Similar to the US American discourse, this trope allows the Spanish American to displace Amerindian communities into the past while also laying the ideological groundwork for the aggressive land grab campaigns of the mid to late nineteenth century such as Argentina's Conquest of the Desert (Shumway, *The Invention of Argentina,* 144).

156. Harrison, *The Dominion of the Dead,* ix.

157. *Jicoténcal,* 3.

158. Ibid., 117.

159. Ibid., 140.

160. Ibid., 125.

161. Olmedo, *Obras poéticas de d. José Joaquín Olmedo,* 30.

162. Ibid., 42.

163. *Jicoténcal,* 6.

164. Walker, "The Patriotic Society: Discussions and Omissions about Indians in the Peruvian War of Independence," 276.

165. Said, *Reflections on Exile,* 176.

166. Mbembe, "Necropolitics," 11.

167. I find this approach very succinctly expressed in Jane Tompkins's reading of Eva's death in *Uncle Tom's Cabin.* In these powerfully sentimental death scenes, Tompkins writes, death itself becomes "the supreme form of heroism . . . it brings an access to power, not a loss of it" through its requirement of response or responsibility (*Sensational Designs,* 127). See chapter 3 for further elaboration of this sentimental power.

Chapter 3

1. The author describes the witnesses as marked by a "quietud estúpida" (*Jicoténcal,* 132). See chapter 2 of the current study for a detailed reading of this event.

2. Varela, *Jicoténcal,* 138.

3. Cooper, *The Pioneers,* 26.

4. Ibid., 27–28.

5. Ibid., 85.

6. Ibid. See chapter 4 of the current study for a discussion of this work of renaming as a "translation" of Indigenous personhood for the purposes of creole nativism.

7. Ibid., 416.

8. Ibid., 405.

9. Ibid., 85.

10. Ibid., 410.

11. Ibid., 421.

12. Ibid., 419.

13. Ibid., 421.

14. Ibid., 451.

15. Ibid., 452.

16. Ibid.

17. *The Prairie,* 381.

18. Ibid., 383.

19. Ibid., 384.

20. Ibid., 386.

21. *The Dominion of the Dead,* 24.

22. Ibid., 19.

23. Ibid., 28.

24. Ibid., 34.

25. Fiedler, *Love and Death in the American Novel,* 181.

26. Ibid., 194.

27. Cooper, *The Prairie,* 384.

28. Ibid., 386.

29. A note on terminology is due here for the dependence on the term "miscegenation," which for the purposes of this study references those romances whose central marriage plot involves an interracial couple whose coupling produces an interracial child. *Mestizaje* and *mestiçagem,* the equivalent terms in Spanish and Portuguese, did not carry the same negative weight that accompanies the term "miscegenation." Doris Sommer, in explaining the role of this interracial ideal in national formation, declares that in Latin America they were "practically a slogan for national consolidation" and laments that the terms are "so pejoratively rendered in English as miscegenation." See Sommer, *Foundational Fictions,* 22, 78. I use the term here as a reflection of those nationally minded projects incorporated into its Spanish and Portuguese equivalents but I do not divorce the negative connotative development attached to the English, instead arguing throughout that such conciliatory expressions hold within them the violent exclusion implied in the negative term it has become in English.

30. Fiedler, *Love and Death in the American Novel,* 208.

31. Richter, *Facing East from Indian Country,* 154.

32. "Yamoyden (Review)," 480.

33. Ibid., 480–81.

34. Sydney Smith wrote in the *Edinburgh Review:*

> The Americans are a brave, industrious, and acute people; but they have hitherto given no indications of genius, and made no approaches to the heroic, either in their morality or character. They are but a recent offset indeed from England; and they should make it their chief boast, for many generations to come, that they are sprung from the same race with Bacon and Shakespeare and Newton. . . . During the thirty or forty years of their independence, they have done absolutely nothing for the Sciences, for the Arts, for Literature. . . . In the four quarters of the globe, who reads an American book? Or goes to an American play? ("Statistical Annals of the United States of America. Review," 79).

Of note is his insistence that when he declares the United States to be a "cultural wasteland," as Samuel French described it, Smith means that they should cling to their British patrimony. Cultural independence is thus set up as a filial reimagining. His comments sparked several conversations about the need for this independent national culture in the United States and the *Yamoyden* review referenced here formed a part of that discussion.

35. Quoted in Karcher, "Introduction," xviii.
36. *Hobomok,* 3.
37. Ibid.
38. Ibid., 4.
39. Baym, *American Women Writers,* 11–28.
40. Ibid., 17.
41. Quoted in ibid.
42. Ibid., 14.
43. Ibid., 23.
44. Quoted in ibid.
45. Ibid., 155.
46. Renan, "What Is a Nation," 56.
47. Berlant describes this as "a particular form of liberal sentimentality that promotes individual acts of identification based on collective group membership." In the United States, she argues, this sentimentality "has been conventionally deployed to bind persons to the nation through a universalist rhetoric not of citizenship but of the capacity for suffering and trauma at the citizen's core" ("Poor Eliza," 636). In focusing on mourning instead of alliances of pain, I differ from Berlant in locating this bind within the consuming work of identification, in which the ego accretes around the kernel of loss, rather than the narcissistic wound of trauma and pain.
48. Quoted in Mailloux, "The Rhetorical Use and Abuse of Fiction," 134.
49. Quoted in ibid.
50. Ibid., 136.
51. "Miscellaneous Notices: Hobomok," 263.
52. "Recent American Novels," 87.
53. Ibid.
54. Tompkins, *Sensational Designs,* 127.

55. Ibid.
56. Ibid., 128.
57. Freud, "Family Romances," 298.
58. Ibid., 299–300.
59. Hirsch, "Jane's Family Romances," 170.
60. Freud, "Family Romances," 300.
61. Ibid.
62. Ibid.
63. Hirsch, "Jane's Family Romances," 171.
64. Child, *Hobomok,* 16.
65. Ibid., 58.
66. Ibid.
67. Ibid., 65.
68. Ibid., 110.
69. Ibid.
70. Ibid., 97.
71. Vaux, "But Maria, Did You Really Write This?" 135.
72. Child, *Hobomok,* 7.
73. Ibid.
74. Ibid., 112.
75. Ibid.
76. Ibid.
77. Cooper, *The Pioneers,* 16.
78. Ibid., 450.
79. Cooper, *The Prairie,* 386.
80. Child, *Hobomok,* 126.
81. Tompkins, *Sensational Designs,* 132.
82. Child, *Hobomok,* 109.
83. Ibid., 131.
84. Ibid., 119.
85. Ibid., 131.
86. Ibid., 119. This valuation of the performance of grief, that is, the act of crying itself, reflects a larger contemporary shift in acceptable standards of mourning. In her study of nineteenth-century modes of grief, Dana Luciano cites the increasingly acceptable presence of tears, seen as "natural" expressions of sensibility rather than a pathological attachment to those lost. See *Arranging Grief,* 30.
87. Child, *Hobomok,* 109.
88. Ibid., 119.
89. Ibid.
90. Ibid., 108.
91. Ibid., 119.
92. Ibid.

93. Ibid., 126.
94. Ibid., 109, emphasis added.
95. Ibid., 149.
96. Ibid., 58.
97. Mills, *Cultural Reformations,* 17.
98. Ibid.
99. Ibid., 13.
100. Ibid., 17.
101. Ibid., 16.
102. Child, *Hobomok,* 6.
103. Mills, *Cultural Reformations,* 13.
104. As I have previously noted, the narrative as a whole relocates the native community to the white settlement. When I refer to nativism, it is identification with this foundational white community, not the Native American population.
105. Baym, *American Women Writers,* 155.
106. Child, *Hobomok,* 3.
107. Ibid., 4.
108. Ibid., 5.
109. Certeau, *The Writing of History,* 23.
110. Ibid., 31.
111. Ibid., 46.
112. Ibid.
113. Child, *Hobomok,* 40.
114. Ibid., 7.
115. Ibid., 139–40.
116. Ronell, *Crack Wars,* 97.
117. Child, *Hobomok,* 84.
118. Ibid., 124.
119. Ibid., 130.
120. Ibid., 135, emphasis added.
121. Ibid., 136.
122. Ibid., 137.
123. Bergland, *The National Uncanny,* 22.
124. Harrison, *The Dominion of the Dead,* x.
125. The deployment of *mestiçagem* as a trope of national unification, while still popular in contemporary discourse, can be traced to the consciously national cultural projects embarked upon in Brazil that mirror that call made by the *North American Review* described earlier in the chapter. One of the most famous of these incidents was the contest for defining national historiography sponsored by the newly founded Instituto Hisórico e Geográfico Brasileiro (see E. Bradford Burns, *Perspectives on Brazilian History* [New York: Columbia University Press, 1967], 21–41). The winning essay, by the German Karl Friedrich Philipp von Martius, was titled "Como se Deve Escrever a Hisória do Brasil [How One Should Write the

History of Brazil]." In that essay, the author writes: "Anyone who undertakes to write the history of Brazil, a country which promises so much, should never lose sight of the elements which contributed to the development of man there. These diverse elements come from the three races, namely: the copper-colored, or American; the white, or Caucasian; and the black, or Ethiopian. Because of the reciprocal and changing relations of the three races, the present population consists of a novel mixture, whose history therefore has a very particular stamp" (Quoted in Burns, 23).

126. Renata Wasserman notes that Cooper's work was available in translation and Alencar himself goes so far as to deny this charge in his "Como e porque sou romancista" (1893). Sergio Bellei notes that "as referências ao relacionamento Cooper-Alencar são relativamente frequentes na crítica do século XIX: Joaquim Nabuco, Antônio Henriques Leal, Pinheiro Chagas. São também geralmente etnocêntricas, registrando antes um débito do que um ganho original [references to the Cooper-Alencar relationship are relatively frequent in criticism written in the nineteenth century. . . . These are also in general ethnocentric, registering an original advantage (over Cooper) rather than a debt]" (Bellei, *Nacionalidade e literatura,* 23).

127. Ibid., 26.

128. Fitz, *Brazilian Narrative Traditions in a Comparative Context,* 65.

129. Wolfe, "Settler Colonialism and the Elimination of the Native."

130. Alencar, "Carta," 129.

131. Sommer, *Foundational Fictions,* 39.

132. Doniger, "Foreword," viii, emphasis in original.

133. Wasserman, "The Red and the White," 818.

134. Doniger, "Foreword," viii.

135. Duarte, "O signo de Eva," 195.

136. Da Costa, *The Brazilian Empire,* 172–201.

137. Duarte, "O signo de Eva," 198.

138. Kadir, "The Commons of History," 600.

139. Kadir, *Columbus and the Ends of the Earth,* 60.

140. Certeau, *The Writing of History,* xxv–xxvii.

141. Alencar, "Carta," 129.

142. *Iracema,* 36, 104. Iracema is also referred to as "virgem do sertão," the virgin of the forest or jungle. The equivalence or confusion with the landscape is aggravated by this second environmental moniker, since it is very similar to the common description of the untouched land as virginal, as in the *floresta virgem.*

143. The relationship between Martim and his blond virgin that waits for him is never explicitly articulated but many critics have claimed her as his fiancée. The effect of his longing, whether nostalgia for an actual relationship or simply a sexual fantasy, is to marginalize his Indian lover by projecting his desire in racial terms.

144. Alencar, *Iracema,* 64.

145. Ibid., 67.

146. We can map this isolation of Iracema from her tribe as a form of the assimilationist "elimination of the native" traced by Patrick Wolfe. By isolating private individuals from tribal identity, settler colonial states created a "kind of death" for these subjects. "Without the tribe

... for all practical purposes they were no longer Indians" ("Settler Colonialism and the Elimination of the Native," 397).

147. Duarte, "O signo de Eva," 199.

148. Ibid.

149. Ibid.

150. Douglas defines "dirt" as "all the rejected elements of ordered systems" (*Purity and Danger,* 35).

151. Ibid., 8.

152. Ibid., 16.

153. Alencar, *Iracema,* 65.

154. Ibid., 24.

155. Ibid., 66.

156. In other words, being "on drugs" (under the influence of the sacred *jurema*), outside the realm of the Law and legal sanction, Martim ceases to guard against the abject.

157. Alencar, *Iracema,* 67.

158. Ferreira-Pinto, *Gender, Discourse, and Desire,* 14.

159. Duarte, "O signo de Eva," 199.

160. Alencar, *Iracema,* 119.

161. As in the United States, writers in Brazil frequently elevated maternal labor as a service to the future health of the republic, an idea that came to be known as "republican motherhood." One can see this idea reflected in Brazilian writings of the period including that of Nísia Floresta (1810–1885), whose writings in defense of women's rights often centered on their role in educating their children. The growing popularity in Brazil of domestic manuals that included children's education as well women's participation in domestic reform, such as the racialized protests against the "ama de leite," or wet nurse, demonstrate a similar commitment to the social work of child rearing. Sonia Roncador discusses this latter movement in the period of the first republic in "O demônio familiar."

162. One could read the whitening of these two mixed-race children as a product of the dominant racial discourse as well. In Brazil, positivist racial science contributed to the popular idea that mixing races would generally *whiten* the population. In Child's context, Hobomok's conversion offered hope to those reformers who declared in what Roy Harvey Pearce calls a "doubled discourse," that the only way for the Native to survive was for him to become more white, or more civilized, an assertion that almost always was accompanied by the mournful acknowledgment that such conversions were in fact impossible (*Savagism and Civilization,* 65–67).

163. The liminoid is related to yet separate from the liminal stage of the rite of passage. For an elaboration of the term, see Turner, *From Ritual to Theatre.*

164. Wasserman, *Exotic Nations,* 13–14.

165. Douglas, *Purity and Danger,* 45.

166. Wasserman, *Exotic Nations,* 30.

167. Duarte, "O signo de Eva," 199.

168. Alencar, "Carta," 126.

169. Alencar, *Iracema,* 122.

Chapter 4

1. Alencar, *Iracema*, 121.

2. Ibid., 112 n.117.

3. Ibid., 121.

4. Ibid.

5. Ibid.

6. Ibid., 122.

7. Wasserman, "Re-Inventing the New World," 134.

8. Renan, "What Is a Nation," 16.

9. Moaçir thus functions in a similar way to Follen's "Sachem," whose hill becomes incorporated in the name Massachusetts (See chapter 3).

10. Ballacay, "Andrés Bello y la conciencia del idioma," 123; Blanch, "El problema de la lengua española en América," 12–23.

11. Quoted in Wells, *Dictionaries and the Authoritarian Tradition,* 56.

12. Lepore, *A Is for American,* 17. Tim Cassedy has recently shown that literary histories tend to ignore the unpopular nature of Webster's early linguistic nationalism. If language was imagined as a repository of the self, Cassedy argues, then many early national language projects actually argued for the positive cultural claims of British English. If "revolutionary Americans were enthusiastic about overturning their political environment," he writes, "[they were] far less enthusiastic about the prospect of overturning their cultural or mental environment" (*Figures of Speech,* 111). Cassedy notes that this skepticism shifts dramatically by 1826, when Webster's dictionary was nearly complete. This period, notably after the conclusion of the war of 1812, was marked by the rise of the national historical romance, aided in part by what Cassedy sees as an attempt to erase all prior ambivalence about the Revolution. Sean Harvey notes that the conclusion of the war in 1815 initiated a period of "surging nationalism and millennialism," what the current study identifies as the national discourse of loss and fulfillment that produces the nation (*Native Tongues,* 115).

13. "Language," Anderson writes, "had never been an issue in the American nationalist movements . . . on the whole, any attempt to give historical depth to nationality via linguistic means faced insuperable obstacles" (*Imagined Communities,* 196–97).

14. Ibid., 42–46.

15. Ibid., 44.

16. Ibid., 45.

17. Cooper, *Last of the Mohicans,* 8.

18. Ibid.

19. Anderson, *Imagined Communities,* 43.

20. Harrison, *The Dominion of the Dead,* 76.

21. Ibid., 81–82.

22. Ibid., 86.

23. Niranjana, *Siting Translation,* 2.

24. Cheyfitz, *The Poetics of Imperialism,* xix.

25. Ibid., xii.

26. Cooper, *Last of the Mohicans,* 12.

27. Ibid., 8.

28. Harrison, *The Dominion of the Dead,* 86.

29. Quoted in Jobim and Acízelo de Souza, *Iniciação à literatura brasileira,* 107.

30. Ribeiro, *Mulheres de papel,* 219.

31. Gonçalves Dias, *Diccionario da lingua Tupy.*

32. Von Martius, "Como se deve escrever a historia do Brasil," 445. This twentieth-century reprint of the essay standardizes the spelling of the original, which was published in *Jornal do Instituto Historico e Geographico Brazileiro* 24 (Janeiro de 1845): 381–403. For more on von Martius and the work of the Instituto Histórico e Geográphico Brasileiro in directing the development of national history, see Guimaraes, "Nação e civilização nos trópicos"; Burns, *Perspectives on Brazilian History.*

33. Alencar, "Carta," 126.

34. Ibid.

35. Ibid.

36. Ibid., 129.

37. Rothwell, "Shit, Shrimps, and Shifting Sobriquets," 289.

38. Alencar, *Iracema,* 66.

39. Ibid., 66 n.67.

40. Rohter, "Language Born of Colonialism Thrives Again in Amazon."

41. Campbell, *American Indian Languages,* 23.

42. Certeau, *Heterologies,* 227.

43. Rothwell, "Shit, Shrimps, and Shifting Sobriquets," 288.

44. Ibid., 289.

45. Ibid., 293–94.

46. Brunet, "Linguisters on the Prairie," 239.

47. Cooper, *The Prairie,* 75.

48. Ibid., 77.

49. Ibid., 85.

50. Brunet, "Linguisters on the Prairie," 248.

51. Ibid., 255. "La traduction intralinguistique joue également un rôle important, notamment autour du docteur Battius [Intralinguistic translation plays an equally important role, notably around Dr. Battius]."

52. Cooper, *The Prairie,* 69.

53. Ibid., 98.

54. Ibid., 71.

55. Ibid., 76–77.

56. Cooper, *Last of the Mohicans,* 57.

57. Cooper, *The Prairie,* 98.

58. Ibid., 96.

59. Ibid., 97.

60. Ibid., 98.

61. Ibid., 99.

62. Ibid., 100.

63. The differend described by Jean-François Lyotard is a site of difference in which there is no determining power of an absolute code of knowledge. It is instead the "negative presentation of the indeterminate" (*The Differend,* 56).

64. Cooper, *The Prairie,* 100.

65. Brunet, "Linguisters on the Prairie," 248.

66. Benjamin, "Die Aufgabe des Übersetzers," vii.

67. Benjamin, "The Task of the Translator," 70.

68. Lefevere, *Translating Literature,* 6.

69. de Man, "Conclusions," 87.

70. Ibid., 80. This failure is akin to what Avital Ronell names as the "ineluctable disrepair" of the translation (which exists always with its pair, the original to which it refers). See her translator's note in Derrida, "The Law of Genre," 230–31.

71. de Man, "Conclusions," 80.

72. Ibid.

73. Jacobs, *In the Language of Walter Benjamin,* 87–88.

74. de Man, "Conclusions," 84. For more on this essential failure, see the Coda to this study.

75. Brodie, *No Man Knows My History,* 61. Joseph Smith's sacred translations are not limited to *The Book of Mormon.* Beginning in June 1830, Smith started an "inspired" translation of the King James Version of the Bible, a project designed (like *The Book of Mormon*) as a restoration of the "many plain and precious things taken away from the book" (1 Nephi 13:28). Smith would continue producing and revising this translation until his death in 1844.

76. Cooper, *The Prairie,* 385.

Coda

1. I have used the contemporary spellings of Pequot and Mashpee. Apess used the common spellings Pequod and Marshpee. Apess had served as a spokesman for the Mashpee in their petition for self-government and had been arrested for inciting a riot. See Lepore, *The Name of War,* 215–17.

2. Apes, *Indian Nullification.* In his biography of Apess, Philip Gura notes that the publication of *Indian Nullification* "kept the now-settled controversy in the public eye, for given their wide coverage of the Mashpee petition, New England newspapers and the periodical press noticed this book more than any of his others" (*Life of William Apess,* 102). His increased notoriety due to this involvement with and publication about the Mashpee Revolt likely contributed to his enlarged public platform in Boston. Maureen Konkle describes Apess as enjoying a period of notoriety in Boston, a city she describes as "the center of white involvement in the antiremoval effort" (*Writing Indian Nations,* 104).

3. Apess, *Eulogy on King Philip,* 6.

4. For more on representations of Philip in early national literature and culture, see Lepore, *The Name of War,* 186–90, 191–226; Deloria, *Playing Indian,* 64–65; Sayre, *Indian Chief as Tragic Hero,* 80–125. Lepore notes that the Odeon, where Apess delivered his *Eulogy,*

was just a few blocks from the Tremont Street Theater, which featured the drama of Philip's life *Metamora* (217).

5. Apess, *Eulogy on King Philip,* 21.

6. Gerald Vizenor defines survivance as "an active sense of presence, the continuance of native stories, not a mere reaction or a survivable name." For more on survivance as presence above and beyond figuration or signification, see the second section of this Coda (Vizenor, *Manifest Manners,* vii).

7. Apess, *Eulogy on King Philip,* 21.

8. Ibid., 6.

9. Ibid., 20.

10. The full title of the 1829 text is *A Son of the Forest. The Experience of William Apes, a Native of the Forest. Comprising a notice of the Pequod Tribe of Indians. Written by Himself.* Apess changed the spelling of his name in his revision of the text. I have retained this later spelling here, although all citations refer to the first edition unless otherwise noted.

11. Samuel Gardner Drake, the bookseller and antiquarian whose work also served as a resource for Apess's revisionary history, famously corrected Apess's collapsing of Pequot and Wampanoag tribal identity through the figure of Philip, saying he needed to "enlarge the boundaries of his knowledge of Indian history" (Gura, *Life of William Apess,* 45, 103–4). Contemporary scholars frequently repeat this correction, although Barry O'Connell suggests that Apess might have made the elision between the Pequot War and King Philip's War intentionally, but O'Connell also offers his suspicion that Apess has "just confused them" (*On Our Own Ground,* 4 n.2). In tracing the performances of Apess's *Eulogy on King Philip,* Daniel Radus has recently made the provocative connection between this tie to Philip and what Robert Warrior has described as the already-transnational relations of Native American community and identity. Radus connects this conflation of tribes to Apess's later work under the name of Handsome Lake (Radus, "Apess's Eulogy on Tour"; Warrior, "Native American Scholarship and the Transnational Turn").

12. Apess, *A Son of the Forest,* 7. All spellings and emphasis reflect that in the text unless otherwise noted.

13. Ibid., 8.

14. This opening displacement of a post-colonial history into the colonial past is rearranged in the revised autobiography published in 1831. In the revised text, Apess begins with the location and date of his birth, reversing the structure in the original that begins from the twinned acts of dispossession and defilement only then to move on to his immediate family history and eventually arrive at his own birth (9). Scholars connect the appearance of this revised edition to Apess's reconciliation with the Methodist Episcopal Church; in this later edition, as Philip Gura notes, Apess "removed his criticism of and reasons for withdrawal from the Methodist Episcopal church. He also claimed to have 'improved' the book's style and arrangement" (*Life of William Apess,* 45).

15. Apess, *A Son of the Forest,* 15, emphasis added.

16. Ibid., 18.

17. Ibid., 27–28.

18. Ibid., 28–29. Apess is recounting a childhood illness that Phillip Gura has suggested

might be whooping cough. When Apess refers to the strange noise that accompanies and makes difficult his breathing, Gura notes that "it was perhaps that of whooping cough or croup, but because of his newfound fear of death, it caused him irrational fright" (*Life of William Apess,* 15). By highlighting its narrative connection to these other touchstone moments in the opening of his life story, I do not mean to argue that his illness was invented but rather to highlight how the choices made in arranging his story make death itself present as a looming figure in his story (both presently threatening but also as a sign of futurity).

19. Apess, *A Son of the Forest,* 27.

20. Ibid., 23.

21. Ibid., 21.

22. Ibid., 23.

23. In reflecting on the same passage, Mark Rifkin notes that here "Apess gestures toward the existence of another way of framing the past" ("Shadows of Mashantucket," 694).

24. Apess, *A Son of the Forest,* 23, emphasis added.

25. Brooks, "Turning the Looking Glass on King Philip's War," 726.

26. Round, *Removable Type,* 150.

27. "Especially damaging to Native authors' chances of engaging in unmediated public writing," Round writes, "was the Court's insistence on the Indians' need for guardians. The relationship of the United States to Native people was framed by the language of paternalism; its relationship to copyrighted authors, in contrast, focused on 'exclusive right[s]' and 'concrete labor'" (ibid., 157).

28. Ibid., 155.

29. Ibid., 160. Gura notes that the inclusion of the portrait signals Apess's reconciliation with the Methodist Episcopal Church, along with the removal of some of the autobiography's original condemnation of the group's decision not to issue Apess a license to preach. He names the painter of the portrait as one John Paradise, notes the cost of including such material and Paradise's previous work for Methodist publications, and concludes "Apess's patronage of him—or more likely, that of someone in the Methodist hierarchy who thought that an engraved portrait from such a painting should grace Apess's publication—parallels Apess's more forgiving tone toward the Methodist Episcopal Church in this edition" (*Life of William Apess,* 45).

30. See chapter 3 of the current study for a more extended discussion of the connection between the historical romance and history/biography.

31. Round notes that Black Hawk does not own the copyright to his autobiography. "Copyright is owned by J.B. Patterson, who is listed as the 'editor and proprietor' on the 1834 edition's title page" (162).

32. Conn, *History's Shadow,* 49–50.

33. Drake, *Indian Biography,* 268.

34. Lepore, *The Name of War,* 218.

35. Rifkin, *Beyond Settler Time,* 16.

36. Barlow makes this connection explicit in his footnotes to the text. Art historian Samuel Edgerton further notes that this renaming might have been inspired by an earlier

poem by Philip Freneau in which McCrea is named "Lavinia" (the poem, "America Independent," 1786, does not describe the moment of her death but rather refers to "Lavinia of the vale" as one of the "mouldering on the plain"). I owe the connection between Apess's image and the McCrea visualization to Clayton Zuba's presentation "Apess' Eulogy, Native Visualcy, and the Shapes of Sovereignty," later published as "Apess's Eulogy on King Philip and the Politics of Native Visualcy." Zuba privileges the salon painting "The Death of Jane McCrea" by John Vanderlyn (1804) as the source for the frontispiece, while Edgerton's study of the McCrea figuration uses Barlow's correspondence and personal writings to trace the image from its origin in Robert Fulton, its subsequent takeover by Vanderlyn, and its final actualization for the *Columbiad* in Smirke. Edgerton remarks that, while the original Fulton piece does not remain, the similarity between the Vanderlyn painting and the Smirke illustration indicates not only the precision of Barlow's instructions but also the likelihood that the later work copied a structure already present in the missing original. It is Barlow's *Columbiad,* then, that furnished "a simplified but poignant arrangement for the subsequent visualization of the Jane McCrea legend" ("The Murder of Jane McCrea," 483). Following Edgerton, I have chosen to focus on the Smirke illustration in large part because its inclusion in Barlow's text meant that it circulated broadly and it is much more likely that Apess had seen this image and not Vanderlyn's painting while preparing his work using Samuel Drake's resources.

37. Edgerton, "The Murder of Jane McCrea," 483. Apess cites Drake directly in his *Eulogy* (*Eulogy on King Philip,* 8). Many scholars have commented on the relationship between these two figures, including Sayre, *Indian Chief as Tragic Hero;* Gura, *Life of William Apess;* Konkle, *Writing Indian Nations.*

38. Truettner, "Picturing the Murder of Jane McCrea," 231.

39. William Apess includes a notice of errata at the end of his *Eulogy* that offers the following correction: "In the Frontispiece, the man at the head of Philip, should be an Indian" (60). Barry O'Connell has suggested that this error might indicate that the scene is supposed to describe Philip's later dismemberment, but Apess's correction seems to insist that the image is indeed the moment of his death.

40. O'Connell, "Introduction," xv.

41. O'Connell, "'Once More Let Us Consider.'" O'Connell attributes the discovery of an 1839 inquest into William Apess's death to Reginald Pitts. Despite this discovery, the idea of Apess's vanishing seems difficult to dislodge. Tracing later performances of the *Eulogy,* Daniel Radus points out this critical commonplace: "That Apess disappeared from public life after January 1836 has become the conventional analysis, persisting nearly to the present day" ("Apess's Eulogy on Tour," 81). Contemporary works that continue this idea include Round's 2010 book where he writes that Apess "disappears from the historical record in 1838 when the Barstable Court of Common Pleas attached his household goods and estate for debt" (*Removable Type,* 172). J. Gerald Kennedy seems to acknowledge obliquely the fact of Apess's death but he also repeats this idea of disappearance or amnesia (eliding three years of his life as well). In his 2016 study *Strange Nation* he writes: "[The 1836 *Eulogy*] would be Apess's last bow; for reasons that remain unclear, he soon moved to New York and disappeared himself, perishing in oblivion in 1839" (*Strange Nation,* 204). This idea of "oblivion"

stands in stark contrast to Robert Warrior's offer of "speculations" and what I develop as the tracing of and through "remains." For a provocative study of the ways in which oblivion framed the project of cultural memory and the development of antiquarianism in the early national period, see DiCuirci, *Colonial Revivals.*

42. O'Connell, "'Once More Let Us Consider,'" 176.

43. Warrior, "Eulogy on William Apess," 2.

44. Ibid. Some examples include: "Why Apess would have moved from Massachusetts to New York City is still not known and may never be" (3), "no record shows Apess as being part of any larger community" (3–4), "conjecturing that his and Mary's marriage split up is not a stretch. Or even possibly, he maintained two marriages at once. The possibility exists that Mary and Elizabeth are the same person going by different names" (7).

45. O'Connell, "Introduction," xv.

46. Ibid., xvi.

47. Ibid., xvii.

48. Brooks, "Turning the Looking Glass on King Philip's War," 726.

49. Lazo, "The Invention of America Again," 761.

50. Ibid., 762.

51. Lazo, "Accounting for Textual Remains," 181.

52. Ibid., 186. More recently, Mark Rifkin's *Beyond Settler Time* has made a persuasive case for the ways in which dominant modes of temporality marginalize or render illegible other ways of being-in-time, particularly Indigenous temporalities that cannot (and should not) be reconciled with hegemonic reckonings of time. "Settler time," Rifkin writes, "reduces the unfolding and adaptive expressions of Indigenous peoplehood to a set of points—the supposedly shared now of the present, modernity, and national history—within a configuration that is positioned as the commonsensical frame in ways that deny the immanent motion of indigeneity." Instead of recognizing the Native Americans as modern, thereby reconciling Indigenous peoples to the settler time of modernity, Rifkin proposes temporal multiplicity as a way to make possible "the copresence of varied ways of living time, the coexistence of temporal formations that cannot be assessed against a presumptively modern present—a singular background for a necessarily shared history" (*Beyond Settler Time,* 26, 16).

53. Parker, *The Sound the Stars Make Rushing through the Sky,* x–xii.

54. Ibid., xiii–xiv. "I have tried," Parker writes, "to let the mysteries and uncertainties remain mysterious and uncertain rather than impose a false assurance. When I do not know and the records do not tell us, then I have acknowledged that plainly" (xiii).

55. Ibid., 2, emphasis added. In his list of "first knowns," Parker makes a distinction between what he qualifies as *literary writing* from the sermons, testimony, and personal writings of Native American writers who predate Schoolcraft.

56. Parker's search still remains rooted in a privileging of the text as the material that should/can be recovered, framing the exigence of his project as his belief that "American Indian people left a much larger written record than historians usually realize, and early Indian writers left far more writing than historians imagine" (ibid., ix). As I discuss in the section that follows, this is distinct from the archival work that addresses oratory, oral tradition,

and performance artifacts that can *only* be traced through "remains," as Lazo names it, or what Gerald Vizenor names "intransitive shadows" (Vizenor, *Manifest Manners*).

57. Knapp, *Lectures on American Literature,* 2.

58. Ibid., 10.

59. Ibid., 9.

60. Ibid., 25. "The Indians themselves," Knapp declares, "are becoming philologists and grammarians, and exciting the wonder of the world, by the invention of letters."

61. Ibid., 28. Knapp spells Sequoyah as "See-quah-yah" and refers to the syllabary as the "Cherokee alphabet."

62. Ibid., 29.

63. *Lettre du Comte de Mirabeau à ses commettans,* 498. In this Mirabeau seems to be citing Locke, who famously declared that a "great *abuse of Words is, the taking them for Things*" (*An Essay Concerning Human Understanding,* 497). William Keach describes this complaint as "the Enlightenment paradigm that, variously developed and inflected, remains central to the philosophy of language into the nineteenth century," saying that within this paradigm "the claim that language is 'arbitrary' depends on understanding words as signs—primarily of ideas, secondarily of things" (*Arbitrary Power,* 23). The collection of Mirabeau's assembly speeches referenced here are named as his letters, although the prefatory "Avis du libraire éditeur" indicates that the writings were "composé sous sa direction, n'étoit pas de sa plume [composed under his direction but not from his pen]." Translations of these writings refer to them in English as his "speeches" (see reference below). Mirabeau died in April of 1791, making even this early collection a posthumous publication.

64. "We shall soon have occasion to examine this theory of the three powers, which, when exactly analysed, will perhaps shew the aptitude of the human mind to take words for things, formularies for arguments, and follow the routine of a certain order of ideas, without ever stopping to consider the intelligible definition which it hath taken for an axiom" (Mirabeau, *Speeches of M. de Mirabeau,* 133–34).

65. Quoted in Keach, *Arbitrary Power,* 24, 41.

66. Locke, *An Essay Concerning Human Understanding,* 3.2.

67. In marking this shift, I offer a way to read Apess from within the scryptural economy of nineteenth-century nativist writings but also as a discursive rupture that resists the terms of recognition provided him. Glen Sean Coulthard has argued that "instead of ushering in an era of peaceful coexistence grounded in the ideal of *reciprocity* or *mutual* recognition, the politics of recognition in its contemporary liberal form promises to reproduce the very configurations of colonialist, racist, patriarchal state power that Indigenous peoples' demands for recognition have historically sought to transcend" (*Red Skin, White Masks,* 3).

68. Vizenor, *Manifest Manners,* 63.

69. Ibid., 72, 73.

70. Robin D. G. Kelley attaches a revolutionary possibility or optimism to this idea of the trace, which he sees as an "assault on settler rule." "The 'trace,' then, is both the refusal to accept the permanence and terms of settler domination, and the memory/dreams/fantasy of life before and beyond invasion" ("The Rest of Us," 274).

71. Vizenor, *Manifest Manners,* 69.

72. Gura, *Life of William Apess,* 106.

73. Lepore, *The Name of War,* 225. Placing Apess's *Eulogy* in conversation with other Philip-centered performances, Lepore notes: "Oratory was central to Forrest's performance ("Speak, Metamora, Speak!"), to Brougham's and other parodies ("Death or my nation's glory, that's the talk"), and to Apess' *Eulogy* (complete with spurious Philip speech)."

74. Cassedy, *Figures of Speech,* 150.

75. The "intransitive shadows" remark upon what Daniel Radus describes as the "shrouded" field of knowledge encountered when moving "from the page to the stage" ("Apess's Eulogy on Tour," 81). We might call Radus's work on performance history a kind of shadow play in which the scholar must extrapolate from what Lazo describes as the archive's remains to make present what that the institution does not (or cannot).

76. Apess, *Eulogy on King Philip,* 5, 18, 21, 24.

77. Ibid., 24.

78. Ibid., 28, 45.

79. Apess, *A Son of the Forest,* 107.

80. Apess, *Eulogy on King Philip,* 5.

81. Vizenor, *Manifest Manners,* 70.

82. Quoted in Konkle, *Writing Indian Nations,* 99.

83. Deloria, *Playing Indian,* 90, 91. Patrick Wolfe has called this erasure of Indigenous identity "repressive authenticity" and locates it within a "logic of elimination" ("Settler Colonialism and the Elimination of the Native").

84. Rifkin, *Beyond Settler Time,* 39–40.

85. Gura, *Life of William Apess,* 104.

86. Quoted in ibid. This aggressive attachment to figurations of Indian life can contribute to the Native invisibility that fragments the archive, as previously discussed. Whether one was "seen" or counted *as Indian* seemed to vary substantially, as can be seen in Gura's account of the various categorization of Apess and his family in censuses.

87. Derrida, "Mnemosyne," 6.

88. Quoted in Lepore, *The Name of War,* 220.

89. Ibid.

90. Patricia Bizzell says that Apess "preached the Christian gospel to New England Indians in Algonquian," although no evidence is provided to support this claim and I have been unable to find record of this in other studies of his work (Bizzell, "(Native) American Jeremiad," 36). In his recent biography, Philip Gura asserts early on that we have no positive knowledge of Apess's ability to speak anything other than English, although he later uses this section of the *Eulogy* as possible evidence to the contrary ("Apess even promised to 'give a specimen of Philip's language,' which suggests that he still could use the Massachusetts tongue," 107). My argument here is not that Apess spoke only English. Although it is unclear what language was spoken in his parents' house, from which he was removed at age four and educated only in English, there is a possibility if not a probability that he maintained ties with other Pequots in the area. A few scholars have also noted his later conversations with Pequot speakers as evidence that he retained some of his tribal language but most recently Sean Harvey has claimed that "neither [Apess] nor most of the rest of his nation knew any

Pequot" (*Native Tongues*, 93), tracing the beginnings of Pequot language extinction to the destruction of Native-language materials in the seventeenth and eighteenth centuries and English-only schooling from 1803 (117).

91. While *Ethnologue* catalogs the two under distinct language codes (xpq for Mohegan-Pequot and wam for Wampanoag, also known as Massachusett(s), Natick, or the autonym Wôpanâak), it also notes that the two languages are "reportedly similar" in its notes on Pequot dialects (Simons and Fennig, "Mohegan-Pequot"; Simons and Fennig, "Wampanoag"). Sean Harvey traces the work of early philologists who claim a commonality so strong among coastal Indigenous languages that they assumed a common root, while others offered contradictory assessments, finding instead "no compelling similarities (*Native Tongues,* 52). In table 1 (pages 186–87), you can see the distinction not only between different versions of the Lord's Prayer in Massachusett, but also compare these to a record of the Lord's Prayer in Pequot. The comparison is offered as potential although not conclusive evidence of their distinction, since "collecting" language samples sometimes varied in terms of phonetic transcription, the translation being offered, and was frequently affected by misunderstandings and mistranslations of its own.

92. Apess, *Eulogy on King Philip,* 56. In all my time spent considering the proliferation of meaning in this brief passage, this "we" still remains provocative and yet is not addressed here. Apess's statements of action immediately previous are framed as an "I" statement ("I shall pronounce him the greatest man that was ever in America"), as are many of those that precede and follow the prayer. While he uses "we" in the speech, it is usually in reference to an event of witnessing ("we often hear"). While I identify one potential "we" in what follows (Drake), the openness here in this "we" is productively vexing, given my argument about this passage's unreadability.

93. Ibid., 32.

94. Lepore, *The Name of War,* 40.

95. Apess, *Eulogy on King Philip,* 33.

96. Lepore, *The Name of War,* 28.

97. Quoted in ibid., 29.

98. Apess, *Eulogy on King Philip,* 49.

99. Drake, *Book of Indians of North America,* III, 40. Lindsay DiCuirci has traced Drake's concern for "specimens" to his larger project of preservation, citing his criticism of "modernized" colonial texts such as John Winthrop's journal in order to show Drake's commitment to archiving the material character of the text as part of its historical significance (*Colonial Revivals,* 73).

100. Derrida, "Mnemosyne," 38.

Works Cited

"7 April, 1844 (2) (Sunday Afternoon)." Religious Studies Center, Brigham Young University, n.d. https://rsc.byu.edu/archived/words-joseph-smith-contemporary-accounts-nauvoo-discourses-prophet-joseph/1844/7-april-18-0.

"Accounts of the 'King Follett Sermon.'" The Church Historian's Press, March 18, 2014. The Joseph Smith Papers. josephsmithpapers.org.

Agamben, Giorgio. *State of Exception*. Translated by Kevin Attell. Chicago: University of Chicago Press, 2005.

Ahearne, Jeremy. *Michel de Certeau: Interpretation and Its Other*. Stanford, CA: Stanford University Press, 1995.

Alencar, José de. "Carta ao Dr. Jaguaribe (1865)." In *Iracema*, 123–30. Alegre: L & PM, 2006.

———. *Iracema*. Alegre: L & PM, 2006.

Allen, Michael J. "'Sacrilege of a Strange, Contemporary Kind': The Unknown Soldier and the Imagined Community after the Vietnam War." *History & Memory* 23, no. 2 (Fall/Winter 2011): 90–131.

Allen, Thomas M. *A Republic in Time: Temporality & Social Imagination in Nineteenth-Century America*. Chapel Hill: University of North Carolina Press, 2008.

Anderson, Benedict. *Imagined Communities: Reflections on the Origin and Spread of Nationalism*. Revised ed. New York: Verso, 1991.

Apes[s], William. *Indian Nullification of the Unconstitutional Laws of Massachusetts, Relative to the Marshpee Tribe: Or, The Pretended Riot Explained*. Boston: Jonathan Howe, 1835.

Apess, William. *Eulogy on King Philip, as Pronounced at the Odeon, in Federal Street, Boston, by the Rev. William Apes, an Indian*. Boston: Published by the author, 1836.

———. *A Son of the Forest*. New York: Published by the author, 1829.

Appleby, Joyce Oldham. *Inheriting the Revolution : The First Generation of Americans*. Cambridge, MA: Belknap Press, 2000.

Balderston, Daniel, ed. *The Historical Novel in Latin America: A Symposium*. Gaithersburg, MD: Ediciones Hispamérica, 1986.

Ballacay, Andres Gallardo. "Andrés Bello y la conciencia del idioma." In *From Romanticism to Modernismo in Latin America*, edited by David William Foster and Daniel Altamiranda, 123–36. New York and London: Garland, 1997.

Bancroft, George. *History of the United States from the Discovery of the American Continent*. Vol. 3. 10 vols. Boston: Little, Brown, & Company, 1844.

Baquero Arribas, Mercedes. "La conquista de América en la novela histórica del romanticismo español: El caso de Xicotencal, príncipe americano." *Cuadernos Hispanoamericanos* 480 (1990): 125–32.

Barthes, Roland. *Michelet.* Translated by Richard Howard. Berkeley and Los Angeles: University of California Press, 1992.

Baudrillard, Jean. *America.* Verso, 1989.

Bauer, Ralph. "Hemispheric Studies." *PMLA* 124, no. 1 (January 2009): 234–50.

———. "The 'Rebellious Muse': Time, Space, and Race in the Revoultionary Epic." In *Creole Subjects in the Colonial Americas: Empires, Texts, Identities,* edited by Ralph Bauer and José Antonio Mazzotti. Chapel Hill: University of North Carolina Press, 2012.

Baym, Nina. *American Women Writers and the Work of History, 1790–1860.* New Brunswick, NJ: Rutgers University Press, 1995.

———. "Putting Women in Their Place: The Last of the Mohicans and Other Indian Stories." In *Feminism and American Literary History: Essays,* 19–35. New Brunswick, NJ: Rutgers University Press, 1992.

Bell, Michael Davitt. *Hawthorne and the Historical Romance of New England.* Princeton, NJ: Princeton University Press, 1971.

Bellei, Sérgio Luiz Prado. *Nacionalidade e literatura: Os caminhos da alteridade.* Florianópolis: Editora da UFSC, 1992.

Bellin, Joshua David. "Apostle of Removal: John Eliot in the Nineteenth Century." *New England Quarterly* 69, no. 1 (March 1996): 3–32.

Benítez-Rojo, Antonio. "The Nineteenth-Century Spanish American Novel." In *Cambridge History of Latin American Literature,* edited by Roberto González Echevarría and Enrique Pupo-Walker, 1:417–89. Cambridge: Cambridge University Press, 1996.

Benjamin, Walter. *The Arcades Project.* Translated by Howard Eiland and Kevin McLaughlin. Prepared on the Basis of the German Volume Edited by Rolf Tiedemann. Cambridge, MA and London: Harvard University Press, 2002.

———. "Die Aufgabe des Übersetzers." In *Tableaux Parisiens,* by Charles Baudelaire, vi–xvii. Heidelberg: Verlag Von Richard Weissbach, 1923.

———. *Illuminations.* Translated by Harry Zohn. New York: Schocken Books, 1968.

———. "The Task of the Translator. An Introduction to the Translation of Baudelaire's Tableaux Parisiens." In *Illuminations,* edited by Hannah Arendt, translated by Harry Zohn, 69–82. New York: Schocken Books, 1968.

Bergland, Renée L. *The National Uncanny: Indian Ghosts and American Subjects.* Hanover, NH: University Press of New England, 2000.

Berlant, Lauren. "Poor Eliza." *American Literature* 70, no. 3 (September 1998): 635–68.

Bernal Medina, Rafael. "Analisis comparativo de las críticas de Bolívar y de Bello." In *La victoria de Junín: canto a Bolívar (Facsímile de la edición Londinense, 1826),* 115–22. Bogotá: Litografía Arco, 1974.

Bhabha, Homi K. "DissemiNation." In *Nation and Narration,* edited by Homi K. Bhabha, 291–322. New York: Routledge, 1990.

Bitton, Davis. "Guide to Mormon Diaries and Autobiographies," 1977. http://lib.byu.edu/sites/mormonstudies/files/2008/09/bittons-guide.pdf.

Bizzell, Patricia. "(Native) American Jeremiad: The 'Mixedblood' Rhetoric of William Apess." In *American Indian Rhetorics of Survivance,* edited by Ernest Stromberg, 34–49. Pittsburgh, PA: University of Pittsburgh Press, 2006.

Blanch, Juan M. Lope. "El problema de la lengua española en América." *Nueva Revista de Filología Hispánica* 43, no. 1 (1995): 17–36.

Blanchot, Maurice, and Jacques Derrida. *The Instant of My Death/Demeure: Fiction and Testimony.* Translated by Elizabeth Rottenberg. Stanford, CA: Stanford University Press, 2000.

Bloom, Harold. *The American Religion.* New York: Simon & Schuster, 1992.

Borch-Jacobsen, Mikkel. *The Emotional Tie: Psychoanalysis, Mimesis, and Affect.* Stanford, CA: Stanford University Press, 1993.

Brading, D. A. *The Origins of Mexican Nationalism.* Cambridge: University of Cambridge Centre of Latin American Studies, 1985.

Brennan, Timothy. "The National Longing for Form." In *Nation and Narration,* edited by Homi K. Bhabha, 44–70. London: Routledge, 1990.

Brickhouse, Anna. *Transamerican Literary Relations and the Nineteenth-Century Public Sphere.* Cambridge: Cambridge University Press, 2004.

Brodie, Fawn McKay. *No Man Knows My History: The Life of Joseph Smith, the Mormon Prophet.* Second ed. New York: Vintage Books, 1995.

Brooks, Lisa. "Turning the Looking Glass on King Philip's War: Locating American Literature in Native Space." *American Literary History 25, no. 4 (2013): 718–50.*

Brown, John. "An Idea of Things in Kansas (1857)." In *John Brown's Raid on Harpers Ferry: A Brief History with Documents,* edited by Jonathan Earle, 58–62. Bedford Series in History and Culture. Boston and New York: Bedford/St. Martin's, 2008.

———. "Selected Prison Letters (October 21–December 2, 1859)." In *John Brown's Raid on Harpers Ferry: A Brief History with Documents,* edited by Jonathan Earle, 88–103. Bedford Series in History and Culture. Boston and New York: Bedford/St. Martin's, 2008.

Brown, Samuel Morris. *In Heaven as It Is On Earth: Joseph Smith and the Early Mormon Conquest of Death.* New York: Oxford University Press, 2012.

Browne, C. A. *The Story of Our National Ballads.* New York: Crowell, 1960.

Brunet, François. "Linguisters on the Prairie." *Revue Française d'Etudes Américaines* 37 (July 1988): 238–66.

Bryant, William Cullen. "Thanatopsis." In *Poems of William C. Bryant.* New York: Thomas Y. Crowell & Co., 1893.

Burns, E. Bradford. *Perspectives on Brazilian History.* New York: Columbia University Press, 1967.

Bushman, Richard L. *Joseph Smith and the Beginnings of Mormonism.* Urbana: University of Illinois Press, 1984.

———. "Mormon Persecutions in Missouri, 1833." *Brigham Young University Studies* 3 (1960): 11–20.

Bustamante, Carlos Maria de. *Cuadro histórico de la revolución mejicana.* 3rd ed. Vol. II. Mexico: Juan R. Navarro, 1854.

Byrd, Jodi A. *The Transit of Empire: Indigenous Critiques of Colonialism.* Minneapolis: University of Minnesota Press, 2011.

Cabot, James Elliot. *A Memoir of Ralph Waldo Emerson.* Boston and New York: Houghton, Mifflin & Company, 1887.

Campbell, Lyle. *American Indian Languages: The Historical Linguistics of Native America.* Oxford: Oxford University Press, 2000.

Cassedy, Tim. *Figures of Speech: Six Histories of Language and Identity in the Age of Revolutions.* Iowa City: University of Iowa Press, 2018.

Castiglia, Chris. *Interior States: Institutional Consciousness and the Inner Life of Democracy in the Antebellum United States.* Durham, NC: Duke University Press, 2008.

Castro-Klarén, Sara. "The Nation in Ruins: Archaeology and the Rise of the Nation." In *Beyond Imagined Communities: Reading and Writing the Nation in Nineteenth-Century Latin America,* edited by Sara Castro-Klarén and John Charles Chasteen, 161–95. Washington DC: Woodrow Wilson Center Press, 2003.

Castronovo, Russ. *Necro Citizenship: Death, Eroticism, and the Public Sphere in the Nineteenth-Century United States.* Durham, NC, and London: Duke University Press, 2001.

"Celebrant." *Oxford English Dictionary Online.* Oxford University Press, 1989.

Certeau, Michel de. *Heterologies: Discourses on the Other.* Translated by Brian Massumi. Theory and History of Literature. Minneapolis: University of Minnesota Press, 1986.

———. *The Practice of Everyday Life.* Translated by Steven Rendall. Berkeley and Los Angeles: University of California Press, 1984.

———. *The Writing of History.* Translated by Tom Conely. New York: Columbia University Press, 1988.

Chasteen, John Charles. "Introduction: Beyond Imagined Communities." In *Beyond Imagined Communities: Reading and Writing the Nation in Nineteenth-Century Latin America,* edited by Sara Castro-Klarén and John Charles Chasteen, ix–xxv. Washington DC: Woodrow Wilson Center Press, 2003.

Chatterjee, Partha. "Anderson's Utopia." *Diacritics* 29, no. 4 (Winter 1999): 128–34.

Cheyfitz, Eric. *The Poetics of Imperialism: Translation and Colonization from The Tempest to Tarzan.* Expanded ed. Philadelphia: University of Pennsylvania Press, 1997.

Child, Lydia Maria. *Hobomok and Other Writings on Indians.* Edited by Carolyn Karcher. American Women Writers. New Brunswick, NJ, and London: Rutgers University Press, 1986.

Clavijero, Francisco Javier. *Historia antigua de México: Sacada de de los mejores historiadores españoles, y de los manuscritos y pinturas antiguas de los indios.* Edited by José Joaquín de Mora. Vol. 1. 2 vols. México: Departamento Editorial de la Dirección General de las Bellas Artes, 1917.

Clerke, Agnes M. *A Popular History of Astronomy during the Nineteenth Century.* 2nd ed. Edinburgh: A. & C. Black, 1887.

"Conference Minutes." *Times and Seasons,* August 15, 1844. The Joseph Smith Papers (Church Historian's Press).

Conn, Steve. *History's Shadow: Native Americans and Historical Consciousness in the Nineteenth Century.* Chicago and London: University of Chicago Press, 2004.

Cooper, James Fenimore. *The Last of the Mohicans; A Narrative of 1757.* 1826. Edited by James Franklin Beard, James A. Sappenfield, and E.N. Feltskog. Albany: State University of New York Press, 1983.

———. *The Pioneers, or the Sources of the Susquehanna. A Descriptive Tale.* 1823. Edited by

James Franklin Beard, Lance Schachterle, and Kenneth M. Anderson Jr. Albany: State University of New York Press, 1980.

———. *The Prairie: A Tale.* 1827. Edited by James P. Elliott. Albany: State University of New York Press, 1985.

Cotler, Julio. *Clases, estado y nación en el Perú.* 2nd ed. México: Universidad Nacional Autónoma de México, Instituto de Investigaciones Sociales, 1982.

Coulthard, Glen Sean. *Red Skin, White Masks: Rejecting the Colonial Politics of Recognition.* Minneapolis and London: University of Minnesota Press, 2014.

Coviello, Peter. *Intimacy in America: Dreams of Affiliation in Antebellum Literature.* Minneapolis and London: University of Minnesota Press, 2005.

Da Costa, Emilia Viotti. *The Brazilian Empire: Myths and Histories.* Revised ed. Chapel Hill and London: University of North Carolina Press, 2000.

Dahl, Curtis. "Mound-Builders, Mormons, and William Cullen Bryant." *New England Quarterly* 34, no. 2 (1961): 178–90.

Daniell, David. "John Rogers." *Oxford Dictionary of National Biography.* Oxford University Press, 2009–2004.

Davies, Douglas. *The Mormon Culture of Salvation.* Aldershot, England, and Burlington, VT: Ashgate, 2000.

Debray, Regis. "Marxism and the National Question." *New Left Review* 105 (September/October 1977): 25–41.

Deloria, Philip J. *Playing Indian.* New Haven, CT, and London: Yale University Press, 1998.

De Man, Paul. "Conclusions: Walter Benjamin's 'The Task of the Translator.'" In *The Resistance to Theory,* 73–105. Minneapolis and London: University of Minnesota Press, 1986.

Derrida, Jacques. *The Gift of Death.* Translated by David Wills. Chicago: University of Chicago Press, 1995.

———. "The Law of Genre." Translated by Avital Ronell. *Glyph* 7 (1980): 202–32.

———. "Mnemosyne." In *Memoires for Paul de Man,* translated by Cecile Lindsay, 3–43. New York: Columbia University Press, 1986.

———. *Paper Machine.* Translated by Rachel Bowlby. Stanford, CA: Stanford University Press, 2005.

DiCuirci, Lindsay. *Colonial Revivals: The Nineteenth-Century Lives of Early American Books.* Philadelphia: University of Pennsylvania Press, 2018.

Dippie, Brian W. *The Vanishing American: White Attitudes and U.S. Indian Policy.* Middletown, CT: Wesleyan University Press, 1982.

Doctrine and Covenants of the Church of the Latter Day Saints: Carefully Selected from the Revelations of God, and Compiled by Joseph Smith Junior, Olivery Cowdery, Sidney Rigdon, Frederick G. Williams [Presiding Elders of Said Church.]. Kirtland, OH: F. G. Williams & Co., 1835. http://www.josephsmithpapers.org/paper-summary/doctrine-and-covenants-1835/.

Doniger, Wendy. "Foreword." In *Myth and Meaning: Cracking the Code of Culture,* by Claude Lévi-Strauss, vii–xv. New York: Schocken Books, 1995.

Douglas, Mary. *Purity and Danger: An Analysis of the Concept of Pollution and Taboo.* London and New York: Routledge Classics, 2002.

Drake, Samuel G. *The Book of Indians of North America: Comprising Details in the Lives of about Five Hundred Chiefs and Others, the Most Distinguished among Them. Also, a History of Their Wars; Their Manners and Customs; Speeches of Orators [. . .].* Boston: Josiah Drake, 1835.

———. *Indian Biography, Containing the Lives of More than Two Hundred Indian Chiefs: Also Such Others of That Race as Have Rendered Their Names Conspicuous in the History of North America [. . .].* Boston: Josiah Drake, 1832.

Duarte, Eduardo de Assis. "Iracema: A expansão portuguesa sob o signo de Eva." In *Literatura e Feminismo: Propostas Teóricas e Reflexões Críticas,* edited by Christina Ramalho, 195–214. Rio de Janeiro: ELO Editora, 1999.

Earle, Rebecca. "Creole Patriotism and the Myth of the 'Loyal Indian.'" *Past and Present Society* 172 (2001): 125–45.

Echevarría, Roberto González, ed. *Historia y ficción en la narrativa hispanoamericana: Coloquio de Yale.* Caracas: Monte Avila Editores, 1984.

Edgerton Jr., Samuel Y. "The Murder of Jane McCrea: The Tragedy of an American Tableau d'Histoire." *Art Bulletin* 47, no. 4 (December 1965): 481–92.

Emerson, Ralph Waldo. "Speech by Ralph Waldo Emerson." In *Echoes of Harpers Ferry,* edited by James Redpath. Boston: Thayer & Eldridge, 1860.

Ferreira-Pinto, Cristina. *Gender, Discourse, and Desire in Twentieth-Century Brazilian Women's Literature.* West Lafayette, IN: Purdue University Press, 2004.

Fiedler, Leslie A. *Love and Death in the American Novel.* Normal, IL: Dalkey Archive Press, 1997.

Fisher, John Robert. *Bourbon Peru, 1750–1824.* Liverpool: Liverpool University Press, 2003.

Fitz, Earl E. *Brazilian Narrative Traditions in a Comparative Context.* World Literatures Reimagined. New York: Modern Language Association of America, 2005.

Flanders, Robert. "To Transform History: Early Mormon Culture and the Concept of Time and Space." *Church History* 40 (1971): 108–17.

Follen, Eliza Lee Cabot. *Poems.* Boston: W. Crosby & Company, 1839.

Forsberg, Clyde Revere. "In Search of the Historical Nephi: The Book of Mormon, 'Evangelicalism' and Antebellum American Popular Culture." PhD dissertation, Queen's University, 1994.

Freud, Sigmund. "Family Romances." In *The Freud Reader,* edited by Peter Gay, 297–300. New York: W. W. Norton, 1989.

———. "Mourning and Melancholia." In *The Standard Edition of the Complete Psychological Works of Sigmund Freud,* edited by James Strachey, Vol. XIV (1914–1916). London: Hogarth Press and Institute of Psycho-Analysis, 1957.

———. *Reflections on War and Death.* Translated by A. A. Brill and Alfred Kuttner. New York: Moffat, Yard & Company, 1918.

Gellner, Ernest. *Nations and Nationalism.* 2nd ed. Ithaca, NY: Cornell University Press, 1983.

Genette, Gérard. *Narrative Discourse: An Essay in Method.* Translated by Jane E. Lewin. Ithaca, NY: Cornell University Press, 1980.

Glissant, Edouard. *Caribbean Discourse: Selected Essays.* Translated by J. Michael Dash. Charlottesville: University Press of Virginia, 1989.

Gold, Peter J. "'Indianismo' and 'Indigenismo.'" *Romance Notes* 14, no. 3 (Spring 1973): 460–64.

Gonçalves Dias, Antônio. *Diccionario da lingua Tupy chamada lingua geral dos indigenas do Brazil.* Lipsia: F. A. Brockhaus, 1858.

Gould, Philip. *Covenant and Republic: Historical Romance and the Politics of Puritanism.* Cambridge and New York: Cambridge University Press, 1996.

Gruesz, Kirsten Silva. *Ambassadors of Culture: The Transamerican Origins of Latino Writing.* Princeton, NJ, and Oxford: Princeton University Press, 2002.

Guerra, François-Xavier. "Forms of Communication, Political Spaces, and Cultural Identities in the Creation of Spanish American Nations." In *Beyond Imagined Communities: Reading and Writing the Nation in Nineteenth-Century Latin America,* edited by Sara Castro-Klarén and John Charles Chasteen, 3–32. Washington, DC: Woodrow Wilson Center Press, 2003.

———. "Identidad y Soberanía, Una Relacíon Compleja." In *Revoluciones Hispánicas: Independencias Americanas y Liberalismo Español,* edited by François-Xavier Guerra, 207–42. Madrid: Editorial Complutense, 1995.

Guimaraes, Manuel Luis Salgado. "Nação e civilização nos trópicos: O Instituto Histórico e Geográfico Brasileiro e o projeto de uma história nacional." *Estudos Históricos* 1 (1988): 5027.

Gura, Philip F. *The Life of William Apess, Pequot.* Chapel Hill: University of North Carolina Press, 2015.

Gutjahr, Paul. "The Golden Bible in the Bible's Golden Age: The Book of Mormon and Antebellum Print Culture." *American Transcendental Quarterly* 12, no. 4 (1998): 275–93.

Hansen, Klaus J. *Mormonism and the American Experience.* Chicago: University of Chicago Press, 1981.

Harrison, Robert Pogue. *The Dominion of the Dead.* Chicago: University of Chicago Press, 2003.

Hart, James David. *The Popular Book: A History of America's Literary Taste.* Westport, CT: Greenwood Press, 1976.

Harvey, Sean P. *Native Tongues: Colonialism and Race from Encounter to Reservation.* Cambridge, MA, and London: Harvard University Press, 2015.

Hawthorne, Nathaniel. "Chiefly about War Matters by a Peaceable Man." *Atlantic Monthly,* July 1862.

Hirsch, Marianne. "Jane's Family Romances." In *Borderwork: Feminist Engagements with Comparative Literature,* edited by Margaret R. Higgonet, 162–85. Ithaca, NY: Cornell University Press, 1994.

Holland, Sharon Patricia. *Raising the Dead: Readings of Death and (Black) Subjectivity.* Durham, NC, and London: Duke University Press, 2000.

Howe, Julia Ward. *Reminiscences, 1819–1899.* Boston and New York: Houghton, Mifflin & Company, 1899.

Howells, William Dean. "Reviews and Literary Notices: Melville's Battle Pieces and Aspects of War." *Atlantic Monthly,* 1867.

Hutchison, Anthony. "Representative Man: John Brown and the Politics of Redemption in Russell Banks's Cloudsplitter." *Journal of American Studies* 41, no. 1 (2007): 67–82.

Ianes, Raúl. *De Cortés a la huérfana enclaustrada: La novela histórica del romanticismo hispanoamericano.* New York: Peter Lang, 1997.

Irving, Washington. *The Sketch Book of Geoffrey Crayon, Gent.* Vol. 2. London: John Murray, 1820.

Jackson, Andrew. "First Annual Message, December 8, 1829." *The American Presidency Project,* n.d. http://www.presidency.ucsb.edu/ws/?pid=29471.

Jackson, Thomas J. ("Stonewall"). "Letter to Mary Anna Jackson," December 2, 1859. Virginia Military Institute Archives.

Jacobs, Carol. *In the Language of Walter Benjamin.* Baltimore and London: Johns Hopkins University Press, 1999.

Jefferson, Thomas. *Notes on the State of Virginia.* Richmond, VA: J. W. Randolph, 1853.

"Jicotencal. Filadelfia. Imprenta de Guillermo Staverly. Two Volumes. 1826." *United States Review and Literary Gazette* 1, no. 5 (February 1827): 336–46.

Jobim, José Luis, and Roberto Acízelo de Souza. *Iniciação à literatura brasileira.* Rio de Janeiro: Ao Livro Técnico S.A., 1987.

Kadir, Djelal. *Columbus and the Ends of the Earth: Europe's Prophetic Rhetoric as Conquering Ideology.* Berkeley: University of California Press, 1992.

———. "The Commons of History." In *Do the Americas Have a Common Literary History,* edited by Barbara Buchenau and Annette Paatz, 599–616. Interamericana. Frankfurt: Peter Lang, 2002.

Karcher, Carolyn L. "Introduction." In *Hobomok and Other Writings on Indians, by Lydia Maria Child,* ix–xlv. New Brunswick, NJ, and London: Rutgers University Press, 1986.

Keach, William. *Arbitrary Power: Romanticism, Language, Politics.* Princeton, NJ: Princeton University Press, 2004.

Kelley, Robin D. G. "The Rest of Us: Rethinking Settler and Native." *American Quarterly* 69, no. 2 (June 2017): 267–76.

Kennedy, J. Gerald. *Strange Nation: Literary Nationalism and Cultural Conflict in the Age of Poe.* Oxford: Oxford University Press, 2016.

Kimball, Spencer. "Listen to the Prophets." *Ensign* May (1978): 76.

Kipp, Laura Maffley. "Introduction." In *The Book of Mormon.* New York: Penguin, 2008.

Knapp, Samuel L. *Lectures on American Literature, with Remarks on Some Passages of American History.* New York: Elam Bliss, 1829.

König, Hans-Joachim. "El indigenismo criollo ¿proyectos vital y político realizables, o instrumento político?" *Historia Mexicana* 46, no. 4 (1997): 745–67.

Konkle, Maureen. *Writing Indian Nations: Native Intellectuals and the Politics of Historiography, 1827–1863.* Chapel Hill and London: University of North Carolina Press, 2004.

Lacoue-Labarthe, Philippe, and Jean-Luc Nancy. "The Unconscious Is Destructed Like an Affect." *Stanford Literature Review* 6 (Fall 1989): 191–209.

Langlois, Charles-Victor, and Charles Seignobos. *Introduction aux études historiques (1898).* Lyon: ENS Éditions, 2014.

Lazo, Rodrigo. "Accounting for Textual Remains." *J19: The Journal of Nineteenth-Century Americanists* 2, no. 1 (2014): 178–86.
———. "The Invention of America Again: On the Impossibility of an Archive." *American Literary History* 25, no. 4 (2013): 751–71.
———. *Letters from Filadelfia: Early Latino Literature and the Trans-American Elite.* Charlottesville: University of Virginia Press, Forthcoming.
Lee, Maurice. "Writing through the War: Melville and Dickinson after the Renaissance." *PMLA* 115, no. 5 (2000): 1124–28.
Lefevere, André. *Translating Literature: Practice and Theory in a Comparative Literature Context.* New York: Modern Language Association of America, 1992.
Lepore, Jill. *A Is for American: Letters and Other Characters in the Newly United States.* New York: Alfred A. Knopf, 2002.
———. *The Name of War: King Philip's War and the Origins of American Identity.* New York: Vintage, 1998.
Lewis, R. W. B. *The American Adam; Innocence, Tragedy, and Tradition in the Nineteenth Century.* Chicago: University of Chicago Press, 1955.
Lindstrom, Naomi. *Early Spanish American Narrative.* Austin: University of Texas Press, 2004.
Ljungquist, Kent. "'Meteor of the War': Melville, Thoreau, and Whitman Respond to John Brown." *American Literature* 61, no. 4 (1989): 674–80.
Locke, John. *An Essay Concerning Human Understanding.* Edited by Peter H. Nidditch. Oxford: Oxford University Press, 1975.
Longfellow, Henry Wadsworth. *The Song of Hiawatha.* Boston: Ticknor & Fields, 1860.
López García, José Ramón. "Visiones de la conquista en el teatro del exilio: 'El regreso de Quetzalcóatl. La epopeya Azteca' de Álvaro Custodio y 'El gran Tianguis' de José María Camps." *Anales de la literatura española contemporánea* 37, no. 2 (2012): 573–95.
Loughran, Trish. *The Republic in Print: Print Culture in the Age of U.S. Nation Building, 1770–1870.* New York: Columbia University Press, 2007.
Luciano, Dana. *Arranging Grief: Sacred Time and the Body in Nineteenth-Century America.* New York and London: New York University Press, 2007.
Lynch, John. *The Spanish American Revolutions, 1808–1826.* London: Weidenfeld & Nicolson, 1973.
Lyotard, Jean-François. *The Differend: Phrases in Dispute.* Translated by Georges Van den Abbeele. Minneapolis: University of Minnesota Press, 1989.
Mailloux, Steven. "The Rhetorical Use and Abuse of Fiction: Eating Books in Late Nineteenth-Century America." *Boundary 2* 17, no. 1 (1990): 133–57.
"Marcha patriótica (himno nacional)." In *El redactor de la Asamblea (reimpresión facsimilar),* 107–8. Buenos Aires: Compañía sud-americana de billetes de banco, 1913.
Marshall, Zach. "Signs in the Heavens and the Distress of Nations." *J19: The Journal of Nineteenth-Century Americanists* 6, no. 2 (Fall 2018): 285–306.
Mbembe, Achille. "Necropolitics." Translated by Libby Meintjes. *Public Culture* 15, no. 1 (2003): 11–40.
———. "The Power of the Archive and Its Limits." In *Refiguring the Archive,* edited by

Carolyn Hamilton, Verne Harris, Jane Taylor, Michele Pickover, Graeme Reid, and Razia Saleh, translated by Judith Inggs, 19–26. Dordrecht, Netherlands: Kluwer Academic Publishers, 2002.

McCormick, John O. "Notes on a Comparative American Literary History." *Comparative Literature Studies* 5 (1968): 167–79.

McDonald, John J. "Emerson and John Brown." *New England Quarterly* 44, no. 3 (1971): 377–96.

McPheeters, D. W. "Xicoténcal, símbolo republicano y romántico." *Nueva Revista de Filología Hispánica* 10 (1956): 403–11.

Melville, Herman. *The Battle-Pieces of Herman Melville.* Edited by Hennig Cohen. New York, London, Toronto: Thomas Yoseloff, 1963.

Méndez, Cecilia. "Incas Sí, Indios No: Notes on Peruvian Creole Nationalism and Its Contemporary Crisis." *Journal of Latin American Studies* 28, no. 1 (1996): 197–225.

"Message of the President of the United States to Both Houses of Congress on the Commencement of the Second Session of the Twenty-First Congress. December 7, 1830" (Andrew Jackson). *The Register of Debates* 21st Cong., 2nd sess. (1830): ii–xiii.

Michelet, Jules. *Œuvres Complètes.* Edited by Bernard Leuilliot. Vol. XXI (1872–1874). Paris: Flammarion, 1982.

Mills, Bruce. *Cultural Reformations: Lydia Maria Child and the Literature of Reform.* Athens: University of Georgia Press, 1994.

Minguet, Charles. "El concepto de nación, pueblo, estado y pátria en las generaciones de la independencia." In *Recherches sur le monde hispanique au dix-neuvième siècle,* edited by Jean René-Aymes, 58–71. Lille, FR: Université de Lille, 1973.

Mirabeau, Honoré-Gabriel Riqueti. *Lettre du Comte de Mirabeau à ses commettans. Pendant la tenue de la première législature.* Paris: Lavillette, 1791.

———. *Speeches of M. de Mirabeau the Elder, Pronounced in the National Assembly of France.* Translated by James White. London: J. Debrett, 1792.

"Miscellaneous Notices: Hobomok, a Tale of Early Times." *North American Review* 19, no. 44 (July 1824): 262–65.

"Mitote." Diccionario de la lengua española, edición del tricentenario. *Real Academia Española.* http://www.rae.es.

Montemayor, Carlos, Enrique Garcia Escamilla, Enrique Rivas Paniagua, and Librado Silva Galeana, eds. *Diccionario del náhuatl en el español de México.* 2nd ed. México, D. F.: Universidad Nacional Autónoma de México, Programa Universitario México Nación Multicultural, 2013.

Muller, Gilbert H. *William Cullen Bryant: Author of America.* Albany: State University of New York Press, 2008.

Murphy, Gretchen. *Hemispheric Imaginings: The Monroe Doctrine and Narratives of U.S. Empire.* Durham, NC, and London: Duke University Press, 2005.

Niranjana, Tejaswini. *Siting Translation: History, Post-Structuralism, and the Colonial Context.* Berkeley, Los Angeles, and London: University of California Press, 1992.

Noll, Mark A. *America's God: From Jonathan Edwards to Abraham Lincoln.* Oxford and New York: Oxford University Press, 2002.

Nudelman, Franny. "'The Blood of Millions': John Brown's Body, Public Violence, and

Political Community." In *The Afterlife of John Brown,* edited by Andrew Taylor and Eldrid Herrington, 27–55. New York: Palgrave Macmillan, 2005.

Nyman, Monte S. *I, Nephi Wrote This Record.* Orem, UT: Granite, 2003.

O'Brien, Jean. *Firsting and Lasting: Writing Indians Out of Existence in New England.* Minneapolis and London: University of Minnesota Press, 2010.

O'Connell, Barry "Introduction." In *On Our Own Ground: The Complete Writings of William Apess, a Pequot,* xiii–lxxvii. Amherst: University of Massachusetts Press, 1992.

———. "'Once More Let Us Consider': William Apess in the Writing of New England Native American History." In *After King Philip's War: Presence and Persistence in Indian New England,* edited by Colin G. Calloway. Hanover, NH, and London: University Press of New England, 1997.

Olmedo, José Joaquín de. *Obras poéticas de d. José Joaquín Olmedo. Única colección completa, revista y correjida por el author, y ordenada por J.M.G.* Valparaíso: Imprenta Europa, 1848.

Olson, Christa J. *Constitutive Visions: Indigeneity and Commonplaces of National Identity in Republican Ecuador.* University Park: Pennsylvania State University Press, 2014.

Orians, George Harrison. *The Cult of the Vanishing American: A Century View, 1834–1934.* Toledo, OH: H. J. Chittenden, 1934.

Parker, Robert Dale, ed. *The Sound the Stars Make Rushing through the Sky: The Writings of Jane Johnston Schoolcraft.* Philadelphia: University of Pennsylvania Press, 2007.

Pearce, Roy Harvey. *Savagism and Civilization: A Study of the Indian and the American Mind.* Berkeley, Los Angeles, and London: University of California Press, 1988.

Pérez Vejo, Tomás. "La construcción de las naciones como problema historiográfico: El caso del mundo hispánico." *Historia Mexicana* 53, no. 2 (December 2003): 275–311.

Pratt, Lloyd. *Archives of American Time: Literature and Modernity in the Nineteenth Century.* Philadelphia: University of Pennsylvania Press, 2010.

Pratt, Parley. *The Autobiography of Parley Parker Pratt.* One of the Twelve Apostles of the Church of Jesus Christ of Latter-Day Saints, Embracing His Life, Ministry and Travels, with Extracts, in Prose and Verse, from His Miscellaneous Writings. New York: Russell Brothers, 1874.

———. "The Latter-Day Saints Millennial Star." W. Shackleton & Son, 1841. Tom Perry Special Collections, Brigham Young University.

Preston, John T. L. "Letter to His Wife," December 2, 1859. Virginia Military Institute Archives.

Quinn, D. Michael. *Early Mormonism and the Magic World View.* Salt Lake City: Signature Books, 1987.

Radus, Daniel. "Apess's *Eulogy* on Tour: Kinship and the Transnational History of Native New England." *Studies in American Indian Literatures* 28, no. 3 (Fall 2016): 81–110.

"Recent American Novels." *North American Review* 21, no. 48 (July 1825): 78–104.

Redfield, Marc. "Imagi-Nation: The Imagined Community and the Aesthetics of Mourning." *Diacritics* 29, no. 4 (Winter 1999): 58–83.

Renan, Ernest. "What Is a Nation?" In *Nation and Narration,* edited by Homi K. Bhabha, translated by Martin Thom, 8–22. New York: Routledge, 1990.

Reynolds, David S. "Cultural Biography: Reflection, Transcendence, and Impact." *Biography and Source Studies* 7 (2003): 83–99.

———. *John Brown, Abolitionist: The Man Who Killed Slavery, Sparked the Civil War, and Seeded Civil Rights.* New York: Alfred A. Knopf, 2005.

Ribeiro, Luis Filipe. *Mulheres de papel: Um estudo do imaginário em José de Alencar e Machado de Assis.* Niterói, RJ: Editora da Universidade Federal Fluminense, 1996.

Richter, Daniel K. *Facing East from Indian Country: A Native History of Early America.* Cambridge, MA: Harvard University Press, 2003.

Ricœur, Paul. *Memory, History, Forgetting.* Chicago: University of Chicago Press, 2004.

Rifkin, Mark. *Beyond Settler Time: Temporal Sovereignty and Indigenous Self-Determination.* Durham, NC, and London: Duke University Press, 2017.

———. "Shadows of Mashantucket: William Apess and the Representation of Pequot Place." *American Literature* 84, no. 4 (December 2012).

Roach, Joseph. *Cities of the Dead: Circum-Atlantic Performance.* New York: Columbia University Press, 1996.

Rogers, Samuel. *Autobiography of Elder Samuel Rogers: Toils and Struggles of the Olden Times.* Cincinnati: Standard Publishing Co., 1880.

Rohter, Larry. "Language Born of Colonialism Thrives Again in Amazon." *New York Times,* August 28, 2005.

Romero, Lora. "Vanishing Americans: Gender, Empire, and the New Historicism." *American Literature* 63, no. 3 (1991): 385–405.

Roncador, Sonia. "O demônio familiar: Lavadeiras, amas-de-leite e criadas na narrativa de Júlia Lopes de Almeida." *Luso-Brazilian Review* 44, no. 1 (2007): 94–119.

Ronell, Avital. *Crack Wars: Literature, Addiction, Mania.* Urbana: University of Illinois Press, 2004.

Rosaldo, Renato. *Culture and Truth: The Remaking of Social Analysis.* Boston: Beacon Press, 1989.

Rothwell, Phillip. "Shit, Shrimps, and Shifting Sobriquets: Iracema and the Lesson in Lost Authority." *Portuguese Literary and Cultural Studies* 6 (Spring 2001): 285–95.

Round, Phillip H. *Removable Type: Histories of the Book in Indian Country, 1663–1880.* Chapel Hill: University of North Carolina Press, 2010.

Said, Edward W. *Reflections on Exile and Other Essays.* Cambridge, MA: Harvard University Press, 2000.

Santner, Eric L. *On Creaturely Life: Rilke, Benjamin, Sebald.* Chicago: University of Chicago Press, 2006.

Sayre, Gordon. *The Indian Chief as Tragic Hero: Native Resistance and Literatures of the America, from Moctezuma to Tecumseh.* Chapel Hill: University of North Carolina Press, 2005.

———. "The Mound Builders and the Imagination of American Antiquity in Jefferson, Bartram, and Chateaubriand." *Early American Literature* 33, no. 3 (1998): 225–49.

Scheidenhelm, Richard Joy. *The Response to John Brown.* American History Research. Belmont, CA: Wadsworth, 1972.

Scholnick, Robert. "Politics and Poetics: The Reception of Melville's Battle-Pieces and Aspects of War." *American Literature* 49, no. 3 (1977): 422–30.

Sedgwick, Catharine Maria. *Hope Leslie, or, Early Times in the Massachusetts.* Two vols. New York: White, Gallaher, & White, 1827.

Sedgwick, Catharine Maria, and Mary E. Dewey. *Life and Letters of Catharine M. Sedgwick.* New York: Harper & Bros., 1871.

Seed, Patricia. *American Pentimento: The Invention of Indians and the Pursuit of Riches.* Minneapolis: University of Minnesota Press, 2001.

Shimeall, Richard C. *Age of the World: As Founded on the Sacred Records, Historic and Prophetic: And the "Signs of the Times," Viewed in the Aspect of Premonitions of the Speedy Establishment on the Earth of the Millenial State, by the Second, Personal, Pre-Millenial Advent of Christ.* New York: Swords, Stanford & Co., 1842.

Shipps, Jan. *Mormonism: The Story of a New Religious Tradition.* Urbana: University of Illinois Press, 1985.

Shumway, Nicolas. *The Invention of Argentina.* Berkeley: University of California Press, 1991.

Silverberg, Robert. *Mound Builders of Ancient America: The Archaeology of a Myth.* Greenwich, CT: New York Graphic Society, 1968.

Simons, Gary F., and Charles D. Fennig, eds. "Mohegan-Pequot." *Ethnologue: Languages of the World.* Dallas, TX: SIL International, 2018. www.ethnologue.com.

———, eds. "Wampanoag." *Ethnologue: Languages of the World.* Dallas, TX: SIL International, 2018. www.ethnologue.com.

Skousen, Royal, ed. *The Book of Mormon: The Earliest Text.* New Haven, CT, and London: Yale University Press, 2009.

Smith, Carolyn F. "The Sacred-Historical Role of the Inca in Olmedo's 'Canto a Bolívar.'" *Hispania* 56 (1973): 212–16.

Smith, Joseph. *The Book of Mormon, 1830.* Church Historian's Press, josephsmithpapers.org/paperSummary/book-of-mormon-1830.

———. *Doctrine and Covenants of the Church of Jesus Christ of Latter-Day Saints. Given to Joseph Smith, Jun., The Prophet for the Building Up of the Kingdom of God in the Last Days.* Liverpool: William Budge, 1879.

———. *History of the Church of Jesus Christ of Latter-Day Saints.* Period I: History of Joseph Smith, the Prophet, by Himself. Salt Lake City: Deseret News, 1902.

———. Smith, George Albert. *Documentary History of the Church.* Vol. 6. Salt Lake City: Deseret Book Co., 1950.

———. *Teachings of the Presidents of the Church: Joseph Smith.* Salt Lake City: Church of Jesus Christ of Latter-day Saints, 2007.

Smith, Joseph, and Dean C. Jessee. *The Personal Writings of Joseph Smith.* Rev. Salt Lake City, UT; Provo, UT: Deseret Bk. : Brigham Young University Press, 2002.

Smith, Sydney. "Statistical Annals of the United States of America. Review." *Edinburgh Review* 33, no. 65 (1820): 69–80.

Sommer, Doris. *Foundational Fictions: The National Romances of Latin America.* Berkeley and Los Angeles: University of California Press, 1991.

Southerton, Simon G. *Losing a Lost Tribe: Native Americans, DNA, and the Mormon Church.* Salt Lake City: Signature Books, 2004.

Spicer, W. A. *Our Day in the Light of Prophecy.* London: Review & Herald Publishing Association, 1917.

Stoler, Ann. *Along the Archival Grain: Epistemic Anxieties and Colonial Common Sense.* Princeton, NJ: Princeton University Press, 2010.

Thoreau, Henry David. "A Plea for Captain John Brown." In *John Brown's Raid on Harpers Ferry: A Brief History with Documents,* edited by Jonathan Earle, 110–21. Bedford Series in History and Culture. Boston and New York: Bedford/St. Martin's, 2008.

———. *The Writings of Henry David Thoreau.* Edited by H. G. O. Blake. Riverside Press. Vol. 6. 11 vols. Boston and New York: Houghton Mifflin Company, 1884.

Tompkins, Jane P. *Sensational Designs: The Cultural Work of American Fiction, 1790–1860.* New York: Oxford University Press, 1986.

Truettner, William H. "Picturing the Murder of Jane McCrea: A Critical Moment in Transatlantic Romanticism." In *Transatlantic Romanticism: British and American Art and Literature, 1790–1860,* edited by Andrew Hemingway and Alan Wallach. Amherst: University of Massachusetts Press, 2015.

Turner, Victor. *From Ritual to Theatre: The Human Seriousness of Play.* New York: PAJ Publications, 1982.

Underwood, Grant. "Early Mormon Millenarianism: Another Look." *Church History* 54 (June 1985): 215–29.

Unzueta, Fernando. "Scenes of Reading: Imagining Nation/Romancing History in Spanish America." In *Beyond Imagined Communities,* edited by Sara Castro-Klarén and John Charles Chasteen, 115–60. Washington, DC: Woodrow Wilson Center Press, 2003.

Van Orden, Bruce A. "I Have a Question." *Ensign* 24, no. 1 (January 1994): 54–55.

Varela, Félix. *Jicoténcal. 1826.* Recovering U.S. Hispanic Literary Heritage. Houston: Arte Público, 1995.

Vaux, Molly. "'But Maria, Did You Really Write This?': Preface as Cover Story in Lydia Maria Child's Hobomok." *Legacy* 17, no. 2 (2000): 127–40.

Vizenor, Gerald. *Manifest Manners: Narratives of Postindian Survivance.* Lincoln and London: University of Nebraska Press, 1994.

Von Martius, Karl Friedrich, and José Honório Rodrigues. "Como se deve escrever a historia do Brasil." *Revista de Historia de América* 42 (December 1956): 433–58.

Wald, Priscilla. *Constituting Americans: Cultural Anxiety and Narrative Form.* Durham, NC, and London: Duke University Press, 1995.

Walker, Charles F. "The Patriotic Society: Discussions and Omissions about Indians in the Peruvian War of Independence." *The Americas* 55, no. 2 (October 1998): 275–98.

Warren, Robert Penn, ed. *Selected Poems of Herman Melville.* New York: Random House, 1971.

Warrior, Robert. "Eulogy on William Apess: Speculations on His New York Death." *Studies in American Indian Literatures* 16, no. 2 (2004): 1–13.

———. "Native American Scholarship and the Transnational Turn." *Cultural Studies Review* 15, no. 2 (September 2009): 119–30.

Wasserman, Renata. *Exotic Nations: Literature and Cultural Identity in the United States and Brazil, 1830–1930.* Ithaca, NY: Cornell University Press, 1994.

———. "The Red and the White: The 'Indian' Novels of José de Alencar." *PMLA* 98, no. 5 (1983): 815–27.

———. "Re-Inventing the New World: Cooper and Alencar." *Comparative Literature* 36, no. 3 (1984): 130–45.

Webster, Noah. *An American Dictionary of the English Language: Exhibiting the Origin, Orthography, Pronunciation, and Definitions of Words.* Harper & Brothers, 1848.

Wells, Ronald A. *Dictionaries and the Authoritarian Tradition. A Study in English Usage and Lexicography.* The Hague: Mouton, 1973.

Wertheimer, Eric. *Imagined Empires: Incas, Aztecs, and the New World of American Literature, 1771–1876.* Cambridge: Cambridge University Press, 1999.

White, Ed. "Early American Nations as Imagined Communities." *American Quarterly* 56, no. 1 (2004): 49–81.

White, Hayden. *Metahistory: The Historical Imagination in Nineteenth-Century Europe.* Baltimore and London: Johns Hopkins University Press, 1973.

Whitman, Walt. "Leaves of Grass (1867)." *Whitman Archive,* http://www.whitmanarchive.org.

Whittier, John Greenleaf. "Brown of Ossawatomie." In *The Complete Poetical Works of John Greenleaf Whittier,* 258. Boston and New York: Houghton, Mifflin & Company, 1892.

Wolfe, Patrick. "Settler Colonialism and the Elimination of the Native." *Journal of Genocide Research* 8, no. 4 (2006): 387–409.

"Yamoyden, a Tale of the Wars of King Philip, in Six Cantos. By the Late Rev. James Wallis Eastburn, A.M. and His Friend (Review)." *North American Review* 12, no. 31 (April 1821): 466–88.

Yaremko, Jason M. "'Obvious Indian': Missionaries, Anthropologists, and the 'Wild Indians' of Cuba. Representations of the Amerindian Presence in Cuba." *Ethnohistory* 56, no. 3 (2009): 449–77.

Zuba, Clayton. "Apess's Eulogy on King Philip and the Politics of Native Visualcy." *Early American Literature* 52, no. 3 (2017): 651–77.

Index